New Perspectives On Public Ser

New Perspectives on Public Services

Place and Technology

Christopher Pollitt

OXFORD
UNIVERSITY PRESS

OXFORD
UNIVERSITY PRESS

Great Clarendon Street, Oxford, OX2 6DP,
United Kingdom

Oxford University Press is a department of the University of Oxford.
It furthers the University's objective of excellence in research, scholarship,
and education by publishing worldwide. Oxford is a registered trade mark of
Oxford University Press in the UK and in certain other countries

First Edition published in 2012

First published in paperback 2013

Impression: 1

Published in the United States of America by Oxford University Press
198 Madison Avenue, New York, NY 10016, United States of America

British Library Cataloguing in Publication Data
Data available

ISBN 978–0–19–960383–1
ISBN 978–0–19–967736–8 (pbk.)

Printed and bound by CPI Group (UK) Ltd, Croydon, CR0 4YY

For Cayba, Rosie, Otto, and Konsta
Each in Their Own Times and Places

Preface

> It is seeing which establishes our place in the surrounding world; we
> explain that world with words, but words can never undo the fact that
> we are surrounded by it. The relationship between what we see and
> what we know is never settled.

(Berger 1972: 7)

This book is written on the bold assumption that there is a hugely important aspect of modern government that most of the professional scholars
who write and teach about public policy and management have largely
ignored. It is the aspect of 'place' and 'space'. I find very little of this in the
standard works on public policy and management (including my own past
efforts). In recent years scholarly interest in this 'angle' (which was never
great) actually seems to have shrunk. There is a lot of talk about how e-
government and the Net have diminished the importance of time and
space, as though we do not need to worry about such things any more.
Yet (I will argue) place is crucial to both the understanding and the organization of many public programmes, and can also sometimes be a significant
influence on citizens' attitudes towards their government(s). To make the
point rather crudely, one might say that as citizens we live and work
in *places*, not in policies. In John Berger's terms, places are what we *see*,
and our explanations for them are never settled or complete. Both theory
and evidence support this broad position, as I will attempt to demonstrate
in the chapters that follow.

The main focus will be on three inter-related questions. First, how
and why does the provision of public services shape places? Second, and
conversely, how do the characteristics of particular places influence how
public services are organized? Third, how do the locations/sites of public
service provision influence citizens' wider attitudes towards, and engagements with, the state? The first question entails a discussion of how we can
conceptualize, research, and understand the overall impact that public
authorities have on spatial relationships. This is in part, but not entirely,

a question about modalities of action (decisions, policies, routines, techniques). The second, reciprocal question seeks understanding of how the manifold particularities of place act back to influence both the ways in which public policies are formulated and the manner of their implementation. The third addresses the issue of effects on citizens—does it matter to citizens where and how they interact with their public authorities? This set of questions will be explored, and refined, as the book proceeds.

I will come at these questions from a particular angle. My background, training, and interests are mainly in the concrete workings of public service organizations—schools, hospitals, police forces, and so on. So that is where my main focus will lie. I will not be attempting to scale the abstract heights of fashionable contemporary debates about 'rescaled' state power and globalization, or 'the virtual state' or the 'network society', or even 'governmentality'. But I will most certainly be looking at the effects of some of these grand processes in so far as they are (or are not) visible within the frames of specific organizational, local, and national contexts.

My father was a geographer, and I nearly became one too. As a teenager I studied a subject called 'political geography' (although I preferred geomorphology), but then my studies abruptly changed direction and I left geography behind. For many years now I have been a public policy and management academic, and, until recently, I thought mainly about the phases and cycles of the policy process, models of management, and the consequences of using particular organizational structures and technical tools in specific political and cultural contexts. None of this involved much cogitation about space and place. As my work progressed, however, I became more and more suspicious of generic management theory (or of generic democratic theory for that matter). I grew convinced that 'context' was often crucial, and that perception has informed many of my publications (e.g. Pollitt 2003a; Pollitt et al. 2004; Pollitt and Bouckaert 2009, 2011). Of course, I am only one of many who have in various ways resisted the push for 'six steps'-type universal 'solutions'. For me the next stage was to disentangle some of the key elements in that enormously vague-but-useful term 'context'. The national political system was the first element out of the bag, and that seemed to help one understand a good deal about why reforms went down one trajectory in country A and another in country B (Pollitt and Bouckaert 2009, 2011). Then I thought I saw two key elements even further 'behind the scenes' and even more protean with respect to context. These were time and place, both of which appeared to be widely ignored in many of the most popular management texts.

So I tackled time first (Pollitt 2008; Pollitt and Bouckaert 2009), and now, in this work, I come to place.

Such explorations are frequently fraught with surprises (at least for the traveller), and this one was no exception. I had not got very far with place before I realized that it was also going to be necessary to examine the effects of changing technologies. Technologies of transport and communication play central roles in how places and spaces are shaped. The role of technologies, therefore, features strongly in the book. In recent years public managers have begun to write quite extensively about technology—or at least about e-government—so it is not such a conspicuously neglected topic within the public administration community as is place. Nevertheless, its treatment tends to be rather ghettoized (Pollitt 2011), whereas here I want to connect the issue of technology to mainstream concerns about the placing and organization of public services. None of this, incidentally, is meant to imply that place and technology have unvarying, deterministic effects, or that they outweigh all other influences, or even that it is feasible to construct a general model of how they 'work'. (I will get on to 'theory' in Chapter 2.)

It is scarcely possible to write an academic book without being interrogated about its disciplinary identity. During early discussions of the proposal for this book some geographers said it did not adequately cover modern political geography, and a couple of political scientists said it did not embrace the full range of relevant ideas in contemporary political science. Some public administrationists said time and space sounded interesting, but how was I going to relate them to the debates in their field about governance, innovation, networks, partnerships, public value, post-New Public Management (NPM) (and a few other things)? The gentle reader may by now have guessed my response—that I am going to disappoint each and every one of these questioners. For this book is not intended to survey the state of any discipline, or, indeed, to import one or more disciplines, lock, stock, and barrel, into my own interdisciplinary field of public policy and management. My purpose has been more magpie-like—to carry off attractive and glittering objects from wherever I might find them, and then put them together to see if they could add lustre to my own topic. Not everything fits—and certainly not everything fits with everything else—but the basic approach, though constrained by some general precepts of social science epistemology (epistemological and logical coherence, some kind of correspondence with available empirical evidence), is eclectic. The focus is on the spatial and 'platial' dimensions of public service organizations, how these have changed, and how they are continuing to change. If this interdisciplinary promiscuity generates discomfort among disciplinary guardians, so be it. I comfort myself with the thought that interdisciplinary magpies have played a most honourable and fertile role in the history of my field (and many others). Consider, for example, the amazing range of literatures raided by Charles T. Goodsell, for his half-forgotten, but fascinating, *The Social Meaning of Civic Space* (1988), or the melding of architecture, history, political science, and other things in Paul Hirst's *Space and Power: Politics, War and Architecture* (2005). My biggest regret is that such a broad and eclectic approach, while in important respects appropriate for a foray into only partly charted territory, inevitably means that I treat some fascinating literatures in a 'smash and grab' manner—I do not do justice to their intrinsic complexity or subtlety. At the micro-level, the design of public buildings and 'civic spaces' would be one example, while at the meso-level the evolution of models of spatial planning would be another.

What I hope to offer, at least on my optimistic mornings, is a new way of thinking about public service organizations—more concrete and practical than long analyses of abstract management tools and concepts, and more rooted in the locational specificity of everyday life. One possible ambition would be that most graduate and postgraduate courses in public policy and/or administration would invite their students to pay attention to conceptualizing, theorizing, or even just *noticing* spatial issues. This would be rather a big change from the status quo. During my more pessimistic afternoons I see such aspirations as, though justifiable, nevertheless somewhat pretentious. A more modest goal would perhaps be to convince at least a healthy proportion of the readers of this book that places and technologies are practically important to governments (as they are to citizens), and that we policy and management academics could and should do much more to theorize and investigate them. There is a place for place, one might say, and the study of public management and policy-making has been the poorer for the recent underestimation of this dimension of public life.

Christopher Pollitt

Vanha Rajatie
Pohjankuru
Finland
2011

Acknowledgements

To be trite, all books are to varying degrees collective efforts, not excluding those that have only one nominal author.

First on my list of those to thank is undoubtedly my research assistant at the Katholieke Universiteit Leuven in 2009–2010, Liesbeth op De Beeck. Although it was her first job in research, she was always quick and efficient, and usually succeeded in hiding her astonishment at some of my working habits. She found lots of good stuff that I would probably never have found myself. I am also indebted—not for the first time—to two outstanding secretaries: Anneke Heylen and Inge Vermeulen.

Second, I want to express my continuing gratitude to a group of friends and colleagues who have often suffered my pestering with questions and drafts in the past, and must surely hope that this is my last book. They include Geert Bouckaert (Leuven), John Clarke (Open University), John Halligan (Canberra), Steve Harrison (Manchester), Ed Page (LSE), Peter Roberts (Darlington Borough Council), Colin Talbot (Manchester), and Roger Wettenhall (Canberra). In addition to these hardened advisers, my research on Canberra and Brasília benefited enormously from the apparently limitless generosity of a number of denizens, especially Helen Moore and Alastair Greig (Australian National University), Frederico de Holanda and Brasilmar Ferreira Nunes (University of Brasília), and Evelyn Levy (World Bank, Brasília). These kind and tremendously well-informed individuals made my time in those places socially enjoyable as well as intellectually stimulating. Others who have helped with particular requests include Christina Andrews (University of São Paulo), David Flannery (University of Canberra), Peter Humphreys (formerly of the Irish Institute of Public Administration), John Mohan (University of Southampton), and Tom Pollitt.

Third, this book also draws on the Brighton Leuven project, the first stage of which was described and reported in Pollitt and Bouckaert (2009: see especially pp. 195–7). During that project I received immense help from many managers and clinicians at the Brighton and Sussex University Hospitals Trust (see Chapter 6) and from senior officers in the Sussex Constabulary, the National Police Improvement Agency, and elsewhere (see Chapter 8). Despite the relentless pressures of life at or near the top of their respective organizations, more than thirty individuals willingly gave time to be interviewed—in some cases more than once. Add another fifty, subsequently interviewed for the Time, Place and Task (TPT) project on which much of this book is based, and you will appreciate why I cannot list all my creditors here.

Fourth, I am grateful to four anonymous reviewers of the first version of a proposal for this book. I did not like some of their observations, but they imposed necessary clarity on certain matters, and, in one way or another, I have endeavoured to accommodate most of their suggestions. As usual, it was the least welcome comments that demanded the closest attention.

Fifth, I would like to express my deep appreciation of the honour that Katholieke Universiteit Leuven did me by awarding me a BOF/ZAP research professorship in 2006. The ensuing period—free to do my own research in an ancient university in a beautiful city—has been profoundly satisfying.

Sixth, and finally, I am running out of novel ways to acknowledge the huge and unceasing contribution made by my wife, Hilkka Summa-Pollitt. By words, thoughts, and deeds she quietly improves me and my writings, though she never, ever, exhibits that special moral fervour that can so easily make 'improvers' objectionable.

Contents

List of Figures

List of Tables

Abbreviations

Abbreviations specific to this research

GAP   government as placemaker
TPT   Technology, Place, and Task

See the Appendix to this volume for more information on the research and for details of all TPT interviews.

Other abbreviations and acronyms

ACPO   Association of Chief Police Officers
ACT   Australian Commonwealth Territory
AHA   Area Health Authority
ANPR   automatic number plate recognition
BCU   Basic Command Unit
CCTV   closed circuit television
CSI   crime scene investigation
DIG   Decentralization Implementation Group
DRG   Deputy Registrar General
GLC   Greater London Council
GP   general practitioner
GRO   General Register Office
HMIC   HM Inspectorate of Constabulary
ICT   information and communications technology
NCDC   National Capital Development Commission
NFLMS   National Firearms Licensing Managing System
NHS   National Health Service
NPIA   National Policing Improvement Agency
NPM   New Public Management
NPT   Neighbourhood Policing Team
NSW   New South Wales
OECD   Organization for Economic Cooperation and Development
OGC   Office of Government Commerce
PCT   Primary Care Trust

PIC	Personal Identity Code
PT	Partido dos Trabalhadores (Workers' Party)
PNC	Police National Computer
RSCH	Royal Sussex County Hospital
SIS	Schengen Information System
SOCA	Serious Organized Crime Agency
SOCO	Scene of Crime Officer
TPT	Technology, Place, and Task
UNESCO	United Nations Educational, Scientific, and Cultural Organization
VFM	value for money
VISOR	Violent and Sexual Offenders Register

1

Introduction: Where Is the Government?

The state contains two dualities: it is place and persons and center and territory.

(Mann 1993: 56)

An understanding of public space is imperative for understanding the public sphere.

(Low and Smith 2006: 6)

The key innovation and decision-making processes take place in face-to-face contacts, and they still require a shared space of places, well-connected through its articulation to the space of flows.

(Castells 2010: p. xxxvi)

1.1 Where Was It, and How Has It Moved?

Many of us have enjoyed summer holidays visiting those idyllic central and southern French villages. As the morning sun beats down and we amble across the village square in search of croissants and morning coffee, or the cheap local wine, there can be little doubt about where the government is. It is in the *mairie* (town hall), the most formal and impressive building in town, standing there right next to the church and the post office. Similarly, in the very different circumstances of northern English industrial towns, we can hardly fail to notice the magnificent Victorian town hall (Manchester, Leeds, Bradford, and others). In both France and England these are not just temporary containers for actors in the ephemeral dramas of party politics; they are permanent and prominent symbols of a continuing state. In some other countries it is not merely buildings but whole cities that symbolize government—cities that were created specifically as hubs for national rule, such as Brasília, Canberra, or Washington DC.

Consider also the typical user of public services, in, say, the 1960s. For the main part using public services meant going to an office and (eventually) speaking face-to-face with an official: an employment office, a local government tax office, a registrar of births, marriages, and deaths, a police station, a school or hospital reception counter. Routine and unproblematic exchanges would be handled by letter—the immediately recognizable official buff envelope flopping onto the mat at home as the postman (or woman) retreated down the front path.

Government, therefore, had a face, and a place—or a variety of such. And these were not just the presidents or prime ministers in their (now) incessantly televised official residences, or even the national parliaments, busy with our babbling representatives. Indeed, for many citizens the town hall, the employment office, the register office, and the local hospital were probably more 'meaningful' (slippery term) than the national leaders. Such local, material faces and places of government were woven into *la vie quotidienne*, and they were tangible, human faces and solid, seldom-changing buildings.

But that has all begun to change—and rather fast. Our typical contact with government now is via the Internet or a telephone. We navigate through websites and call centres that have no human face and (for most of us) no known place. They may not even be in the country. They are sometimes, unbeknown to the vast majority of callers, operated by private, for-profit companies, not the government agency the citizens think they are calling (Schuppan 2009). Our primary relations with government have become (to use an overworked term that we will have to discuss later) 'virtual'. Changing technologies (and not only computers and the Internet) have clearly played an important part in all this, and must be incorporated in any convincing analysis. Organizational change has also done its bit—spatial relationships shift when public services such as refuse collection, facilities management, water supply, or the maintenance of the public transport infrastructure are contracted out to national—or international—firms.

Some take the view that this is all Progress. Things are faster now, and available 24/7. From the government's point of view, they are also usually cheaper. Fewer staff, more websites. Call centres or deconcentrated agencies sited in parts of the country with high unemployment, with a relatively plentiful supply of workers who need not be paid as much as in the over-heated labour markets of the capital cities. Or even call centres in another country, with a far cheaper workforce than could possibly be imagined anywhere at home. Or perhaps the service user him- or herself can be exported? In the early years of the twenty-first century some of the UK National Health Service's (NHS's) elective surgery patients were sent to France for their operations so that they would not have to wait so long (a decade and a half ago some foresighted academics were already writing about the 'globalization' of public services (Dunleavy 1996)). Citizens who are travelling can access the services they need from wherever they happen to be; they do not have to be at home. These are powerful reasons for moving even further down the road towards a virtual, 'de-territorialized' government.

But that is not the whole of the story. There are other aspects to these changes, including some that have received limited attention in either the academic literature or the popular media. One large question is whether the decline in 'real', local, face-to-face contacts with the public authorities influences the citizen's more general attitudes towards the reliability, trustworthiness, and, ultimately, legitimacy of government. After all, some public services invested considerable energies over the past two decades training their front-line staff to behave in customer-friendly, customer-focused ways. Presumably, if the front line now becomes a website, some at least of the value created by this more citizen-sensitive set of face-to-face behaviours will be lost. A more general reflection would be that non-verbal communication (most of which is lost in telephone or Internet interactions) is usually considered more powerful than words themselves in establishing a sense of trust or distrust (see, e.g., Argyle et al. 1970).

Preceding, and subsequently running alongside, this 'virtualization' of citizen–government relationships there has been—particularly in the Anglo-Saxon countries, but elsewhere too—a massive shift towards the provision of public services in contracted-out, or partnership forms (see, e.g., Koppell 2010; Osborne 2010; Pollitt and Bouckaert 2011). This means that even when Joe Public actually meets a service-provider face-to-face, the chances are that they may not be a state employee. If this 'hollow state' is put together with the 'virtual state', it is thus possible to argue that the average citizen's contacts with government have 'thinned out' very considerably within the space of just one generation. Yet very little thinking—academic or otherwise—seems to have been addressed to this issue.

Also, how far do the new arrangements create new 'winners' and 'losers'—some who find it easier to access what they need, and others who find it more difficult? Why is it that, despite all the new mobility and communication, poverty, crime, and ill health (among other things) still seem to be concentrated in very specific (and often quite small) locales? And why does the supply of public services frequently fail to match this pattern of localities? In a recent study, Allard demonstrates that, in the fragmented, contracted-out American welfare state, the provision of vital services 'varies substantially from place to place and neighborhood to neighborhood. High poverty areas have access to about half as many social services as low-poverty areas' (Allard 2009: 7). 'As anyone who provides services to low-income populations can attest, place matters', he writes. 'In this book I describe the safety net as out of reach or mismatched from need' (Allard 2009: p. x).

Against this, we must weigh the claims made by the techno-optimists to the effect that the Net will become a vehicle for new forms of political and community participation. We will subject such claims to closer scrutiny in later chapters, but for the moment we can just note this pungent observation by an early commentator on e-democracy:

Technological optimists think that computers will reverse some of this social atomisation, touting virtual experience and virtual community as ways for people to widen their horizons. But is it really sensible to suggest that the way to revitalize our community is to sit alone in our rooms, typing at our networked computers and filling our lives with virtual friends?

(Turkle 1995: 235)

This is not at all to argue that using the Net is valueless in civic or community terms. Rather it is to suggest that such activities *complement* more traditional forms of engagement and will rarely, by themselves, *substitute* for those older types of activity.

Further, on the side of the public services themselves, do the new ways and places of working affect the attitudes and behaviours of public servants? It is often said that the coming of high-tech warfare loosened certain constraints, in the sense that a bomber pilot over Nagasaki could release a weapon that, unseen to him, instantly killed tens of thousands of civilians below, whereas in earlier times face-to-face combat tended to induce a different relationship with 'the foe'. Does this also apply to our modern public services, beginning, perhaps as early as the 1960s, when the 'bobby' (police officer) left his 'beat' and climbed into his patrol car? And what of the increased mobility of citizens themselves, combined with their constant access to the international news media and computational and communication devices? Does the footloose character of much modern employment, and the international spread of more and more families, reduce the propensity for citizens to become involved in local government—because fewer and fewer of us can still call anywhere 'our town'? Do the changes in the communications media mean, for example, that parents lose respect for local schools because they read in the newspaper that the UK's PISA score (an international educational test for 15-year-olds) has fallen further behind those of Finland and South Korea? Do they become wary of their own primary-care providers after seeing TV reports of an incompetent (or downright murderous) doctor or nurse in another town (or even country)?

Of course, not all public services need to have face-to-face contact with their users (indeed, for reasons hinted at above, fewer do than previously). Others have always been in a sense 'remote' or at least impersonal—from street lighting to the marking of state examinations to the testing of air quality. Yet these too often exhibit interesting spatial and/or technological dimensions. The lighting of public spaces, for example, appears to be a significant factor in certain types of crime (and some parts of town are much less well lit than others). In England, public discontent over the late and irregular marking of school-leaving examinations intensified when it was revealed that the problem had arisen after the government had contracted out the marking to an American educational consultancy (Sutherland Inquiry 2008). The testing of air quality became less of a public monopoly and more challengeable by citizen action as technological improvements put simple, easily portable air-testing kits within reach of environmental activists and concerned residents.

This book will pose questions about the place and face of public services. Because this is an underexplored subject, what is launched here is an *exploration* rather than the delivery of a neat new theory. The exploration will yield some answers but also many further questions. Along the way it will derive and propose a working model of governments as multiple-limbed placemakers, which is intended to serve as a heuristic device for organizing what would otherwise be some rather disparate fragments of scholarly activity. Some familiar and some (probably) unfamiliar concepts and theories will be introduced—some borrowed from other disciplines and rarely applied within public management and policy-making. They will be used in the analysis of a range of empirical material, local, national and international, and implications will be drawn. International comparisons will also be presented.

1.2 The Plan of the Book: Inclusions, Omissions, Motivations

The book is intended to have a four-part trajectory:

1. First, I journey quickly round the topic to identify the key questions I mean to pursue, to give a taste of the scale and nature (of some) of its many empirical manifestations, and generally to set up some of the dynamic links between place, space, and technology (this chapter).

2. Second, I move to three more conceptual and theoretical chapters. These are designed to set up the necessary framework of concepts and theories before putting them to work with the chosen empirical material. Thus Chapter 2 assembles a menu of promising theories, models, and concepts from a variety of disciplines and fields. It reviews the answers theorists have given to basic questions about the relationships between place, space, time, technology, and organizations, and then draws out the implications of these for governments and public authorities. Chapter 3 builds on this review by developing the technological theme—showing in concrete terms the variety of ways in which changes of technology have consequences for places, but also for public-service staff, the distribution of tasks, company profits, public budgets, patterns of regulation, and even our deeper perceptions of time and space. Chapter 4 then draws the material of the previous two chapters together by constructing an integrative, heuristic model. The model incorporates those government actions (and inactions) that are particularly significant for placeshaping in respect of public services. To this model of *modalities* there is then added some patterns of typical *effects* (consequences). How do particular locations—or changes of location—influence both the providers and the users of public services?

3. The third part of the book takes the form of four empirical chapters (5, 6, 7, and 8) in which some of the concepts introduced in Chapters 2 and 3, together with the model of governments as placemakers set out in Chapter 4, are applied to a wide range of empirical material concerning public services, mostly by means of international comparisons.

4. The final part (Chapter 9) offers a reflective overview and a set of conclusions.

The book covers a lot of ground, and, because the scope is ambitiously framed, it is inevitable that all manner of important things are left out. The pattern of inclusions and omissions was partly determined strategically, but partly also by accidents of previous knowledge and practical convenience.

Most importantly, *this is a book about public services, not about everything to do with space and place*. Thus, for example, it would have been perfectly possible—and probably very valuable—to have had empirical chapters on the relationships between subnational governments, central governments, and international organizations such as the European Commission or the World Trade Organization (what is now sometimes referred to as 'multi-level governance'), but this did not seem a good moment to launch myself into yet another large new territory of specialist literature. Or, again, the book could have benefited from a learned analysis of the history and contemporary evolutions of urban and spatial planning, but—for much the same reasons—this was not an excursion I attempted to make. (Disappointed readers are invited to turn to Cullingworth and Nadin 1994, Pennington 2000, Brenner 2004, Booth et al. 2007, or Marcuse et al. 2009.) There are certainly a number of references to spatial planning in this book, including some to those works recommended above, but they are, to reiterate the earlier metaphor, magpie-like. I would certainly not claim that they added up to a balanced or synoptic treatment of the subject. Their purpose is narrower—to illuminate the specifically spatial aspects of public services.

1.3 Key Questions

Before too many more words flow, the reader deserves a preliminary summary of the focal questions for the book. These are three in number:

1. How and why does the provision of public services shape places?
2. Conversely, how do the characteristics of particular places influence how public services are provided?
3. How do the locations/sites of public-service provision influence citizens' wider attitudes towards, and engagements with, the state?

In each case the question will be posed in a dynamic rather than a static way. That is to say, in respect of (for example) the first question, I shall enquire how *changes* in the provision of public services over time alter the placeshaping effects of government actions. In each case, also, I will take a particular interest in the role played by *technological change* in the equation under scrutiny. Thus, for the third question, for example, I will look at how technological changes have shifted many of the sites at which citizens and public services interact.

The three questions are interrelated. They all refer to place, of course. Beyond that, however, they connect in a variety of ways, some of which are to be discovered, or hinted at, rather than confidently stated. For example, governments shape places, but then the places that are so formed subsequently feed into questions 2 and 3. They feed into question 2 by creating places, however remote or inconvenient, that then have to be 'serviced'. Thus Russian 'science cities', located by the Soviet regime in the vastnesses east of the Urals, still require electricity, postal services, transportation, and so on—even if much of their original purpose has disappeared (Thubron 1998). In the UK, military and technologically sensitive installations put in relatively out-of-the-way places such as the nuclear campus at Sellafield (previously Windscale, Cumbria) or the Royal Air Force base at Kinloss (Morayshire) become major employers in otherwise economically feeble regions. Schoolteachers have to be found for them. Post offices have to be kept open. Doctors have to be persuaded, by a variety of inducements, to set up local practices. Bus schedules have to include them. Their possible closures or rundowns are then no longer simply military or business decisions—they become political battlegrounds for all sorts of interests. Government placemaking also feeds into question 3, by a variety of mechanisms, both positive and negative. An 'abandoned' or 'placeless' place (Carmoma et al. 2010: 123–5) may help convince residents and passers-through that the public authorities either do not care or are impotent. A capital city, stuffed with important public buildings, galleries, monuments, and parks, may, conversely, impress the visiting citizen with the symbolism of the power and history of the state.

1.4 Empirical Choices

The logic of the empirical selections was geared to, first, the model of governments as placemakers, and, within that, specifically to the role(s) of governments' provision and regulation of public services. Subsidiary to this, I was also pragmatically drawn to topics where I could build on my previous comparative research projects and international networks. Thus Chapter 5 focuses on the most obvious and direct way in which governments affect places—by locating their own buildings and people in them (or by removing those buildings and people and placing them somewhere else). It is concerned with the idea of 'deconcentration'—the movement of staff and facilities out from the centre—and it compares the histories of such efforts in the UK and Ireland. Later in that chapter we examine two cases of what might be thought of as the most radical version of deconcentration—the movement of entire governments to fresh, 'greenfield' sites. Here Canberra and Brasília provide our examples (and reveal fascinating contrasts in terms of the political and analytical processes that led up to the founding of these two new capital cities, and that shaped their subsequent development). Chapters 6, 7, and 8 then focus on how changing technologies influence *where* activities are carried out, *what* those activities actually are, and *how* the public experiences them. Again, the approach is historical and internationally comparative. I chose three very basic public services—one from the welfare state (hospitals), one fundamental piece of state data-gathering (population registration), and one from the maintenance of law and order (the police). For each of these I surveyed the relevant literature but also conducted extensive empirical research in several European countries (details of this Technology, Place, and Task (TPT) research programme are given in the Appendix to this volume). The first of these services attempts to heal you when you are ill, the second registers you as a denizen and citizen, and the third protects you from harm and/or may deprive you of your civil liberties if you are considered to have transgressed the law. These three services were selected because, prima facie, I expected them to be very different. My anticipation was that population registration would turn out to be a slowly changing, traditional kind of service, firmly rooted in each locality and only gradually accepting of new technologies. By contrast I expected both the hospital service and the police to be technologically transformed services in which the significance of particular locations to their operations had probably diminished. Readers may refer to Chapters 6, 7, and 8 to discover how far these expectations were confirmed.

Earlier it was suggested that, in large part, this book was an exploration of a new territory (or, at least, new to most students of public policy and management—geographers, for instance, may regard some of this as old hat, although hopefully there will be other elements that they will find novel). In that spirit, one might describe the four empirical chapters not as anything like a comprehensive map of the territory, but as the cartographic records of four expeditions to the interior. They show what has happened along these particular routes and raise questions about whether the patterns, processes, and outcomes identified on these journeys are particular, or whether they can perhaps be found more widely, throughout the territory as a whole.

1.5 New Perspectives?

The book's title refers to 'new perspectives'. This claim has to be carefully presented. My belief is that the book is, to a worthwhile degree, 'new' in its examination of the interactions between, first, places, second, changing technologies, and, third, public services. It is also tolerably novel in insisting that these interactions are important enough to deserve to be a regular part of the mainstream public-management/public-policy curricula. However, it is definitely *not* new in recognizing the general importance of place in administration, or in studying the use of new technologies in government. The former has been recognized since the Domesday Book (1086), if not ancient Mesopotamia (where the first accounts, *c.*2500 BC, scored into clay tablets, seem to have been organized by localities). Much more recently, since the early 1990s, information technology has formed a main focus for several groups of public-administration scholars (see, e.g., Bellamy and Taylor 1998; Snellen and Van de Donk 1998), but their efforts have only recently begun to penetrate into the mainstream of the field— which is where I want to locate my own account (Pollitt 2011).

Finally, I need to justify my concentration on public services. Why are they important enough to deserve separate, book-length treatment? Why not, for example, simply offer a comprehensive analysis of spatial planning? One preliminary reason was again pragmatic—I lack the background to tackle such a huge subject, and others, far better equipped, seem already to have done a good job (see, e.g., Cullingworth and Nadin 1994; Brenner 2004; Booth et al. 2007). A deeper reason, however, is my conviction that public services are basic to the legitimacy and stability of modern government—a view that, again, opens up new perspectives. This argument deserves a few lines of its own.

A first, and obvious, point is that public services form the centre of gravity for governments, in terms of both expenditure and personnel. Social security, health care, and education are the biggest public spending programmes in most EU member states, and in the USA: 'evidence from studies of trends right across the OECD make it clear that the overall trend of social expenditure as a percentage of GDP has been modestly upwards since the early 1980s, and that global market pressures have played a negligible role compared to domestic factors in shaping cross national spending differences' (Castles 2007: 3). The average expenditures for twenty-six OECD member states, expressed as percentages of GDP in 2006, were 6.5 for health, 5.6 for education, and 15.2 for social protection.

Thus the average public spend on these three areas represented more than a quarter of these countries' entire economies (OECD 2009: 55). These pro-grammes were also the employers of the majority of public servants, includ-ing many of the most highly qualified and professionalized (doctors, teachers, nurses, and so on). In 2005 general government employment for the OECD twenty-six averaged almost 15 per cent of total employment, with France and the Nordic countries topping 20 per cent (OECD 2009: 67). The much-discussed remodelling of the welfare state since 1980, although very important in several ways, has not transformed these basic dimen-sions, although the fiscal crisis since 2008 has began to put these huge budgets and workforces under severe pressures. For the moment, however, one might say that these core public services are almost bound to have a major influence in shaping places, because they represent such a large slice of both employment and expenditure.

A second point is both more subtle and more debatable. Rhetorically, at least, our governors crave legitimacy, and to this end they constantly tell us that they are going to be more transparent, accountable, responsive, participative, efficient, and effective. The public services are central to this debate, for several reasons. They are the most visible and far-reaching part of the state, as far as most citizens are concerned. Few, if any, of us can manage without, or at least avoid, public services. We must register our births and deaths, pay our taxes, obey legitimate requests from police officers, educate our children, seek health care when we need it, and so on. (Even in the so-called private US health care system, since the 1960s more than 40 per cent of the money spent has come from the public purse.) For many people, whose direct interest in formal 'politics' may be negli-gible, the public services are the primary interface with government, and therefore a prime site at which attitudes and opinions concerning govern-ment are formed. The Australian Minister for Human Services, recently announcing a reform of service delivery, put it like this: 'The agencies within the Human Services portfolio—their staff, their shopfronts and their websites—are the face of government for many Australians. For many Australians these *are* "the Government"' (Bowen 2009: 4; emphasis in original). A series of careful surveys in Canada also shows that citizens' experiences with public services influence their overall view of government and the public sector (Institute for Citizen-Centred Service 2005). A series of comparative studies in Europe indicate that satisfaction with public services holds up much better than trust in government, and that 'providing superior public services may be a step towards achieving that trust and strengthening civil society' (Vigoda-Gadot et al. 2010: 296).

Citizen disillusionment with the school system or the police is, therefore, arguably, more harmful than disillusionment with the particular political leaders of the day. Following from this, although the evidence is patchy and occasionally contradictory, a case can be made to the effect that the principal welfare state services are a main influence on citizen perceptions of government and, ultimately therefore, on trust and legitimacy. Although citizen-initiated individual contacts with local public services tend to be 'routine' and 'invisible' (and therefore understudied), they are nevertheless 'a significant form of political behavior' (Sharp 1986: 3–5). Being treated fairly and impartially by teachers, doctors, nurses, police officers, and social workers is a central component of the 'quality' of government (Rothstein and Teorell 2008). A comparison of Israel and five European countries found that 'the legitimization of the democratic system, as reflected in citizens' trust in governance, may be highly dependent on the quality of policy outcomes and managerial success in implementing public initiatives wisely' (Vigoda-Gadot et al. 2010: 304). In the USA, a major study found that the degree of 'civic engagement' (often with local public services) was the biggest single long-run influence on citizen trust in government (Keele 2007: 251). Another—rather famous—study found that the degree of civic engagement varied enormously between different Italian regions, and that the best explanations for those differences called upon place-specific social and political processes stretching back over hundreds of years (Putnam 1993). Corruption and unfair treatment on the part of public officials played an important part in sustaining the low trust and low civic engagement that had long characterized southern regions such as Puglia and Basilicata. In principle this finding seems to be extendable to many other parts of the world that suffer from poor governance (Kaufmann et al. 2009).

Civic, or citizen, 'engagement' can, of course, take very many different forms. Millions seek health care, but only a small fraction of that number attend the public meetings of the hospital trust or look for active participation as non-executive directors, parent members of school governing bodies, or probation boards. Yet such is the scale of the public services that even this small, 'active' fraction adds up to quite a large number in absolute terms. Simmons et al. (2007: 459) suggest that, in the UK, almost half a million citizens serve as lay 'governors' of one kind or another.

Therefore, it may not be a coincidence that the alleged 'golden age' of citizen trust in government (roughly 1950–70) was also the age of welfare-state expansion. It was an era when politicians promised major new programmes that would benefit all citizens—better universal education, more comprehensive and accessible health-care services, decent state pensions, new forms of social care. (It should also be mentioned that it was an age with a much smaller and more deferential mass-media sector, so the hunt for 'scandals' and failures was far less intense.) Our biggest public services are, in a sense, the monuments of that era, and in most countries they remain enduringly popular. Despite a quarter century of politicians' attempts to curb social expenditure—cutting back on entitlements, increasing co-payments, contracting out many particular activities, and so on—the aggregate totals continue to rise. Dismantling the welfare state turns out to be a politically formidable task, as its numerous beneficiaries—and its many employees (often well-organized professionals)—defend it resourcefully. Faced with the challenge of making major cutbacks, most OECD politicians have, in the period since 1980, opted instead to increase public borrowing, or to cash in the post Cold War 'peace dividend' by cutting defence expenditure, or to reduce other elements of non-social 'core' expenditure (Castles 2007). At the time of writing it seems that the Global Financial Crisis (GFC) may have ushered in a new era in which previously 'unthinkable' cuts are forced onto the agenda—but it is too soon to be sure.

If this line of reasoning is substantively correct, then citizen interactions with public services do far more than just generating immediate levels of satisfaction or dissatisfaction with the particular services rendered. They also help to shape larger attitudes to government and public authority. And, if they do this, it matters where and how these interactions take place. Hence a book on public services, place, and technological change.

2

Theories of Place and Technology: A Review

Politics begins with place.

(Therborn 2006: 509)

A map of a geography is no more that geography—or that space—than a painting of a pipe is a pipe.

(Massey 2005: 106)

2.1 Place and Space

This heading should perhaps read 'Place and space *and time*', because time and space have long been (rightly) dealt with as intertwined issues. Thus in this brief introduction to thinking about place and space, we will frequently refer to time as well, in order to draw sometimes a contrast, sometimes a similarity. The role of time in public policy and management has been dealt with at greater length elsewhere (Pollitt 2008; Pollitt and Bouckaert 2009).

Let us begin from a simplistic position, though one shared by many people who are not at all simple. Let us say that *time* is quite an abstract process or flow—an always moving, always dynamic, procession of events—while *space*, by contrast, is an unchanging material dimension or surface—usually conceived of as a kind of three-dimensional container ('French airspace', 'the wide open spaces of the Canadian prairie'). Space has a scale—global, regional, local, and so on—but is nevertheless a neutral and abstract thing, just a dimension, running from very big to very small, from macro to micro, from north to south. Alongside this, we might also say that a *place* is a specific, concrete, and particular bit of space—like the playground at school or the Cocobana beach in Rio de Janeiro. Space in the abstract may be quite a neutral idea, but for each of us particular places will develop special meanings and 'affective' charges, either positive or negative (it was on this corner that I had my first kiss; that was the bar where I was robbed). 'What begins as undifferentiated space becomes place as we get to know it better and endow it with value' (Tuan 1977: 6; Therborn 2006: 517–20).

Since about 1970 almost every aspect of the above position has come under fire from geographers, sociologists, and philosophers (see, e.g., Parkes and Thrift 1980; Gregory and Urry 1985; Massey 1992, 2005; Brenner 2004; Houtum et al. 2005b; Thrift 2006). Some of the major 'moves' in this sustained critique are set out in the following paragraphs.

The recognition that neither time nor space is somehow 'a purely existing dimension' without and beyond us. On the contrary, different civilizations, groups, and even individuals can and do construct and use different versions of time and space and place. In short, each of these is 'socially constructed', although not all such constructions are equally influential (Houtum et al. 2005a: 4). Even the material landscape can be fundamentally reshaped—nowadays technology *can* move mountains (and create new islands), as anyone living in Hong Kong or the United Arab Emirates will be aware. We should also have in mind the example of the Netherlands, whose inhabitants, for almost 1,000 years, have been building dykes and reclaiming land from the sea. In 2000 about 27 per cent of its surface was below sea level, including the most densely populated parts of the country (70 per cent of the population), and much of this enormous engineering accomplishment is controlled by powerful public authorities. Elsewhere, large parts of, *inter alia*, Helsinki, Mexico City, Rio de Janeiro, and Tokyo have been built on reclaimed land. More importantly, however, even if the material landscape is 'natural' or at least relatively stable, the inhabitants can change the *meaning* of that landscape, the *uses* to which it is put, its *profitability* and *desirability*, and its *symbolic role* in relation to other landscapes or places. Thus, socially constructed, space itself soon begins to have real consequences for the people who live in it or depend on it. 'This broad position—that the social and the spatial are inseparable and that the spatial form of the social has causal effectivity—is now accepted increasingly widely, especially in geography and sociology...' (Massey 1992: 71).

This argument also has implications for the distinction between space and place. A number of writers have emphasized the distinction between space (abstract, geometric) and place (specific, loaded with meanings and memories). Some have also mapped this difference onto the binary 'global/local'. Further, some have 'taken sides', arguing that either time or space is the more important thing, and the other one is less so. (For a somewhat pompous and convoluted piece of philosophy favouring place over space, see Casey 1993.) Massey, however, insists that *both* space *and* place are composed of relationships, that the global is just as concrete as the local, and that dualistic thinking (space/place; global/local; abstract/concrete) is misleading and mistaken (Massey 2005: 183–7). 'My argument is not that place is not concrete, grounded, real, lived etc., etc. It is that space is too' (Massey 2005: 185).

It follows that spaces and places are not fixed, and neither are they neutral. Indeed, it is obvious that places are changing all the time. We go back to our birthplace and are surprised to find it has become a slum, or, alternatively, that what had been a slum has become a neat bourgeois enclave; that the ethnicity of the population has changed; that the corner shop has been demolished and replaced by a block of flats; that our old primary school has disappeared beneath a supermarket car park. All these changes are the results of power and money, flowing into or ebbing out of particular activities in particular neighbourhoods. The character of the place today is largely (but not entirely—see below) the result of the current intersections of these flows. There is nothing 'static' about this and nothing 'neutral' either. Much of it is the result of highly purposeful activity and decision-making by politicians, business people, workers, and perhaps even planners—a kind of 'power geometry' (Massey 1992: 81). In contemporary economic development policy-making, 'places are increasingly being reinterpreted, reimaged, designed, packaged, themed and marketed' (Knox 2005: 4). 'Space and time are no longer seen as a passive backdrop to human endeavour' (Thrift 2006: 551). Even outer space is not neutral: 'In particular, the area above the earth—the sky and the first layers of outer space—has histories of representation that are, to a significant degree, constructed around military and national intentions and interests. Space is believed to be a zone of freedom. But . . . that zone is structured by property relations and contests between states and corporations for dominance and wealth' (Kaplan 2006: 400).

By the same tokens, scale is neither neutral nor unchanging—it, too, is socially constructed. 'For, insofar as terms such as local, urban, regional, and so forth are used to demarcate purportedly separate territorial "islands" of social relations, they mask the profound imbrication of all scales' (Brenner 2004: 7). 'Spatial scales are neither simply a conceptual convenience nor simply given, but rather are socially generated in response to and often as solutions to specific social problems and contradictions' (Low and Smith 2006: 7).

Further, if space, place and scale are socially constructed, then it follows that the very way we think about them shifts from one set of social arrangements to another, and over time. Marxist theorists such as Lefebvre speak of the 'production of space', and argue that each different social system produces a different kind of space, thus: 'Capitalism and neocapitalism have produced abstract space, which includes the "world of commodities", its "logic" and its worldwide strategies, as well as the power of money and that of the political state. This space is founded on the vast network of banks, business centres and major productive entities, as also on motorways, airports and information lattices' (Lefebvre 1991: 53). Brenner (2004) argues that space and scale are both processes, and that these processes have recently undergone significant changes as states 'rescale'. Other geographers point out that the dominant concept of space as a kind of abstract three-dimensional container is, historically, a product of modern times, and requires modern techniques of measurement and geometry (Elden 2005). Camille (2000: 9) claims that 'there was no such thing as "space" for medieval people...our modern abstract notion of space...is a postmedieval category'. This line of analysis rather obviously leads to the question of whether all the political, technological, and social changes we see around us are ushering in a new conception of space and, if so, what is it like?

As noted above, *not even the underlying physical landscape—the 'material space'—is unchanging.* Quite apart from the normal long-term processes of erosion and sedimentation—and, more topically, climate change—other more rapid changes are constantly in progress. Even such famous 'natural' open spaces as the English Lake District are not static. Footpaths have to be closed off because of overuse by tourists, leading to erosion. The surface appearance of the hills changes quite suddenly when an epidemic of foot and mouth disease leads to the slaughter of many of the sheep that have hitherto cropped the grassy slopes. Roads must be improved and car parks enlarged to cope with the growing number of visitors. A large tourist industry—much of it located well outside the Lake District, and incorporating both public and private agencies and budgets—toils ceaselessly to promote these particular places and to emphasize their superiority to possible rival destinations. Many of the employees of this industry are probably not aware that at one time, before Wordsworth and the romantic poets, these hills were generally regarded by the polite classes as chaotic and 'wild' in a negative sense—certainly not the kind of place where a respectable family would want to spend their leisure time (if indeed they thought in terms of 'leisure time' and 'work', which is probably a more recent invention in our socially constructed view of time).

It should be noted that many of the key concepts in these debates are themselves 'contested' (Agnew et al. 2008). 'Space', 'territory', 'boundary', 'scale', and 'place' have all been gnawed over by many academics (see, e.g., Houtum et al. 2005b; Howitt 2008; Newman 2008; Paasi 2008; Staeheli 2008). With respect to 'place', for example, Staeheli (2008: 159) distinguishes five main conceptualizations:

1. place as physical location or site
2. place as cultural and/or social location
3. place as a context
4. place as constructed over time
5. place as process.

She declines to choose one as the 'best' definition, seeing some virtues, as well as difficulties, in each of them. It is clear, however, that she sees a particular usefulness in the fifth approach—place as a social process. She quotes Agnew (1987: 28) with approval: 'A key tenet is that the local social worlds of place (locale) *cannot* be understood apart from the objective macro-order of location and the subjective territorial identity of sense of place.'

In Chapter 5 we will examine the history of two national capitals: Brasília and Canberra. There it will be glaringly apparent that those particular places can be understood only in the context of wider national aspirations and power structures.

Given the centrality of the concept of place for this book, Staeheli's own conclusion (2008: 168) is also worth quoting:

Thus place may be mobilized in many ways in any given context. This is what makes it such a messy concept. Place include both subjective meanings and structural locations, and is a process as much as an outcome. Ideas about place, its meanings, and its importance are deeply ingrained in many people. It is this deeply held, and often conflicted, attachment to place that makes it such a powerful motivation for and shaper of political action, and an effective tool or strategy in political struggle.

This *process*—an unceasing series of dynamic interactions between the physical landscape, the built environment, and local, national, and international economic, social, and political forces—poses constant challenges for our focal concern: public services. Consider for a moment the situation of an English secondary school in a socio-economically disadvantaged locality. Compared with schools in more advantaged areas, it may take a much higher proportion of pupils without English as a mother tongue, or with limited language skills, with little possibility to do homework at home, with fewer books or computers at home, and with parents who, on average, interact far less often, less confidently, and less intensively with the school. Further, most of the teachers may choose to live outside the school catchment area, reducing informal contacts and networking between pupils, parents, and the teaching force. What is more, there can be direct effects on the school property—higher rates of crime and vandalism leading to a higher repair and security budget. How the school recruits (both pupils and staff) may also be significantly affected by how many other schools are near by, and what the 'pecking order' is between them (Lupton 2003). The wonders of the Internet may significantly help the school deliver its teaching—in a variety of ways—but it will not help much with most of the above problems of place. Parallel problems face many other public services, especially those that officially aspire to offer an equal service to all citizens, irrespective of location, such as the UK National Health Service, the postal service, or the police. Early in 2010 the news media were full of the horrific consequences of the Haiti earthquake. Over the first few crucial days it became clear that modern ICTs could rapidly bring the rest of the world endless images of the devastation, and could also be used to coordinate a large and complex international aid effort. What these new technologies could not do, however, was move ships to the island more quickly, remove the extreme congestion at Haiti's small airport, unblock the chaotic streets, or substitute for the lack of effective domestic emergency services. In each of these cases, 'old-fashioned' material or physical constraints delayed or prevented prompt emergency relief.

In one way the school example given above is a special case of a much more general question—*where do we put government activity?* Even if the advent of e-government has greatly increased the flexibility of placing bundles of government work, there are still staff and equipment that have to go somewhere. (And 'homeworking' still has to take place somewhere.) In some cases—such as schools, or the post offices mentioned in the previous chapter—facilities still need to be in close proximity to their users. In other cases—such as driving licences or passports—great geographical flexibility is now feasible. Either way, the selection of a location has effects. It brings employment and income to the chosen locality, impacting on local shops and on the use of local educational and leisure facilities (many of which will probably be provided by the local authority). When the UK Meteorological Office was moved from Bracknell to Exeter in 2003, it helped attract other investment to the city, strengthened the local university, contributed to the expansion of the airport, and gave impetus to a scheme for modernizing Exeter's school system (Lyons Review 2004: 36). By doing all these things, relocations create a set of interests that can be expected to fight against any downsizing or withdrawal of the facility in future. In short, the government could not avoid being a placeshaper, even if it wanted to.

A further, rather obvious and direct challenge for public services arises from the growing scale of migration, prompted by the rapidly shifting patterns of economic activity, by wars and welfare, and, most recently, by the effects of climate change. Not so long ago it might have seemed that almost everyone had their own, singular 'place'—somewhere they came from and where they were governed (both in the sense of having rights and of bearing legal obligations). Even criminals—like the police—had their own 'patch'. This was probably never more than an illusion—for example, in Tudor England some parishes were greatly discomforted by 'sturdy beggars' wandering in from other parts of the country, and through the late nineteenth and twentieth centuries the United States famously acted as a giant melting pot for people from many countries who were not 'visitors' but rather 'immigrants' and subsequently 'settlers'. Now, in the twenty-first century, we are again confronted with the governance problems that such large movements of people throw up. Criminals also operate internationally, and there is therefore a need for different national and local police authorities to cooperate, not just by sharing information but also by more and more fast-response operational cooperation. Refugees and economic migrants gathered at the Sangatte camp in north-west France because it was close to the Channel Tunnel and gave them a chance of smuggling themselves on board trains going to England. In 2001 Eurotunnel estimated that perhaps 200 people per night—most of them from the Sangatte camp—tried illegally to board the trains. The train operators intensified security procedures, but the crucial breakthrough came when the British government persuaded the French government to close the facility down. European tax authorities, faced with larger numbers of their nationals living, working, and earning in other countries, or in more than one country, are obliged cooperatively to develop new rules and procedures to lessen the scope for tax evasion.

Of course, public authorities are not concerned only with the placing of their own units and facilities. Usually they also have some kind of overall planning control—authority to constrain or promote the placemaking activities of other actors. Thus Raco (2003) offers the example of the development of a new city-centre shopping complex in Reading during the late

1990s. This development was a vital part of a wider urban regeneration strategy, and the Borough Council, as planning authority, was one of the key players in the complex negotiations around the design and implementation of the scheme (one similar in principle to many other such shopping and leisure redevelopments in English cities over the past few decades). Another important player was the Thames Valley Police, which gave detailed advice on how to avoid the creation of 'dead' or invisible spaces, how to design tunnels and underpasses, and a host of other issues. Both the police and the council worked in partnership with the commercial interests and the architects to ensure that the newly created spaces would be 'safe and seen to be safe' (Raco 2003: 1870).

Places, then, are anything but static or fixed. A travel writer, Paul Theroux, expressed it nicely:

If a place, after decades, is the same, or worse than before, it is almost shaming to behold. Like a prayer you regret has been answered, it exists as a mirror image of yourself, the traveler, who has to admit: I'm the same too, but aged—wearier, frailer, fractured, abused, weaker, shabbier, spookier.

(Theroux 2008: 261)

2.2 The 'Virtual'

Until now we have mainly been discussing 'real', 'material' physical space—national parks, schools, hospitals, and so on. However, it is also necessary to engage with the now considerable amount of writing about *virtual* spaces and places—not least 'cyberspace'. Many books and articles have been written about the 'virtual', and there is neither room nor justification for rehearsing the whole debate again here. Instead I will simply state how I intend to use the term/concept, a usage that, as far as I can tell, is reasonably mainstream/not excessively idiosyncratic.

A virtual world is one that is both removed from reality and simplified from reality. Virtualization involves abstraction and 'modularization'—that is, some parts of reality are represented in a simplified way, and others are not represented at all. At the same time, the virtual image or experience is usually apprehended with less than the full range of human senses—that is, it is reduced to a subset of those senses. Thus, when we converse with our business partners via videophone, we see a two-dimensional image of them, which we apprehend with our sight and our hearing. But we cannot touch them or smell them. The communication has been 'modularized' to certain aspects of sight and hearing.

The encounter with the world with and through technology is only partial when compared with the natural (through our body and senses) encounter with it... Our physical world is one of *reference*... In sharp contrast, *representation*, characterized by technology and virtuality, is an abstraction of the physical world modeled upon rules and regulation decided by the agents designing and implementing technology.

(Sørensen and Pica 2005: 130)

digital living will included less and less dependence on being in a specific place at a specific time, and the transmission of place itself will start to become possible. If I could really look out the electronic window of my living room in Boston and see the Alps, hear the cowbells and smell the (digital) manure in summer, in a way I am very much in Switzerland.

(Negroponte 1995: 165)

If we can smell the digital manure, or even feel the digital breeze, the picture in the electronic window may become more 'realistic', but it is still a *virtual* picture, still a representation of reality apprehended through a technological device capable of receiving and displaying coded messages concerning the visual, olfactory, aural (and so on) aspects of the original phenomena. As Sørensen and Pica suggest, virtuality therefore always invites questions about who has done the coding, and how. Who controls the virtual images with which we are presented, and what purposes are they likely to have?

In some of the relevant literature there is a tendency to portray virtualization as a recent process, and one exclusively concerned with digital technologies. A little thought should indicate that this is not so. Writing itself has always involved a degree of virtualization—my words in a letter or carved into a stone reach readers at times and places from which I myself am absent. They convey meanings 'modularized' into a series of two-dimensional symbols.

It is true, however, that the spread of digital technologies has hugely broadened and deepened this process. In many of our lives virtual interactions now loom larger (at least in terms of minutes per day) than 'real' interactions, and this contrasts with earlier forms of society: 'A locale was in premodern societies also a physical setting for interaction. The field, the homestead, the church and the market were the main contexts for social interactions of presence, of face-to-face interactions, which dominated social life' (Yakhlef 2009: 80). Yakhlef goes on to summarize (*inter alia*) the illustrative case of the introduction of digital signatures for French vets. Apparently French law required that farmers wishing to use certain medicines on their animals must obtain a signed prescription from a vet. Until recently, this meant that a real vet had to visit a (real) farm and write a (real) signature on a (real) piece of paper. Once digital signatures were allowed, however, animal food manufacturing companies who wanted to mix medicines in with their food products were able to appoint 'central vets' who did not need to visit farms but simply added their digital signatures to electronic documents:

With the digital signature, the transaction takes place in the virtual presence of the vet. Needless to emphasize the point that this presence in absence is not only mediated by the digital signature itself but also backed up by legislation and institutions enforcing and controlling the accurate use of digital signatures. Virtualization enlists the efforts of both writing and institutions.

(Yakhlef 2009: 92)

All this is of relevance to our theme, because it is clear that more and more of the citizen's interactions with the state are, in the above sense, virtual. This may, or may not, have large implications for what the citizens thinks of the state—an issue raised at the beginning of the book and one that will be pursued further later. Thus, for example, it could mean that the citizen feels less and less connected to the state, because of the absence of 'real' face-to-face meetings with state officials. If so, it could also mean that the citizen is more alienated and subjectively feels less part of any living, collective community. Some survey data indicated that US citizens were considerably more worried about e-government leading to increasing impersonality and difficulty in getting answers than were the US bureaucrats who were implementing it (Jae Moon and Welch 2005). This, in turn, could lead to greater reluctance to conform with state-legislated requirements and commitments, or to participate in public deliberation or decision-making. On the other hand, the citizen might think: 'Great—now I can do my tax/licensing/healthcare (etc.) business quickly, at any time of day or night, from wherever I can access the net—I like this modern, convenience-oriented state.' Or perhaps some citizens will think one thing and some the other, according to contextual factors?

One piece of research found that among regular American Internet users, more were satisfied or very satisfied with their online dealings with government than were satisfied with face-to-face dealings, *but* that, when one counted all Internet users *and* non-Internet users, the order of preference reversed—38 per cent preferred face-to-face while 25 per cent preferred the Internet (Reddick 2005: 50; see also Welch et al. 2005). Visitors to government websites were found, in the main, to be pleased with their experiences, and thought that government websites were no worse than the commercial counterparts (Thomas and Streib 2003). However, it also needs to be borne in mind that another study found that users of

23

government websites tended to value most highly rather different features from those they valued on business/commercial websites (Morgeson 2011a). Furthermore, citizens look for different things from different agencies, and their satisfaction with these agencies therefore rests on diverse bases—so they may well be prioritizing different aspects in an e-relationship, just as they have done in an 'actual' relationship (Morgeson 2011b). In the case of one agency, the move to e-government was associated with lower satisfaction, but in most cases e-government adoption did not seem to influence satisfaction one way or the other (Morgeson 2011b).

An early review of the evidence (which is accumulating all the time) leaned towards the conclusion that the early effects of Internet use were to reinforce citizens' existing habits (activists became activists on the Net too, but the Net did not recruit a lot of previously passive people suddenly to engage with public affairs (Norris 2001)). A later (autumn 2008) survey concluded:

Whether they take place on the internet or off, traditional political activities remain the domain of those with high levels of income and education. Contrary to the hopes of some advocates, the internet is not changing the socio-economic character of civic engagement in America.

(Smith et al. 2009: 3)

Generally, however, such questions have received relatively little attention from scholars thus far, and most of the American research on 'civic engagement' has referred to party political activity or the expression of political opinions, rather than administrative interactions with public officials.

Other American work found that visiting government websites had no discernible effect on citizen trust, but did tend to improve the citizen's perceptions of the effectiveness of government (West 2004). A later analysis indicated that there was no basis for the optimism of those who saw e-government as an e-panacea, and that adopting e-government systems did not, by itself, have any positive effect on either citizen satisfaction or any broader trust in government as a whole (Morgeson et al. 2011).

A further point is that individual citizens may shift their attitudes according to circumstances, or over time, as they become more accustomed to using the Internet for these purposes. Smith et al. (2009: 5) suggest that the use of social networking sites for forms of civic engagement may turn out to be less stratified by wealth and education, although at the time of their research this was no more than a hint or possibility. Another suggestion is that citizens prefer face-to-face dealings when they need to explain personal circumstances in order to claim a benefit, but for other kinds of transaction may prefer an impersonal screen. Belgian research suggests that those who already use the Internet for government transactions prefer this channel to either the telephone or the office counter, at least for straightforward transactions (Kerschot et al. 2006). Overall, therefore, the picture we have of the effects of a shift to e-government relationships between citizens and public agencies is patchy. On the one hand, there seems to be no evidence that e-government will suddenly transform most citizen attitudes in either a positive or a negative direction. On the other, there is already a good deal of evidence to indicate that many citizens both use and are reasonably satisfied with government websites. Most interesting, perhaps, are the finer-grained studies, now beginning to come though, which indicate considerable variety: that citizens look for different features according to the specific type of service or agency they are dealing with; that there may also be more general differences between what citizens most want from government websites as opposed to commercial ones; and that individual citizens both differ among themselves and develop their opinions and expectations over time.

In the realms of public policy and administration, 'virtuality' has probably received more attention on the providers' side rather than that of the user/citizen (Reddick 2005). There has been much tapping of keyboards about 'virtual organizations'. In one of the pioneering works on IT and public administration, Jane Fountain (2001: 25) had a good deal to say about 'virtual agencies':

As the state becomes increasingly networked through information systems, inter-agency arrangements, public–private partnerships, intergovernmental agreements that join federal, state, local, nonprofit, and private actors, and web-based services that link the websites of hundreds of organizations, we may speak of a virtual state. Virtuality is a function of the apparently seamless integration of disparate, jurisdictionally separate, often geographically dispersed parts.

She points out that joint portals and websites are also highly likely to lead to changes in notions of jurisdiction, accountability, and hierarchical command-and-control (see also Bekkers 2000). Even if a shared portal is at first only 'front office', it tends to prompt subsequent questions that eventually lead to changes in the various 'back offices'. She also argues that such developments directly affect space:

When information is digitized and shared, geographic distance becomes less relevant—in most cases irrelevant—to information flow, making possible geographically distributed partnerships, collaborative problem-solving, and highly coherent organization.

(Fountain 2001: 33)

25

So the virtual seems to have real effects: it can lead to changes in the jurisdictional boundaries, accountabilities, and collaborative arrangements of organizations. It can reach out to citizens who either live in remote locations or are immobilized for some reason. What is perhaps most interesting in Fountain's account, however, is the way in which some of her major propositions are paired with their opposites. For example, she points out that a shift from bureaucratic hierarchies to ICT-facilitated networks *could* reduce the weight of rules and regulations, or, alternatively, it *could* signal a shift to even more rules, but now covertly embedded in the software. Similarly, a shift from face-to-face to virtual interactions *could* increase citizen trust, or it *could* reduce it. In the next subsection we will have something to say about how these apparent contradictions can be conceptualized.

More generally, while it has often been remarked that the Internet has been produced by a process of spontaneous growth, beyond the reach of any government, it should also be pointed out that public organizations played a crucial role in its origins, and that states have taken an increasingly active role in its subsequent governance. Groups of American, government-funded scientists were central to the development of ARPANET, the precursor to the Internet (Castells 2001). Subsequently, 'once the strategic economic and political significance of the internet became clear to states in the late 1990s, efforts were made to assert what were perceived to be national interests of various kinds in Internet communication' (Christou and Simpson 2009: 600). In particular, many states organized themselves to provide inputs to the system for governing Country Code Top Level Domains (ccTLDs)—the familiar suffixes to Internet addresses, such as '.uk', '.de', or '.fi'. More famously, the Chinese government pressed an agreement on the giant Net browser company, Google, that allowed the Chinese authorities to censor its citizens' access to material. Early in 2010 this agreement appeared to become unstuck, as Google publicly declared that 'we have decided we are no longer willing to continue censoring our results on google.cn' (Jacobs et al. 2010).

It is worth noting that the virtual has also expanded our notions of mobility. Previously mainly confined to the idea of physical movement from place to place, mobility has now grown some new meanings (see Pica et al. 2004 for discussion, and Kakihara and Sørensen 2002 for a more abstract treatment):

1. *Locational mobility*: the traditional sense of moving across space. Such movement may now be accompanied by a large range of mobile devices, such as mobile phones, computers, or cameras.

2. *Operational mobility*: using mobile communications devices to co-ordinate daily operations, such as police actions, work of staff within hospitals, political street protests, etc.

3. *Interactional mobility*: using mobile communications devices to achieve intense interactions with diverse people and data sources.

However, this is not pure, unalloyed gain. For example, 'the virtual environment has the potential to divert attention from the physical space of interaction as well as helping it' (Pica et al. 2004: 5). Thus, for example, the driver talking on her mobile phone may be more prone to road accidents, or the police officer at the scene of a crime may seem distant and unsympathetic to the victims of the crime if he is constantly talking on his communicator or checking his laptop.

One interesting aspect (which we shall return to in Chapters 5 and 7) is the effects that changing technologies have had on 'traditional', locational mobility. Obviously faster trains or planes, or better roads, make journeys quicker—and may encourage travellers to travel further. But there is another dimension to this, which is revealed as soon as one asks what travellers are actually doing during their journeys. In brief, new technologies have enabled the traveller both to undertake a wide range of work and to be constantly 'in touch' while in motion. Trains and airliners are nowadays full of people working on their computers and mobile phones, writing, reading, texting, checking, designing, and so on. Even cars may nowadays provide their drivers with a range of communicative and informational devices. Yet since the 1960s the transport economists' standard models have usually treated travelling time as *unproductive* (Lyons and Urry 2005). Indeed, in the cost–benefit analyses that are used to decide whether or not to make major transport infrastructural investments, the heaviest single weighting usually goes to 'savings in travel time' (as it was, for example, in the vast cost–benefit analysis used at the end of the 1960s to try to choose a site for the third London airport (Self 1975)). Thus travelling time is assumed to be equivalent to loss of production time, and is valued (negatively) as the loss of some estimate of average wages. Hence the shortening of the travelling time between A and B results in a large multiple, because all those saved minutes for all those thousands or millions of passengers is converted into new productive, 'working' time according to the prevailing assumptions about average wages. The burden of Lyons and Urry's article is that the whole of this calculative empire, and the government and private decisions that are based upon it, are increasingly unrealistic and out of touch with the technological conditions of contemporary travel.

As a footnote to this brief introduction to the virtual, it may be noted that even the virtual has its roots in particular places. Silicon Valley is a real valley (at least in part). The M4 computer corridor west of London lies along a real motorway (and a real railway line). More generally:

The Internet Age has been hailed as the end of geography. In fact, the Internet has a geography of its own, a geography made of networks and nodes that process information generated and managed from places...The resulting space of flows is a new form of space, characteristic of the Information Age, but it is not placeless: it links places by telecommunicated computer networks and computerized trans-portation systems. It redefines distance but does not cancel geography.

(Castells 2001: 207)

Castells goes on to summarize the geographical distribution of Internet users, Internet equipment manufacturers, and Internet content providers. All are highly unevenly distributed across the globe (although rapid change—particularly in the distribution of users—is quite possible). At the beginning of the twenty-first century, Africa, for example, was virtually (no pun intended) a desert on all three dimensions. Elsewhere, there are 'dense spatial concentrations of major companies and innovative start-ups, as well as ancilliary suppliers, located in a few technological nodes, usually in the periphery of large metropolitan areas...' (Castells 2001: 213). And, as for Internet content, 'provision is increasingly, and overwhelmingly, a metropolitan phenomenon' (Castells 2001: 220).

2.3 The Role of Technologies

If we are to control information technology rather than relinquishing control to fate, evolution, competition, determinism, cyberutopianism, a technocratic elite, or 'the Internet', it will be more important to understand the interplay of technology and institution through human action than to develop dramatic predictions of a future over which we are powerless.

(Fountain 2001: 17)

'Technology' is a large and plastic concept (and information technology is only one part of it). We could easily spend a lot of time probing its many definitions. That is not, however, the purpose of this book. I will therefore take a short cut by opting for a broad definition. This incorporates conceptual distinctions (and warnings) that suit both my general theoretical orientation and my present purposes in writing this book:

A distinction can be made between a *technical device*, conceived of as a material or immaterial artifact, and a *technology*, a concept which refers not just to a device in isolation but also to forms of knowledge, skill, diagrams, charts, calculations and energy which make its use possible.

(Barry 2001: 9; emphasis in original)

And:

The idea that a non-human device or instrument can somehow work autonomously of its multiple connections with other (human and non-human) elements (language, bodies, minds, desire, practical skills, traditions of use) is a fantasy.

(Barry 2001: 9)

Thus technologies are not just objects, divorced from human skills and relationships. Neither can technologies ever be entirely separated from politics or organizations (certainly not by handing them over to 'experts', although for other reasons that may be, at certain points, a sensible thing to do).

Having moved quickly past the definitional debate, we can go on to what is for present purpose the main issue—namely, so far as public services are concerned, *what is the relationship between technological change, place and space?*

There is, of course, a popular answer to this question—an answer that is even popular in many academic articles and books. It is, in essence, that *technological change, by enormously speeding up communications and computations, has shrunk both space and time, and made them less important.* One result is that the actual location—place—of things also becomes less consequential. Cairncross (1997), for example, wrote a book entitled *The Death of Distance: How the Communications Revolution will Change our Lives.* Such claims are usually followed by examples of how suitably equipped individuals can now access vast amounts of data, 24/7, by mobile communication devices, and can communicate in real time with one or many similarly equipped persons anywhere in the world (or, for that matter, in 'outer space'). I do not want to argue that this answer is wholly mistaken—in some senses it is obviously true—but I do wish to suggest that it is far too simple, for various reasons. Although sometimes it is quite a good description of what is happening/has happened, often it is not. The impact of technological change varies with the particular activities under consideration, the institutional context and culture, legal rules and financial

29

considerations, and many other factors. There is usually an interaction—not a one-way flow—between these factors, so that each leaves its mark and none is simply determined by or dependent upon any of the others.

The relevant literature exhibits a spectrum of theoretical positions, ranging from technological determinism (technological change drives organizational change) to a kind of cultural determinism (in which technologies have no independent force, but depend entirely on how they are interpreted in relation to local and current cultural norms and/or political priorities). Neither of these extremes seems tenable. Neither does some of the socio-technical systems literature—full of worthy but distant abstractions—appear to be particularly useful for the examination of concrete government policies (see, e.g., Geels 2004).

A first step, therefore, is to allow for an 'emergent' perspective in which 'the uses and consequences of information technology emerge unpredictably from complex social interactions' (Markus and Robey 1988: 588; Orlikowski and Barley 2001). A second step is to recognize that the very act of drawing a clear line between (on the one hand) 'technology' and (on the other) 'the organization' is highly artificial:

To say that a technology can be political is not to denounce it, or condemn it as a political instrument, or to say that its design reflects particular social or economic interests. Technology is not reducible to politics. Nor is to claim that technical devices and artefacts are 'social constructions' or are 'socially shaped': for the social is not something which exists independently of technology.

(Barry 2001: 9)

Thus we find, for example, that the leading network theorist, Castells, proposes that 'the internet is the technological basis for the organizational form of the Information Age: the network' (Castells 2001: 1). If this at first sounds as though it might be deterministic (that is, the existence of the Internet forces us to switch to network organizations), further reading of Castells shows that this is not his meaning at all. Indeed, he is quite explicit that 'the point of departure of this analysis is that people, institutions, companies and society at large, transform technology, any technology, by appropriating it, by modifying it, by experimenting with it' (Castells 2001: 4).

One implication of this position is that there are no easy formulae. Students looking for the big theory that fits all circumstances; popular academics competing for their places on the airport bookstands; textbook authors looking for the boxed half-page summary—all will be disappointed with this approach. For it rules out the generic, global generalizations and the simple arrow diagrams. It admits that 'making clear distinctions between the technical and the social is always problematic, because each has elements of the other embedded within it' (Sahay 1997: 235). Many case studies of particular technologies have shown how complex and indeterminate the interactions between the technical, the cultural, and the organizational frequently are (for example, for the police, see Chan 2001). Both technologies and institutional/organizational arrangements 'function...as dependent and independent variables' (Fountain 2001: 12). Exactly the same technology can have very different results when introduced to different social contexts, while, equally, a social context can be significantly changed by the introduction of a new technology, whether it is teenage dating behaviour after the introduction of the mobile phone-with-camera, or the disappearance of 'the registry' (the physical home of paper-based files) as the cornerstone of daily divisional/directorate life in government ministries. In the latter case (the move from paper files to electronic databases), certain accompanying organizational and political changes *may* help to produce a better-informed, faster-learning organization. But, equally, it *may* lead to an actual deterioration, rather than an improvement, in the ability of government ministries to document, recall, and analyse their past actions (Pollitt 2009a). There is no deterministic relationship.

There is, however, a further, crucial element, and that is human initiative, creativity, and leadership. Even when a context is favourable for a given mechanism, successful technological change will still require some kind of leadership or, at least, sensible stewardship. This is the 'human action' mentioned in the quotation at the head of this subsection from Jane Fountain. Bad management can mess up even a promising set of circumstances, and, occasionally, good management may achieve something against the contextual odds. Like all actions, these policy and management skills are practised in particular contexts, of which place is often a significant component (Therborn 2006: 520–5). The successful politician or manager is 'in the right place at the right time'.

This has been a brutally brief introduction to a huge topic. In the following chapter we will be able to spell out the effects of technological change on public services in a rather more systematic and extended way.

31

2.4 The Literature on Spatial Planning and Urban Studies

Sections 2.1–2.3 have mainly concentrated on rather general theories concerning space and place and technological change writ large. There is, however, a more specialized, often more pragmatic, and not infrequently more prescriptive literature that is explicitly concerned with spatial planning. It should be of particular relevance to our public services theme, because it usually places the actions of public authorities at its focal point. Spatial planning and urban studies boast a very extensive literature, in many countries, which can only be very superficially and selectively reviewed here.

In the UK, at least, spatial planning had its origins in circumstances that intimately implicated public services. The Industrial Revolution had spawned rapid and largely ungoverned urban growth. This 'eventually resulted in an appreciation of the necessity for interfering with market forces and private property rights in the interest of social well-being. The nineteenth century public health legislation was directed at the creation of adequate sanitary conditions' (Cullingworth and Nadin 1994: 1). The rapid spread of disease originating from the new slums threatened not only the consciences but also the health and the pocket books of the new industrial bourgeoisie. The broad answer appeared to be that these fetid localities required public regulation. 'Town planning' was born.

In other countries spatial planning emerged along different lines and at different periods. (In the mid- and late nineteenth century rather few countries suffered anything like the huge urban concentrations of poverty that disfigured the UK as the first country to undergo full industrialization.) A recent Anglo-French comparison, for example, illustrated the fundamental and enduring differences that stemmed from different legal systems, different conceptions of the respective roles of central and local authorities, and different systems for financing development (Booth et al. 2007). The very titles of the subject differed, 'town and country planning' being a specifically UK discourse, which did not translate easily into other languages (the French *aménagement du territoire* being similarly language-bound (Breuillard and Fraser 2007)). Until recently, although academics occasionally made international comparisons, in the world of practice such national differences continued to reproduce themselves from generation to generation. Now, however, there has begun to be some signs of international initiatives, such as the EU's European Spatial Development

Perspective (Sykes and Motte 2007), though the impact of these can easily be exaggerated.

Whatever the local laws and language, in most countries such planning 'is at its core the intervention of the public interest in the private interests of landowners to control how that land should be used' (Breuillard and Fraser 2007: 2). Or again: 'Planning as a sphere of activity thus finds itself at a crucial interface between public and private action and of necessity represents an "interference" in interests in, and rights to, private property' (Galey and Booth 2007: 34). One would imagine, therefore, that the subject would be absolutely central to this book's focus on the spatial aspects of public services. Alas, often it is not. It does concern the permitted uses of particular places, and, more ambitiously, it sometimes encompasses broad spatial strategies for whole regions or countries. However, it has tended to focus mainly—but narrowly—on specific proposals to develop specific sites, and the rules governing their acceptance and rejection (for example, the huge amount of writing about 'development control' in the UK). Seldom has it taken a broader view, encompassing the public services as whole, and their multifarious impacts on places. Even the planning of public transport—a service one might have thought to have a stunningly obvious relevance to land-use planning—has usually been considered separately, and has sported its own procedures, organizations, and lore (for a brief history, see Cullingworth and Nadin 1994: ch. 10). In other countries, transport planning may have been rather more closely integrated with land use (for France, see Harman et al. 2007), but everywhere the close alignment of these two has proven problematic. As for other public services—health care, education, the police, social services, defence—they feature only rarely in the spatial planning literature (honourable exceptions include Pinch 1985 and Allard 2009). In a passive way, the siting or resiting of individual facilities are usually subject to local planning controls, but the active or strategic planning of their locations so that they might as a set contribute in some systematic way to wider development or land-use goals seems rare. Most of these services have their own spatial planning procedures and routines—hospitals are sited in relation to other hospitals and schools in relation to other schools rather than in relation to any more unified vision of the spatial disposition of the whole suite of public services and their integration with a wider plan for spatial development.

Despite the paucity of its horizontal linkages with other public services, both the theory and the practice of spatial planning do illustrate a number of key considerations with wider relevance to the governance of place and space. The first of these is the great difficulty public authorities have in controlling and channelling private developers. The second is the almost equal difficulty the various public authorities have in coordinating their own goals, rules, and decisions (we will have more to say about this in Chapter 4). The third is that here, too, shifts in technology can have profound effects on assumptions, plans, and the relative attractiveness of different locations. We will now briefly consider each of these.

In the UK, at least, much of the story that is usually told of the evolution of post-war town and country planning is a tale of serial, progressive disappointment with the ability of the planning authorities to control private-sector development. The 1947 Town and Country Planning Act is universally acknowledged as a landmark, making almost all development for the first time subject to planning permission. It looked like a comprehensive reform, one that benefited from the experience of the wartime emergency and that addressed the weak and fragmentary system that had prevailed between the world wars. The broad framework lasted a very long time (and is to a degree still with us). From 1979, however, the Conservative government sought to 'release enterprise' and 'lift the burden (of planning)'. By the mid-1990s the standard text on town and country planning could observe that:

Much private sector development is now 'driven more by investment demand and suppliers' decisions than by final user demand—and even less by any sort of final user needs' [Edwards 1990: 175]. This widening gap between land-use development and 'needs' throws considerable doubt on the adequacy of a planning system which is based on the assumption that land uses can be predicted and appropriate amounts of land 'allocated' for specific types of use.

(Cullingworth and Nadin 1994: 19)

Fifteen years later, an American professor who had spent her whole adult life working for social justice in the city bemoaned: 'Now, the emphasis on economic competitiveness that tops every city's list of objectives causes planning to give priority to growth at the expense of all other values...' (Fainstein 2009: 19). We will hear more about the forces of mobile private capital, and the challenge they represent for public interest-oriented spatial planning in a short while.

The second theme is almost equally pervasive. It is that spatial planning powers are divided between different organizations at different levels, and that these commonly find it rather difficult to coordinate their actions. It is not only that transport tends (forgive the pun) to go down its own track; it is also that, even within the narrower world of land-use planning itself, fragmented authority is the order of the day. In France (which is often credited with having a somewhat more integrated system than the UK), the fragmentation is between large numbers of small communes (which are nonetheless principal players in planning matters), whereas in the UK it is more likely to be a clash of interests between the local authority and the ministry, or between the Countryside Commission or English Heritage, the local authority and, perhaps, an Urban Development Corporation, or a local community development project (Booth et al. 2007; Baldersheim and Rose 2010). (The names of such bodies have changed constantly over the past few decades, but the existence of friction has not.) The underlying problem, of course, is that the state executive, far from being merely a 'committee for managing the common affairs of the whole bourgeoisie' (as Marx had it in the *Communist Manifesto*) is actually a disparate collection of organizations and cadres, embodying an equally diverse range of goals and interests. 'The bureaucracy' is not singular, it is multiple, as every public administration student knows.

The third point brings us back to the influence of changing technologies. A long view makes this very obvious—for example, in the link between urban sprawl, on the one hand, and, on the other, the growth of motor-car ownership and/or urban transport systems like the London tube or the Paris metro. It does not have to be a new technology, such as the motor car, but simply the development of an existing technology, such as the steam-driven, steel-built ship. In the twenty-first century, London, Liverpool, Rotterdam, and a number of other cities display derelict or redeveloped docks near their centres. These docks are no longer used, partly because of shifts in the types of maritime traffic, but partly also because ships have become so much bigger that the old city-centre docks are now too small and inaccessible. Some, however, have been profitably converted for use by a growing economic sector—leisure. So old docks become marinas and old dock warehouses become smart shops or apartments.

Alongside, and somewhat overlapping, the spatial planning literature, there is a rather different body of academic material, usually trading under the name of 'urban studies'. Where many spatial planning books and papers are quite close to public administration, at least in the sense that they focus on the detail of specific organizational structures and procedures, much of the work in urban studies has a more sociological and overtly theoretical flavour. Specific developments are explained in relation to broad—often international or even global—socio-economic trends. For example:

Globalization, like Taylorism and Fordism before it, is creating a new man [*sic*] and a new society, by transforming states, markets, labor processes, aesthetics, goods, habits, values, culture, social and individual subjectivity, and the production of space and environmental relationships.

(Maricato 2009: 194)

There is usually precious little discussion of actual planning procedures or regulations—the academic division of responsibilities with the town planners seems somewhat rigid. The urban studies community's publications appear to be dominated by a group of big 'critical-left' names, and, in so far as they analyse planning *per se*, it tends to be in fairly negative terms (planning as yet another instrument of capitalistic forces):

Planning powers (this zoned for commerce, that condemned for insalubrity), edicts to regulate behaviour ('no loitering here'), surveillance (video cameras on every corner), lop-sided service provision (clean streets here, garbage dumps there), and the desperate attempt to impose order, suppress crime and conflict, and bring regularity to daily life in the city—these are everywhere in evidence.

(Harvey and Potter 2009: 42)

One of the most ambitious and sophisticated examples of the genre is Brenner's *New State Spaces* (2004). Here the author offers a Marxian meta-narrative in which he identifies certain policies and processes as characterizing recent trends across Western Europe. From the 1930s to the 1970s, he argues, national policies expressed a form of 'spatial Keynesianism' in which it was government's job to rebalance uneven economic development across the whole of their territories, or at least to ameliorate such disparities. From the 1970s, however, a new 'post-Fordist' regime became dominant, in which the key idea was for government to help selected places to become competitive within an increasingly globalized economy. Thus:

The task of state spatial intervention [up to the 1970s] . . . was to mould the geography of capital investment into a more balanced, cohesive, and integrated locational pattern throughout the national territory. By contrast, with the rescaling of state space and the proliferation of urban locational policies during the post-1970s period, this project of national territorial equalization has been fundamentally inverted: *it is no longer capital that is to be moulded into the (territorially integrated) geography of state space, but state space that is to be moulded into the (territorially differentiated) geography of capital.*

(Brenner 2004: 16; emphasis in original)

This is an interesting and cogent analysis, whether or not the reader 'buys' the overarching Marxian framework. However, despite the claim that the book explores the major role of state institutions, at various scales, in mediating and regulating the interplay between capital investment patterns and the evolution of territorial inequalities (Brenner 2004: 14), very little attention is given to the major public services, to the pattern of their investments, or, for that matter, to any specific body of planning regulations and procedures. The differences between, say, the French and English systems of spatial planning, deemed 'radical' by Booth et al. (2007), pass beneath Brenner's notice. In short, this kind of urban studies analysis is a bit stratospheric, and, further, it shares the same half-blindness to public services that so often characterized its more traditional 'town planning' cousin. Its focus on the role of public authorities is mainly on regulatory bodies and not much at all on the main public-service investors and employers—education, health care, the police, and social security. They do receive brief mention, but only as players in the recent fashion for neighbourhood-based anti-exclusion policies. As one UK government report noted: 'While there is a wide body of research covering the role of the public sector in leading urban regeneration, there appears to be much less on the contribution made by specific relocations to regenerating run down or deprived areas' (Lyons Review 2004: 38).

It should also be said that it is certainly not necessary to subscribe to Marxian theories in order to reach the conclusion that Western governments have retreated from overall spatial planning with some egalitarian flavouring and moved towards policies that support particular, advantaged localities to develop as autonomous growth nodes. Roberts (2010: 75–95) tells a worrying story of how the USA, the UK, and the Netherlands (among others) gave extensive freedoms to their leading 'mainports' (harbours and airports) but how this often eventually resulted in congestion, significant environmental effects, and political controversy. In these cases, governments eventually discovered both that specific *places* were of crucial importance to the expanding global trade flows and that they could not afford to hand over the governance of these places to coalitions of technocratic managers and big business interests.

One final point about the urban studies/urban sociology literature that is particularly worthy of interest is that quite a few of its authors have engaged with the issue of 'public space'. While there has been much agonizing over the 'decline of the public realm' (Carmona et al. 2010: 141), there is, again, a curious partial sightedness concerning the role of public services. Many writers have focused on the police (and private security services) with respect to their new technologies and tactics for the surveillance and control of public streets and squares, but very few seem to have looked at what has been happening to perhaps the most obviously 'public' and intensely citizen-used spaces of all—our schools and hospitals and public offices. Instead, the emphasis has been on the way that (in the USA at least) 'from city parks to public streets, cable and network news shows to Internet blog sites, the clampdown on public space, in the name of enforcing public safety and homeland security, has been dramatic' (Low and Smith 2006: 1). The point for us to take from this branch of the literature is that there is definitely a connection—and a complex one—between 'public space' (however defined) and the 'public sphere' (the area of debate and contestation between civil society and the state apparatus). Low and Smith (2006: 3–6) regret that the development of academic debate concerning public space has for the main part proceeded separately from the development of academic debate concerning the public sphere. While sharing this regret, we add another: that, from the narrower perspective of this book, the role of public-service provision has been greatly understated in *both* literatures. We would like to know more about how the placing and processes of public-service provision (public space) influences citizens' perceptions of government and politics (public sphere). This is *not* to claim that the location of public services is always the most important influence and still less that it acts alone in some one-track way. But it is to argue that public services are frequently powerful placeshapers, and that their role in this regard has been largely ignored by most of the relevant academic literature.

2.5 A Meta-Theoretical Codicil

Some readers may be dissatisfied because, up to this point, there has been plentiful discussion of theory, but no avowment, or confession, of my own meta-theoretical stance. What paradigm am I espousing? What is my underlying ontology and epistemology? My first confession would be that I am somewhat resistant to the demand for such programmatic statements, since my experience is that the most common outcome is that discussion of the matter(s) at hand (in this case, place, technology, and public services) gets put to one side, while mighty battles rage about ultimately irresolvable philosophical profundities—or, at the very least, a chapter or more is consumed in the elaboration of roughly the same meta-theoretical framework that can already be found in a number of other works specifically devoted to these matters. That is why I have delayed until now and, even here, give treatment of the question only the status of a codicil.

My second confession is that my broad orientation could be described as that of a historical institutionalist critical realist. That is itself an ungainly mouthful, but I can think of no shorter but still tolerably accurate label. All I will do with it here is chew a little on the contents—the four words that make up the label. Thus I will try to say what general assumptions and propositions I adhere to, but I will *not* attempt to demonstrate that they are superior to all other possible assumptions and propositions.

Historical institutionalists (unsurprisingly) believe that temporal sequences, durations, paths, and cycles are important explanatory factors, and that institutions help to structure and constrain developments over time (Pollitt 2008: 40–9; Mahoney and Thelen 2010). Critical realists believe that hypothesis testing is not the main or most reliable route to understanding, and that a greater emphasis should be given to 'a relational conception of causality in which causal mechanisms are seen to operate in a highly contingent, contextualized, and non-deterministic manner' (Reed 2009: 435).

Most conventional history takes a narrative form. And later chapters of this book certainly contain some examples of this. It is reasonable to ask, therefore, what role(s) historical narratives play in our descriptions and explanations? First, perhaps, mention of a role they do *not* play. They are *not* intended to test some pre-formed hypothesis about place or technological change. In this, we go with Kay (2006: 63):

We reject here the notion that narratives should be conceived as 'testing' the model, on the grounds that to do so would inevitably render the narrative a 'just so' story where features of the world that are essential and causal in this context are ignored because they do not have, nor could they have, a place in the general model because of the irreducible complexity that characterizes policy processes.

On the other hand, we want go beyond any radical constructivist view that all we have to do is listen to the various stories from the actors involved in the events, place them side by side, and search (somehow) for their (multiple) meanings. We want a narrative to do more work than this, and readily admit that that means that we, as authors, are actively reshaping the evidence that comes from primary sources. We *are* trying to find explanations, and we are perfectly willing to use theories as and when they seem helpful in ordering and making sense of what we read and hear:

In historical narratives, theoretical models are used but they are local or contextual, and sometimes limited to one specific, temporally distinct event within the narrative. Theory is always subordinate to the evidence. The burden of the narrative is to weigh competing models, concepts or metaphors and show that one is the most appropriate in view of the evidence.

(Kay 2006: 612)

This means, of course, that such narratives often have loose ends, and that they seldom confirm or falsify in orthodox, binary fashion. Instead they are used as an analytic dialogue with the evidence, strengthening this interpretation a little and weakening that one. They present a synthesized assessment of the relative appropriateness of a series of explanations for *this* unique body of evidence rather than the (dis)confirmation of the applicability of a general hypothesis to a theoretical instance.

After 'historical', the second word in the title of our orientation is 'institutionalist'. There are, of course, many types of institutionalism, but ours has already been identified as being of the *historical* variety (Peters 1999; Pierre and Peters 2008; Mahoney and Thelen 2010). A useful general definition is that 'an institution is a relatively enduring collection of rules and organized practices that are relatively invariant in the face of turnover of individuals and relatively resilient to the idiosyncratic preferences and expectations of individuals and changing external circumstances' (March and Olsen 2006: 3).

Historical institutionalists typically stress a number of key insights. First, institutions, once set up, often continue to shape the way decisions are made and policies are formed for many years. At one end of the spectrum there can be quite strong 'path dependency', meaning that it is extremely hard for reformers to 'break' existing arrangements and move to a new set-up (Pollitt 2008: 40–51; Pollitt and Bouckaert 2009). However, historical institutionalists also offer examples of gradual change (Mahoney and Thelen 2010) and occasional radical change ('critical junctures' (Pollitt and Bouckaert 2009)). Overall, historical institutionalists have been prominent in stressing the forces for continuity and stability generated by institutionalization, and the complexity of change. In this they contrast themselves with some of the more 'gung ho' management writers who seem to see possibilities for 'transformation' and 'breakthrough' at every corner. Historical institutionalists take an evolutionary rather than a revolutionary stance (Peters 1999: 65). Third, historical institutionalists see a central role for ideas. If institutions are made up of rules, norms, and organizational practices, then most of their members, most of the time, follow a 'logic of appropriateness' (March and Olsen 1998; Pollitt et al. 2004: 47–66). And what is appropriate, in any given situation, is usually defined by a set of prevailing, or dominant ideas (for example, that corruption is normal, or that for-profit organizations are naturally more efficient than public organizations). When these ideas change, then institutions and policies change.

Institutions are thus social structures, but that does not imply that our analyses must be examples of structural determinism. Individual and group agency still play vital parts in explanation, but they usually do so within specific institutional contexts, which are themselves both constraining and enabling: 'Change is seen as the consequences (whether intended or unintended) of strategic action (whether intuitive or instrumental) filtered through perceptions (however informed or misinformed) of an institutional context that favours certain strategies, actors and perceptions over others' (Hay and Wincott 1998: 955).

Turning now to critical realism, critical realists hold that social structures and material factors have a 'real' (ontological) existence, and that they can play a part in causation. Yet at the same time they are to a degree—but not a radical degree—'social constructivists': 'while critical realists see interpretive methods as central to their analyses, they are also skeptical of those interpretive and hermeneutical approaches that assume that actors' perceptions or quoted reasons are the sole and a trustworthy source of analysis' (Kurki 2008: 170).

There is also an important difference from the 'orthodox', hypotheses-and-variables approach, 'because prediction is not necessary for causal accounts, nor are regularities a necessary or a sufficient condition of causation' (Kurki 2008: 169). Instead critical theorists usually work with a wider notion of causation: 'We can conceptualize causes as "constraining and enabling" rather than just as "pushing and pulling" and recognize that the social world is made up by the complex interaction of various different types of cause' (Kurki 2008: 240).

This plurality of types of cause is intended to produce a 'holistic' explanation: 'contra many reflectivists [radical constructivists] we have to recognize that rules, norms and discourses do not, on their own, provide holistic explanations' (Kurki 2008: 237). Equally, '"social (structural) positions" are not just "ideational understandings" that agents possess, but real material positions that carry material as well as formal "constraints and enablements"' (Kurki 2008: 229–30). So being a chief constable or a hospital chief executive is not just a question of how one is seen and understood. It also puts the incumbent in a position where he or she can issue orders, spend money, and launch concrete activities. These powers are, to a critical realist, causal, albeit relational—at least in the sense that they are embodied in specific relationships. The individuals who deploy these powers certainly have their own ideas, beliefs, and reasons. And the use of these powers may well have to be negotiated, just as the conditions under which other stakeholders regard the exercise of such powers as justified may be both complex and changeable. But they are powers—causal powers—nonetheless.

Kurki (2008: 210–34) goes back to Aristotle to find a typology that captures the variety of causes she believes characterize critical realist accounts. She finds four main categories:

- *Material causes*. Social structures are real and have real effects. Hospital chief executives have to stay within or close to their budget ceilings (or find a quite exceptional justification for not doing so), otherwise the institutional structure (governments, supervisory boards) will ensure that they are disciplined or removed. The advent of forensic DNA testing leads to old crimes being solved that could not previously be closed for lack of acceptable evidence—the changing technology, although by no means the 'sole' or 'final' cause, conditions what can be achieved at a given moment. As one chief constable said in interview, 'no cars were stolen in the nineteenth century'.

- *Formal causes*. Individuals are constrained and enabled by ideas, rules, norms, and discourses that surround and pre-exist them and that are difficult to escape or avoid. Many of these constraints are shaped or produced by organizations. Like material causes, they *condition* actors rather than actively bringing about specific effects. The fact that in 1925 the Australian government had embedded Walter Burley Griffin's plan for Canberra in a parliamentary regulation was one important influence in preserving that plan through to the main building effort, which took place only forty years later (see Chapter 5). The professional regulations concerning the minimum numbers of specialist staff with appropriate training who are required before a particular kind of surgical procedure can be carried out have exerted a significant influence on the restructuring and relocation of UK acute hospitals (see Chapter 6).

- *Efficient causes*. Efficient and final causes are the 'extrinsic' or 'active' types of cause. Efficient causes are the prime forces for change, the actions of agents such as voting, handcuffing a burglar, laying a foundation stone, or carrying an injured person to safety. However, 'efficient causes, and hence agency, must always be linked to the material form of causality in the sense that agents' movements and actions are taken within a material environment' (Kurki 2008: 225). Thus (say) doctors performing an operation to save a road accident victim may 'cause' the saving of that patient's life, but they are able to do so only because of the prior material existence of a purpose-built operating theatre with suitable equipment, supporting staff, and so on.

- *Final causes*. This is a more controversial category, which is not used by many critical realists (who, in effect, find the other three categories enough for an explanation). It comprises the intentions of the actors—the reasons why they do what they do. 'If we accept final causes we can ... give intentionality the fundamental role that it deserves in social explanation ... '—this is not to downgrade the other types of causality but to conceive a range of always mutually dependent processes that lead to an outcome (Kurki 2008: 226). One might say that the laying of the foundation stone (efficient cause—see above) came about because certain political leaders had a vision of a new capital city, and of their own popularity, indeed, immortality, if associated with the foundation. Thus the idea of a capital in the empty centre of Brazil was an important one long before Brazilia began to be built in 1956, but President Kubitchek was able to make it his own, and to marshall a whole series of material, formal, and efficient causes in order to get the new city built (see Chapter 5).

One does not have to follow precisely this typology to accept the general point that critical realism embraces a more catholic and diverse concept of causes than either the orthodox variables paradigm or the radical constructivists (who are often uncertain whether they have any time for 'causes' at all).

In another, influential formulation, Pawson and Tilley (1997) present critical realism in a slightly different, though complementary, way. They stress that realist explanations of policy outcomes depend on the interactions between specific mechanisms and particular contexts. Thus it is misguided just to look for mechanisms that have worked (such as neighbourhood policing or CCTV in car parks); mechanisms cannot be sensibly divorced from their contexts (which is a problem for the variables paradigm, which tends to divorce variables from their contexts). Furthermore, contexts are complex. Pawson and Tilley's analysis of mechanisms brings out a number of features that will already sound familiar to those who have read the earlier parts of this section:

we would expect 'program mechanisms' (i) to reflect the embeddedness of the program within the stratified nature of social reality; (ii) to take the form of propositions which will provide an account of how both macro and micro processes constitute the program; (iii) to demonstrate how program outputs follow from stakeholders' choices (reasoning) and their capacity (resources) to put these into practice.

(Pawson and Tilley 1997: 66)

In essence, therefore, the critical realist approach conceives of government actions as mechanisms (or processes) that will produce different outcomes

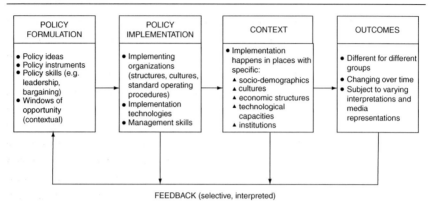

Figure 2.1   A critical realist conception of the policy process

depending on the contexts in which they are deployed—the well-known formula of MECHANISM + CONTEXT = OUTCOMES (Pawson and Tilley 1997: especially 63–78). This is the basic framework for the policy-making schema set out in Figure 2.1.

Note, first, that this figure is something of an oversimplification, since, in critical realist terms, *most policies will contain more than one mechanism* (for example, a regional development policy may involve a financial mechanism—loans or grants—an infrastructural mechanism—constructing new roads—and a communications mechanism, in the shape of an advertising campaign). The logic of realist analysis is that each mechanism will need to be assessed separately—that each will work better in some contexts than in others. Figure 2.1 also makes a distinction between policy formulation (the first box) and policy implementation (the second box). Although this distinction has a long and distinguished history, we readily acknowledge that in the real world implementation can often seem like an actual remake of the policy—it can be anything but a straightforward, mechanical practical spelling-out of the words and ideas in the officially formulated policy statements. Notice, too, that policy formulation is also subject to contextual factors. There is much political science writing about 'windows of opportunity'—those ephemeral moments when many factors, including chance elements such as scandals of accidents, combine to offer an opportunity for policy entrepreneurs to get a radical decision through (see, e.g., Kingdon 1995). The third box represents implementation contexts. These are made up of varying mixtures of socio-demographics, cultures, economic structures, technological capacities, and institutions, and, crucially for our present focus, they frequently vary with *place*. In the fourth box we note that outcomes change over time (policies not infrequently seem like failures at the beginning but later grow to fruition (Pollitt 2008)). There is also the point that different groups will notice different outcomes and/or will evaluate the same outcomes differently. A retired local resident in the redeveloped locality may notice the noise and pollution from the new road by her house. The local farmer may notice that he can get a grant to produce organically reared beef, and can use the road to get his cattle to market more quickly. Both effects may change over time—for example, if the new road becomes congested so that noise and pollution increase while travel time to the market begins to grow again. On the other hand, the financial incentives may be little used at first, and then they become better known, or wider economic circumstances change, so that the take-up rate accelerates. Any or all of these different effects may be seized upon by the media to tell stories of success or failure, and these stories will themselves feed back into the policy-making process.

It is crucial to see that *technology* figures not in just one but in all four boxes. The envisaged policy instruments (the first box) will inevitably involve one or more technologies—if payments are to be made or information is to be communicated or people are to be locked up, which technological instruments are to be considered for carrying out each of these actions? (Making payments to a large and dispersed workforce, for example, is technologically much simpler now than it was in the 1960s.) Also, the policy-makers will bargain and persuade using technologies themselves (websites, blogs, conference calls, SMS to potential supporters, and so on). In the second box the implementing organizations will use a variety of technologies to get the job done. These will interact with specific features of the context (the third box). In one context it will be appropriate to deliver letters to people's homes or offices, warning them of a coming change. In another it may be cheaper and more efficient to telephone them. But neither of these will work when one is dealing with the homeless, or with travellers, or with illegal immigrants who are hiding from the authorities. For these different contexts other communication technologies will have to be found. In one place (the third box) the police can patrol the streets singly, without special equipment or backup. In another the social/cultural make-up of the community will mean that police need to work in pairs and have greater protection. In one community population registrars can assume that local people will already understand—or will be informed in church—that their marriages have to be registered with the state authorities as well as in the church, but in another this assumption will be false, and registrars will have to take extra steps to make sure that marriages are properly registered. There are countless examples of place-based factors influencing how a service is organized, and we will be looking more closely at some of these in the following chapters. Finally, in the fourth box, some of the outcomes are themselves likely to take a technological form. When the police set radar speed traps (a new regulatory mechanism), some motorists buy devices that warn them when they come under radar scrutiny (new defensive mechanism). When organized criminals realize that the police can track their mobile phones, they will begin to communicate through skype, on the Net, because that is encrypted (TPT interview 21). When the vehicle tax on large cars ('gas guzzlers') is raised more than on other types of vehicle, some citizens will begin to take a closer interest in small cars, or hybrids, or whatever. Thus technology is, as indicated earlier, not a separate entity: it is embedded in the social (and political), and vice versa. Fountain (2001) draws a distinction between what she terms 'objective technologies' and 'enacted technologies'. The former represent the full potential of the particular technology and the latter what it actually gets used for. Thus, for example, 'objectively' my PC is capable of many, many things for which I actually never use it, including some that I don't even know how to use it for. The enacted PC is a much more limited, but socially embedded, thing than the objective PC.

We will have more to say about critical realism in Chapter 4.

2.6 The Implications for Public Policy and Administration

When one combines the kinds of empirical changes noted in Chapter 1 with the theoretical and conceptual apparatuses introduced in this chapter, it becomes apparent that there are multiple implications for the theory and the practice of public-service policy-making and management. Yet in many academic texts the traces of such implications are surprisingly faint. 'Through the 1980s and early 1990s, geographers bemoaned the general lack of attention given to place in political studies, or complained that place was understood to be static, fixed, almost a container' (Staeheli 2008: 164). A few very brief examples may indicate the extent of this (continuing) neglect. A casual sample of three mainline scholarly works on the politics and institutions of the European Union shows no indexed references whatsoever to either 'borders' or 'territory' (Richardson 2001; Peterson and Shackleton 2002; Wiener and Diez 2004). Equally, a reading of the four best-known recent handbooks in public administration/public management/public policy—*The Oxford Handbook of Public Management* (Ferlie et al. 2005), the Sage *Handbook of Public Administration* (Peters and Pierre 2003), *The Ashgate Research Companion to New Public Management* (Christensen and Lægreid 2011), and *The Oxford Handbook of Public Policy* (Moran et al. 2006)—reveals almost nothing dealing directly with spatial or locational issues. The Oxford volume on public management has one chapter (26 pages out of 789) that deals with decentralization, but even that does not directly address spatial issues. In the Sage handbook, none of the 49 chapters carries a title suggesting any strong concern with space or place. The Ashgate Research Companion carries 29 chapters and 505 pages, but none of the chapter headings suggests any connection to spatial issues. *The Oxford Handbook of Public Policy* has 44 chapters and 983 pages, but none of its headings is to do with space or place. None of the four handbook indexes—nor any of the three EU studies mentioned above—contains any entries at all for 'borders', 'geography', 'location', 'place', 'space', or 'spatial' (although that in Moran et al. does sport a single entry for 'localism'). The volume edited by Richardson does, however, contain a single one-paragraph reference to the concept of 'geographical spillover', which seems to mean not much more than when a state joins the EU this will have effects not only on the joinee, but on other states that are not members but whose patterns of trade, etc., may be influenced by the shift in status of the joinee.

Furthermore, there is a surprising dearth of public-administration texts dealing with actual, localized interactions between the citizenry and front-line public servants. To take just two examples, a recent major two-volume collection, *The State at Work* (Derlien and Peters 2008), says very little about this subject, concentrating instead on public-employment statistics, human resource management policies, and the like. The one chapter on 'social links' manages a few pages on public opinion polls, but that is mainly about public opinions relating to national institutions. Even a book with the promising title *Service in the Field: The World of Front-Line Public Servants* (Carroll and Siegel 1999) has a disappointingly small amount of systematic material on citizen views—it is overwhelmingly introspective, examining what front-line staff think of themselves, their offices, their bosses, and the constant stream of reorganizations they seem to be subjected to.

Yet, on the other hand, there is a strong, older tradition of political science writing about the state that accords a major role to territoriality. Take Mann, from a quarter of a century or so ago:

The means used by states are only a combination of these [i.e. economic, military and ideological powers], which are also the means of power used in all social relationships. However, the power of the state is irreducible in quite a different socio-spatial sense and organizational sense. Only a state is inherently centralized over a delimited territory over which is has authoritative power. Unlike economic, ideological or military groups in civil society, the state elite's resources radiate outwards from a centre but stop at defined territorial boundaries.

(Mann 1984: 123)

Furthermore: 'Logistical penetration of territory has increased exponentially over the last century and a half' (Mann 1984: 130).

This last comment usefully draws our attention to the fact that, in the developed world at least, modern governments can exercise surveillance and authority *throughout* their territories, unlike medieval governments or even contemporary governments in many developing countries. Technological development has, of course, played a central role in enabling this coverage.

This leads us directly to the issue of oversimplification, which may be an even bigger threat to understanding than the neglect referred to above. Oversimplification replaces silence with an easily remembered phrase, a killer concept, or an apparently powerful model. A currently popular example of this is the idea of a 'borderless world'—an idea Mann would never have accepted. According to this line of analysis, nation states are crumbling, and their borders are fading with them. Increasingly, networks of trade, networks of finance, networks of popular culture, and electronic networks of instant communication reach across these flimsy frontiers with ease. Thus, instead of being confined to a particular nationality, we all become denizens of the 'global village', moving around (either virtually, on the Internet, or actually, on airliners) with ease. Some academics have rather simplistically extracted from the work of Castells (1989) the idea that we are now inhabiting 'a space of flows', not a 'space of places'. We are also said to live in a time of 'deterritorialization', in which spatially bounded concepts are becoming steadily more and more feeble, politically and administratively.

This kind of thinking is seductive, because it convincingly identifies certain real and important trends, but nevertheless it misrepresents or exaggerates their place in the 'big picture'. 'From a geographer's point of view', says Newman (2008: 133) of the 'borderless world' concept, 'this argument is untenable'. 'For romanticisations of mobility are as dangerous to contemporary society as mythologisations of place' (Kaplan 2006: 395). Against the image of a 'borderless world', for example, consider the following: that there are currently many more states than there were either at the beginning or in the middle of the twentieth century; that there are there-fore many more national borders, and that 'there has probably never been a time when so many borderland regions worldwide have become such difficult or dangerous places to live in . . . ' (Paasi 2005: 26). Indeed, modern technologies enable states to project their virtual borders well beyond their physical borders:

In recent decades we have witnessed the development of a new type of migration regulation and border control in Europe, North America and Australia. In this system of controls the focus is less on the physical crossing of territorial borders and more on the process as a whole: from airline reservations, ticket-booking and visa applications to monitoring individuals after arriving in the country of destina-tion. The developing mode of border control encompasses a multiplication of borders, a multiplication of actors and a multiplication of data and technology.

(Tholen 2010: 259)

If the nation state is on its last legs—which is extremely doubtful—it certainly retains the ability to reach out to obstruct and punish. More likely, what we are witnessing is not so much some autonomous decline of borders, but a series of shifts in what borders *are* conceptually and functionally, combined with a set of politically driven and technologically facilitated changes in the processes of *how and where* borders are 'acted out'. The borderless world must seem a strange idea to those living close to the new Israeli defence barrier, or the high-tech obstacles and surveillance equipment installed along 2,700 kilometres of the US–Mexican border, or, indeed, even to those millions of air travellers who are currently obliged to surrender any containers of fluids that they may inadvertently have left in their hand luggage. Borders also continue to be strongly articulated *within* some states. In Northern Ireland the public authorities felt themselves driven to erect expensive 9-metre-high barriers down the middle of certain streets in West Belfast in order to insulate the local Protestant and Roman Catholic communities from each other (Murtagh 2002). The facts that they were sometimes painted in pastel shades and were called 'peacelines' did little to reduce the impression of extreme territoriality that had given rise to these structures. In short, the 'space of flows' does not replace the 'space of places'; rather it is superimposed upon it.

After this detour, we should return to the question of the implications of the foregoing for public policy and management. I will cut to the chase by quickly identifying nine main conclusions that can be drawn from the analysis:

- States are responsible for *territories*. Unless they are to be regarded as 'failed states', the normative expectation in the twenty-first century is still that the public authorities will at least maintain public order within that space. But the wealthy liberal democracies of Western Europe and North America are widely expected to do much more than that—to ensure the safety and welfare of all residents. Although the significance of bordered territories is undoubtedly changing, it remains great for most people and many purposes.

- Places have affects as well as effects. Symbolically and functionally they prompt emotional attachments and/or revulsions among most citizens. Some of these attachments may be purely personal but often they have political dimensions as well, both for present residents and for a diaspora (Staeheli 2008; Till 2008). Indeed, some places are sacred, in either a religious or a secular sense (or both). 'Modern nationalism has led to a remarkable sacrilization of national territory, with a great many places that have to be liberated or defended' (Therborn 2006: 519; see also Bin Wong 2006).

- Governments cannot avoid making spatial decisions and having profound spatial effects. Even if they were to back away from 'land-use planning' (as some urban studies academics claim they have), they would still have to decide where to locate their own activities—staff, buildings, and equipment. And in most cases they would still be called upon partly or wholly to finance (and in some cases actually to construct) crucial aspects of the physical infrastructure, especially railways, roads, and airports (look how hard the Conservative governments of the 1980s and 1990s struggled to avoid paying for the new high-speed rail link to the Channel Tunnel, and look how they eventually had to reach into the public purse). These decisions carry substantial social and economic consequences for the localities concerned.

- A substantial range of problems facing public-service providers are specifically and predominantly spatial in character, and, while modern ICTs can assist in the solution of some of these problems (for example, certain kinds of access), they can do little to resolve others (especially those that depend on 'hands-on' or 'face-to-face' services).

- These specifically spatial problems do change their form as social–technological networks change. Just as the telephone began to reduce isolation for some individuals a century ago, so Web-based health-advice systems or shopping software can secure more of the same for, say, some of the single, immobile elderly today. However, these new solutions are never implemented automatically. Their realization depends on a host of institutional, organizational, and cultural factors.

- Changing technologies also have direct impacts on where public services can be sited. Certain kinds of service (particularly the provision of information, the filling-in of forms, and the payment of taxes) can now be sited almost anywhere. Thanks to modern ICTs, the range of activities that are in this sense 'mobile' has increased, but it is still far from comprehensive, and is unlikely ever to become so (as we will see in some of our later empirical material).

- The 'virtualization' of public services may have several, simultaneous, but contradictory effects. On the one hand, it may systemize, standardize, and enlarge the amount of relevant information made available to service providers and service users alike. On the other, it may mean that provider staff gradually lose (or at any rate cannot use) their 'tacit' knowledge and fieldcraft, previously gained by regular direct dealings with the public. Depending on the type of service provided, it may also lead to lower—or higher—user trust and satisfaction.

- Electronic networking may likewise have a variety of effects. Its introduction is likely to be strongly shaped by the pre-existing pattern of organizations, stakeholders, and interests. And yet, once introduced, it is likely, over time, to generate shifts in organizational structures, operating practices, accountabilities, and, eventually, cultures.

- Functional logics increasingly combine with technological possibilities to enhance the political and managerial appeal of international co-operation to deal with increasing international flows. This goes far beyond the obvious cases of crime and terrorism to embrace education, health care, taxation, environmental regulation, and many other public functions.

Beyond these specific implications there are also more general, background processes that may be of large importance. I emphasize the conditional 'may', because this is not a well-researched field, and one must draw connections between a relatively small number of innovatory studies, carried out with various main purposes in mind. The processes I refer to are those in which *both* the supply of locally situated public services *and* the affective attachment of large segments of the population to specific localities are simultaneously reduced. Thus, in the most 'advanced' economies the working population is obliged for economic reasons to become more mobile, while more and more public services can be accessed from many places (including the Internet) rather than one particular place. On the one hand, people have to move where the jobs are—while the jobs move around more rapidly than ever before, and often include working 'unsocial hours' (Sennett 1998, 2005). Those who are left behind tend to be the elderly and the poverty-trapped long-term unemployed, living in their 'sink estates' or ghettoes. On the other hand (partly to cope with the higher levels of mobility), new technologies enable more services to be accessed in more places. All this may be relevant for our theme—not least because trust in government seems to be strongly related to participation in civic engagement (Keele 2007) and civic engagement is itself positively correlated with spending substantial periods in one locality (and is therefore in autonomous decline). Thus the elderly are disproportionately represented in many forms of civic engagement, partly because they are less mobile and they 'have the time'. Another less mobile group—the inhabitants of the sink estates—are not strong candidates for civic engagement because they frequently lack the skills, the resources, and the motives.

The argument can be extended even further. Aldrich's stimulating study of the siting of public 'bads' (nuclear power stations, airports, waste storage facilities) produced evidence that, in Japan, France, and the USA, governments systematically locate these controversial items in areas with low social capital—because these are less likely to generate effective, organized resistance:

Previous studies have shown that rapid population growth increases turnover... breaks apart community connections, and increases alienation... Rapid population changes that are due to events such as economic development are often associated with broad negative impacts, such as increases in crime... increases in gang population... and a breakdown in local networks. Areas where population levels have remained stable are more likely to have intact social networks that allow citizens to overcome collective action problems and to mobilize for such purposes as protesting unwanted facilities.

(Aldrich 2008: 30)

I do not wish to overdraw this picture, but it is possible here to discern a kind of scissors movement between the frequency of citizen engagement with local public services and the difficulty of government. A more mobile citizenry combines with more mobile modes of service delivery to 'delocalize' the main contacts citizens have with 'government'. Mobility goes up, civic engagement and trust go down. And, as they go down, the business of delivering services effectively becomes more difficult, because for many services (education, health care, the police) a modicum of public trust and what one might call stability of clientele are two central ingredients in effectiveness.

There are counter-arguments. Proponents of e-governance point out that mobility is now less of a bar to civic participation than ever before. The digital divide is said to be diminishing (Castells 2010: p. xxv). The fast-moving young executive can log on to blogs and pressure group/movement/collective action websites, and can make her voice heard more widely than ever before. Electronic petitions and public demonstrations can be and sometimes are organized with impressive speed. The decline in membership of the main political parties has been paralleled by an upsurge in single-issue group voluntary activity, much of it electronically facilitated. All this may well be the case, but we should also ask how far this type of activity is really equivalent to the local, face-to-face engagements of yesteryear. Our focus on the importance of place suggests that there may be some differences.

We will conclude the chapter on this speculative note, but this is not the last the reader will hear of these arguments. They will re-emerge regularly throughout the book. Now (Chapter 3) we must explore further the effects that changing technologies have on public services, making the theoretical speculations of this chapter a little more concrete. Once that is accomplished we will be in a position (Chapter 4) to put forward a synthesis of much of this material, advancing the model of governments as—inevitably, but often ineffectively—*placemakers*.

3

Placeshifts: Technologies and the Scale of Change

3.1 Introduction

Chapter 2 rather rapidly reviewed a number of theories and conceptual schemes concerning place, space, virtuality, and technology. This chapter follows directly on from that one. It offers a somewhat more systematic and more concrete picture of the kinds of effects that technological change can have on the public services. While this picture has placeshifts as its focal point, it is also intended to show how a range of other effects are closely related to locational issues. Placeshifts are an important consequence of some technological changes, but certainly not the only one.

While this chapter could be said to be ambitious in terms of its broad scope, at the same time it is modest in several other respects. It does not advance a positive theory. It does not claim to be a solution to any particular problem of government (or governance). It does not even suggest that it is startlingly original or new. It simply aspires to provide a way—one way, a useful way, but not the only way—of thinking about the relationship(s) between technological change and public-service organization. It suggests that these connections can be thought of as a limited number of principal relationships—each of them two-way—between technologies and various groups of actors. In doing this it builds upon a number of earlier approaches, particularly the pioneering work on the 'information polity' by Bellamy and Taylor (1998: 147–70).

Some such general framework seems both useful and necessary. Our major public services are being reshaped by technological change— and not only by the information and communications technologies (ICTs), which get most of the publicity. Yet the academic community in public administration has, with honourable exceptions, opted for a dangerous division of labour. The majority of scholars proceed with their usual business, making few, if any, references to technological change. Alongside them, a specialist minority has long focused on 'e-government' and 'e-governance' (see, e.g., Bellamy and Taylor 1998; Snellen and Van de Donk 1998; Bekkers and Homburg 2005). Some of these works already offer useful ideas for theoretical or conceptual frameworks. Unfortunately, however, to date, communications between this pioneering minority and the majority are somewhat meagre. Mainstream textbooks in public management and administration seldom give more than passing attention to technological change, often contenting themselves with a few paragraphs about the potential for Web-based provision of information and services. This 'ghetto-ization' of technological change has been noted by a number of observers (Lips and Schuppan 2009; Hood and Margetts 2010), and was described by Dunleavy et al. (2006: 9) as 'theoretical neglect'. In what follows I attempt to reconnect the 'ghetto' with some mainstream issues of public policy and administration. This general framework will then be utilized and exemplified in the 'empirical' chapters (Chapters 5–8).

3.2 The Range of Effects of Technological Change

We begin with the citizen's perspective and then move on to other key relationships. The categories are inductively derived from fifty-odd interviews carried out with senior decision-makers in the hospital service, the population registration services, and the police force in several countries— the services that will be analysed in Chapters 6–8. A description of this research can be found in the Appendix to this volume. The categories used here are therefore some of the principal dimensions that make sense to relatively senior officials who are involved in the implementation and application of new technologies in the public services. They talk about the kinds of effects mentioned here under roughly the kinds of headings used here. That is not to say that they would put them all together in precisely the way that is articulated here, and still less that they would use them as a basis for applying social-science theories, which is one of the possible uses of the proposed framework. However, this way of deriving categories does have the advantage that it facilitates discussion between practitioners and academics—it does not shut out or turn off practitioners in the way that some of the wordier theoretical classification systems can sometimes do. More theoretically sophisticated formulations are certainly possible, but these will serve for present purposes.

3.3 Locational Shifts from the Citizen's Perspective

In one adult lifetime the whereabouts of the UK government has shifted considerably. (I use 'government' loosely here—in the English fashion—to include central and local government and other major public services such as the National Health Service and the Post Office.) Whitehall is still Whitehall, but it has undergone at least three major 'deconcentration' exercises intended to shift thousands—tens of thousands—of civil servants out to 'the regions'. Thus, for example, the central records of birth, marriage, and death have moved from Somerset House in central London to Southport in north-west Lancashire, my car is licensed in Swansea (Wales), and my English currency is controlled by the Royal Mint at Llantrisant (also Wales), which moved there in 1968 after 900 years or so in London. Chapter 5 will examine the histories of deconcentration in the UK and Ireland.

Some public services, or parts of public services, have moved outside the country altogether. If I had been a student taking UK National Curriculum tests—SATs—in 2008, I might have been one of the 1.2 million for whom the important results arrived late or not at all. That would have been because, although the tests were national tests, and although I had taken them in a state school, the organization of the marking had been contracted out to a specialist American educational company—Educational Testing Services (ETS)—which a subsequent independent inquiry by Lord Sutherland found to carry the largest share of responsibility for the technical and logistical failures (Sutherland Inquiry 2008). ETS had declined to submit evidence to the inquiry, but there was a good deal of evidence available from other parties to show that the systems installed by ETS had been inadequately tested and were subject to cumulative failure. The government subsequently terminated the ETS contract.

Yet physical relocations and contracting out have not necessarily been the most striking place changes, at least from the perspective of an individual citizen. More significant has been the recent shift to the Internet for many if not most of the public agencies with which the average citizen has to deal. Thus my tax returns, driving licence application, passport renewal, and US visa application—all these and many more no longer require my physical presence in a public office anywhere at all. I can deal with it all from home, or from my office, or from my laptop on a train, or from an Internet café in the high street. (Well, not quite—in 2011 I still have to produce paper documentation for the passport service, but at least I can post it to them after downloading forms and advice.)

Of course the move to the Web has also had direct physical consequences for particular locations. In 2007 the UK Family Records Centre, near Sadler's Wells in London, was closed. It had been a pleasant facility, frequently busy with citizens happily tracing their family histories in the big old ledgers. However, the Office for National Statistics planned an online index of 250 million births, marriages, and deaths, and so judged that this expensive piece of real estate in central London was no longer needed for this purpose (the ledgers were sent off to a storehouse in Dorset). The only problem (apart from the loss of access to the paper records, which gave many users a thrill in itself) was that the closure preceded the availability of the online index. A spokeswoman for the Federation of Family History Societies said: 'It's deplorable. The removal of the paper records and the closure of these facilities is happening ahead of time, but nobody knows when the digital version will be available' (quoted in Kennedy 2007).

A larger-scale and more widely publicized set of closures has been that of small post offices (I use the example of the UK here, but there have also been large numbers of such closures in other countries). In 1979 there were more than 22,000 post offices. By early 2009 this number had been reduced to fewer than 12,000, and many still remained under threat. Behind this decline lay a number of factors, but one important one was the decline in postal volumes, as more and more communications and transactions shifted to the Internet or other media. Even if many post offices clearly lost money, closures on this scale attracted extensive public protest and continuing parliamentary interest and scrutiny (see, e.g., Business and Enterprise Committee 2009). It was frequently pointed out that local post offices had important social and community functions that did not register on their financial accounts. Particularly in rural areas, the closure of the post office sometimes also meant the closure of the last local shop, and the loss of a prime meeting place for local residents. The government committed itself to elaborate access criteria (National Audit Office 2009: 16), but, even so, the chances that, in my old age, I will be able to walk to my local post office will be less than those for my parents' generation. And, if I do manage to get there, I will encounter a different kind of environment from that which prevailed during my youth. Then one queued peacefully in order to receive services—the weighing of parcels, the sale of postage stamps, the payment of state pensions, the getting of various application forms for government services. It did not seem a particularly commercial environment. Now I line up alongside shelving that groans under the weight of DVDs, cookery books, toys, office equipment, and other consumables, while overhead a video screen plays mood music and advertises exotic holidays. This is another sense in which places have changed—many public places have become far more 'retail oriented'/commercially minded than hitherto, including not only post offices but museums, recreation centres, national parks, National Trust preserved buildings, and even some town halls. The typical National Trust country house now sells not only history (in books and DVDs) but also lunches and high teas, tableware, gardening equipment, models, posters, postcards, mementoes, and, of course, jam.

Overall, therefore, the locations of many—probably most—public services have shifted over the years. They have been rationalized, centralized, deconcentrated, co-located, virtualized, and so on. Different patterns of relocation have appeared in different sectors, but virtually all have been affected, in one way or another, by the Internet. What seemed like stability in the 1950s and 1960s has largely evaporated. In Chapters 5–8 we will examine and explain some of these place shifts in more detail.

3.4 Locational Shifts from the Public-Service Provider's Perspective

We began the section on the citizen's perspective by noting how many parts of government were making geographical, physical shifts. Such moves are supposed to achieve several objectives: to reduce costs (in the UK both buildings and staff are cheaper outside the south-east), to improve recruitment (again, certain types of staff are more easily recruited outside London), to boost employment in areas that suffer from relatively high unemployment, and also, it is sometimes claimed, to offer staff a higher 'quality of life'. These moves are crucially dependent on the quality of transportation and communication technologies—how long does the train/plane take to get to the capital for meetings with the minister; can one use videoconferencing to save time and travel; are there secure, encrypted links for message and data transfer? As soon as services can be provided mainly or exclusively online rather than face-to-face, there is a powerful fiscal logic to moving offices away from expensive locations and resiting them in cheaper accommodation. We shall look more closely at some vivid examples of this in Chapter 5.

Then there is the question of databases. Huge databases are required to support major public services such as social security or health care, but when these are computerized they can be sited almost anywhere. As indicated above, when 'family records' meant large paper ledgers, they needed to be somewhere central, but, once they can be put online, who knows where the electronic storage devices may be? When we come to examine the police (Chapter 8), we will look at, *inter alia*, the Schengen Information System (SIS), of which the UK law-enforcement agencies make regular use. The central computer system is in Strasbourg (France), with a backup near Salzburg (Austria). Further, the advent of mobile communication devices means that all sorts of activities that would once have required an office *somewhere* are no longer fixed in that way. As we shall see in Chapter 8, mobile data terminals in English police cars can immediately access a growing range of national databases, giving a single car quick access to much more information than a whole police station would have had a generation ago (Sørensen and Pica 2005). Principal among the data that are accessed is that from the Police National Computer (PNC). And the PNC is the UK contact point for the Schengen Information System.

Staying with the police for a moment, we can also observe that, thanks to burgeoning communications and surveillance technologies, the control room has become a more important location within the police service. In mid-2007 I was shown round the operations room and closed circuit television (CCTV) centre for the Brighton police force. Here, high up in a tower block in central Brighton, mainly civilian staff were able to watch many of Brighton's streets on CCTV, simultaneously communicating with foot and vehicle patrols to direct them to any observed incidents. Already, the screens incorporated automatic vehicle recognition software that signalled as soon as any vehicle with a registration plate logged on the Police National Computer as being of interest passed a camera. Under the overall direction of a chief superintendent, civilian staff sat in a semi-darkened room, in effect moving police officers around the town like pieces on a chess board. Additionally, in the event of a fight or assault, the control room had a visual record against which the statements and claims both of involved citizens and of the police themselves could be checked (various TPT interviews). Not that CCTV cameras always work or are necessarily well maintained. And not that would-be criminals are passive pawns in this new system of surveillance: as indicated earlier, they have developed a variety of ways of defeating the cameras, ranging from wearing hoods, to breaking the cameras (as any devotee of the wonderful Baltimore TV series *The Wire* will remember), to redirecting their activities to other parts of town, where the cameras do not pry (see also Nunn 2001).

One interesting feature of the general shift to Net-based services is that the actual physical location of many government offices has now virtually disappeared. 'Contact us' the websites say, but when a citizen hits that button he or she often gets, not a (postal) street address, but a telephone number and an email enquiries address. Postal correspondence, it seems, is actively discouraged, no doubt for reasons of cost and efficiency or, in some cases, security. Indeed, one extensively discussed (and to some extent practised) model for e-government has been the 'single portal'—a sole electronic window for the whole of government. In this arrangement the entire government (or large sections of it) appears as though it was a unity, a single agency. But this is a virtual agency, behind which the 'real' organizations are as multifarious as ever—and are certainly not in one place.

It is not only computers and the Internet that have affected the location of government activities. Take the invention of the humble home burglar alarm, for example. In 1996 an Audit Commission study of English and Welsh police forces noted:

The activation of an intruder alarm is treated as an immediate response call because it may mean that a crime is in progress, but the vast majority are in fact false alarms. This is a particular concern to police managers seeking to make the best use of their officers' time, and ACPO [Association of Chief Police Officers] recently reviewed its policy of attending alarms that repeatedly malfunction. In 1994 1.1 million activations of remote-signalling intruder alarms were checked by the police, typically by a double-crewed response unit. Some 92% of these activations—just over one million—were false alarms. It takes between 15 and 40 minutes to check a false alarm and thus the minimum opportunity cost to the police was in the region of 500,000 hours.

(Audit Commission 1996: 25)

This is one part—but only one small part—of the long-running story of 'bobbies on the beat' (police officers walking the streets). Public opinion surveys consistently show that a majority of the population place a high value on the visibility of police on patrol—uniforms walking past. However, for a whole variety of reasons—including distractions from malfunctioning intruder alarms—satisfying this public wish is problematic. First, in terms of catching criminals, bobbies on the beat is not a particularly effective way of deploying police resources. Second, as the police force itself has become more specialized, the number of police needed for these specialized duties (computer crime, anti-terrorist squads, child protection, management and planning, and so on) has grown. When the Audit Commission did its study in 1996, it estimated that, in a typical police force of 2,500 officers, only 125 constables would actually be on the street at any one time (Audit Commission 1996: 9–11). Official figures showed that by 2007–8 English police officers spent only 13.8 per cent of their time on patrol (Whitehead 2009: 1). The police are the main subject of Chapter 8.

In many countries, one highly significant shift has been the disappearance of hundreds of smaller hospitals. Three varieties of service-producer rationale—professional logic, financial logic, and technological logic—have intertwined to produce a concentration of acute services at large hospitals, each with a substantial local, regional, or national catchment area. Professional logic has demanded the co-location of a critical mass of different specialists on one site, so as to be able to provide an integrated, twenty-four-hour service. Financial logic has argued against the duplication of services in several smaller units, seeking economies of scale and higher intensities of use with respect to overhead services and high-cost medical equipment. Expensive new technologies such as MRI scanners or computer-controlled radiographic equipment are beyond small hospitals, both financially and in terms of the skilled teams needed to operate them. The overall result, both in England and in other European countries, has been the gradual attrition of many small hospitals. This shift has been supported by a powerful set of official arguments, but that has not prevented it from being, on the whole, deeply unpopular with the citizenry. Many bitter battles have been fought by local residents to save the smaller local facilities, although only a few of these rearguard actions, in the long run, seem to have been successful. Hospitals feature in Chapter 6.

3.5 Changing Technologies Change the Task

Sometimes a change in technology may alter the range of tasks that those providing the service are called upon to perform. This is trivially true in the case of, say, the arrival of police patrol cars in the 1960s, when, within a space of years, virtually all police officers had to learn how to drive, or in the 1980s and 1990s, when most public officials stopped sending their letters to the typing pool and started tapping keyboards themselves. However, it is also true in a more profound sense. Consider the advent of forensic DNA testing, photonics, and other forms of high-tech crime scene investigation. These transformed the tasks to be undertaken at the crime scene, and, to a significant extent, who was going to undertake them. Now the generalist uniformed police officer, or even CID officer, had to share the limelight with an array of specialists. One English chief constable explained to me in interview that he would no longer know what to do at a crime scene, beyond making the area secure (TPT interview 1).

Our earlier example of the post-office network also displays clear inter-actions between changing technologies and changing tasks. In the UK, most state pensions and benefits used to be handed out, in cash, at post offices. Over the years these payments both became electronic and mostly migrated to the commercial banks. Car tax discs were another source of post-office business, but most of these are now obtained online. The attempt to save the post-office network has included the development of new forms of financial service, and the substitution of mobile post offices for fixed buildings in some rural areas (National Audit Office 2009).

However, the picture is not simply that of new technologies 'raising the game' and requiring new breeds of expert. It is much more complicated than that:

The aggregation of tasks, in which operators are given more responsibilities ... using computer-based information processing and 'decision support tools', is often described as 'empowerment' or 'job enlargement' ... But the range of potential choices the 'empowered' operator can make is often limited by the software, thus embedding control formerly exercised by supervisors. Moreover, an operator's decisions are visible to those in charge, and the system may automatically report deviations from standard procedures.

(Fountain 2001: 37–8)

Thus, for example, Belgian police who consult certain national databases now know that their identities are recorded each time they access the data, and a new set of tasks has been created around monitoring the patterns of access of the many police officers using these sources. This can be a powerful tool for monitoring and accountability. In the event of subsequent enquiries, it can show if an investigating officer has failed to look up things he or she *should* have looked up. It can also show if officers have been accessing data that does *not* appear relevant to their responsibilities—possibly for personal or even corrupt motives (TPT interview 20).

Perhaps one of the most important aspects of task-changing is to be found in the role of ICTs in achieving 'joined-up government' and 'cross-cutting services' (6 2004). ICTs hold out the potential for various kinds of 'joining-up', ranging from putting a new joint face on related services (a single portal or gate on the Net) to the progressive linking up of back-office operations and databases (D. Brown 2007; Kernaghan 2007). One-stop shops or single windows/portals on the Web have been a growing trend in many countries, and seem to be popular with the citizens and firms that use them. Almost by definition, they create new tasks, because they require public servants to bring together, standardize, and coordinate activities that were previously separate. To borrow the jargon, they require boundary-spanning skills. We will discuss this further in Chapter 4.

3.6 Changing Technologies Change the Public Official

Since changing technologies change tasks, it is hardly surprising that they eventually change the public officials who perform those tasks. For example, as tasks become more complex, higher levels of education and training may be required of personnel—this would be true, for example, of police, nurses, and schoolteachers, if looked at over the past half century. Interestingly, in each case, as the police officer/nurse/teacher has become a more highly trained, expensive item, new, less-trained, cheaper staff have emerged as ancilliaries—Police Community Support Officers, Nursing Assistants, and Learning Support Assistants (these are the UK terms, but the trend is clearly visible in a number of other EU states). In parallel with this, each profession has also become more dependent on 'experts' from outside their cadre altogether. This is visible in medicine, with the burgeoning variety of para-medical specialists, but perhaps the most salient case is the police, who are increasingly reliant on a range of experts in the various diagnostic and surveillance technologies that they now routinely employ (several TPT interviews).

Technological change may also lead to changes in who is recruited to public-service jobs. When modern ICTs permit functions to be 'deconcentrated' from the capital to regional cities or even rural locations, one result is that the relocated function then draws on the local labour market, not the one in the capital. One senior English civil servant remarked on how much easier it was to recruit good-quality researchers from local universities after his division had been moved out of London in the early 1990s (TPT interview 15).

A further point is that certain types of public official who used to be very common have now virtually disappeared—the typist, the filing clerk, and even the conventional secretary. Typically only very senior staff now qualify for secretaries, and they are called 'executive assistants', or something like that, rather than secretaries, and they perform a changed mix of functions (among which making the tea/coffee may admittedly still be a core task).

3.7 Changing Technologies Change the Public-Service User

A perhaps more subtle point is that changing technologies have their effects on the users of public services as well as the providers. Most obviously, as discussed above, the ability to access the Internet is needed if a citizen is going to reach a wide range of public services, at least in a convenient way. Even if the 'digital divide' is said to be lessening (Castells 2010: p. xxv), it still exists, and means that some sections of the population are increasingly disadvantaged. Others, however, are positively advantaged. For example, those wholly or partly confined to their homes through sickness or disability no longer need to find other people to represent them in many of their dealings with central and local governments. They can do it themselves, from their home Internet connection. They are—to use a frequently abused term—'empowered'. So are those UK citizens who need urgent medical or nursing advice but who, for whatever reason, cannot get to a doctor's office, and instead access the very popular 'NHS Direct' website.

Less obviously, the rapid spread of remote surveillance devices, especially CCTV—both public and private—has changed the way many people feel about being in public spaces:

Emotionally there is a big difference between being looked at by someone directly and being looked at through the lens of a surveillance camera. The variety of feelings surveillance evokes is enormous: those being watched may feel guilty for no reason, embarrassed or uneasy, irritated or angry, or fearful; they may also feel secure and safe.

(Koskela 2000: 257)

Some react to remote surveillance technologies with actions intended to defeat them. These can range from simply wearing a hood or mask to buying devices that will warn their owners when and where they come under surveillance, or will even interfere with the normal working of the surveillance technology. As senior police in both Belgium and England pointed out, there is a never-ending technological race between the police and the criminals—with the expenditures of both sides benefiting those companies who develop the relevant technologies (several TPT interviews).

Beneath many specific examples lies a deeper theoretical debate. How far does use of the Internet actually change the level and/or type of 'civic engagement' undertaken by citizens (Norris 2001)? One 'cyberoptimist' position is that the amazing new possibilities of the Internet will encourage all sorts of people to mobilize and participate in public affairs in new ways. A more cybersceptic view is that 'online resources will be used primarily for reinforcement by those citizens who are already active and well-connected by traditional channels...' (Norris 2001: 218). In this scenario the Internet facilitates a deepening of the divide between the civically engaged and the civically excluded or disenchanted. Some evidence can be deployed on both sides of this argument, and it is also possible that there is a temporal sequence, with reinforcement being the predominant response in the early phases of e-government and more widespread and creative citizen involvement gradually accumulating as systems mature and the younger, Internet-savvy generations grow up. One recent piece of US research concluded that the main effects to date had been to reinforce pre-existing patterns of civic engagement, but that it was possible (but no more than that) that the recently ballooning social networking tools could come to support discussion of public affairs issues across a wider constituency than would previously have engaged with this agenda (Smith et al. 2009).

3.8 Changing Technologies Make Profits

There is a perhaps a tendency for some scholars to become so entranced with the technological possibilities and implications of new devices that they forget the fundamental importance of the *economics* of technological development. New technologies are big business. Advanced industrial states typically spend over 1 per cent of their GDPs on public-sector information technology alone (Dunleavy et al. 2006: 1). So one prominent actor in the dramas of change is usually the contractor or supplier. As Dunleavy et al. have shown, governments have become increasingly—sometimes dangerously—reliant on the big corporations of the global IT industry. Some of the stories of computer consultancies continuing to win large government contracts after being wholly or partially responsible for expensive failures make uncomfortable reading (Craig 2006; Dunleavy et al. 2006).

There are reasons why large-scale government IT contracting is especially difficult—and sometimes very profitable for the contractors (Borins et al. 2007: 29–30). To begin with, the systems are sometimes very large—social security or police or identity systems to cover whole populations, supporting millions of daily transactions. Then there is the tendency (regretted by some commentators) for governments to have 'special requirements', in terms of systems that must be able to be used by anyone, including the most unlearned, and that must incorporate very high standards of security and privacy. Such tailor-made systems are understandably more expensive than off-the shelf, standardized software. Size plus 'specialness' equals complexity, and projects of this kind are so complex that often only a few (usually multinational) companies can realistically bid for them. What is more, once such a project is underway, it is extraordinarily difficult to back out or change contractual horses. All these factors point towards the possibility of big money and substantial profits for the winning companies. Subsequently, when the contract has been won, it may be ferociously difficult for public authorities to change the supplier, even in the face of unsatisfactory service. In a number of cases, governments have persisted with particular companies even after embarrassingly bad performances, because both the costs and the technological risks of changing horses in midstream appeared so great.

3.9 Changing Technologies Make Savings

Governments, always under budgetary pressures, are often drawn to new technologies because they promise savings. 'Cheaper' is often just as important as 'faster' or 'better'. And it is true that there are many cases where a new technology enables savings to be made. Since time is often money, time savings also count here. If a new technology enables staff to complete a given task more quickly, the management can either do more tasks for the same money, or possibly reduce the size of the workforce (thereby making budget savings) without reducing the level of service provided. A recent example would be the Lantern system of mobile identification, tested experimentally by the English police. It enables on-foot police to check identification databases, and therefore avoid having to take suspects back to the station unnecessarily. On the trial, Lantern saved an average of 87 minutes per case in 50 per cent of the cases in which it was deployed (National Policing Improvement Agency, www.npia.police.uk (accessed January 2010)).

Unfortunately, there are two rather important qualifications to the expenditure-saving potential of new technologies. The first is that making savings later on usually requires investment now, up front. With some of the biggest systems (for example, in social security or health care) the initial investment is very large and the period before the innovations pay for themselves and begin to save is quite extended. These initial investments are particularly vulnerable in times of fiscal stress (Borins 2007). When ministries of finance are looking for cuts, expensive future projects, as yet unknown to most citizens, become natural targets. It is politically less painful to postpone or cancel a big computer project than to take existing benefits or programmes away from citizens.

The second qualification is that, even when the investments are made, money is not always saved; indeed, it may be lost. Internationally, the list of major government IT projects that have either failed to work or worked only after enormous, unforeseen budget increases is distressingly long (see, e.g., National Audit Office 2000; Craig 2006; Dunleavy et al. 2006: 72–3). There are many difficulties for governments in managing large-scale IT (or other technological) projects, including lack of internal expertise (the contractors pay higher salaries and are able to commandeer most of the real 'talent'), poorly designed contracts, constant changes of specification coming from the political or senior official level, and the hard-to-avoid risks of being locked into an extended piece of technological development where, after a certain point, it is more expensive to back out than to stay in, even with rising costs and underperforming technology.

3.10 Changing Technologies Collide with the Old Rules

As first-year students are usually taught, a prime characteristic of public-sector bureaucracies is that they are rule-following organizations. Some of those rules are embodied in hard law, some in 'soft law', and some are merely internal administrative procedures. Quite often, new technologies enable new ways of doing things, and the new ways of doing things fit very uncomfortably with the old rules. So the old rules have to be changed, and new rules substituted.

Record-keeping is a very basic requirement for public bureaucracies, and they commonly have many rules concerning what records count as 'official', how they are to be kept, and who is to have access to them. The advent of new communications technologies—especially email, SMS, and mobile phone conversations—have led to reconsiderations of these rules in many countries. In some cases, major controversies have arisen over the lack of order in record-keeping, due partly to the multiplication of media being used. Weighty reports have been produced proposing new rules for record-keeping in the digital age (Pollitt 2009a).

In the case of the police and security services, there have been and continue to be many detailed rule changes in many countries concerning police access to both computer systems and mobile phone records. 'Citizens do not want the police to be unable to listen to terrorists plotting an attack' (TPT interview 21). In Belgium it was the infamous

Dutroux paedophile case that was instrumental in persuading politicians to change the rules and allow the construction of a national criminal database.

A third case involves a double-layering of technological change, putting pressure on a long-standing rule. Since 1974 the Finnish Population Register has issued each newly born Finnish resident with a personal identity code (PIC). This was a centralized computerized system that was generally regarded as ahead of its time. The PIC now serves a variety of purposes, including social security and pension entitlements. One of the characters in the code indicates whether the individual is female (even number) or male (odd). Recently, however, advances in medical technology have made possible more sex changes. Apparently this has led to a small number of cases in which gender-reassigned citizens want their PICs changing—against previously existing rules that the PIC was an unchanging, lifelong identifier (TPT interview 13).

More generally, the creation of more and more Internet-based public services, one-stop shops, multi-organizational portals and gateways, and other kinds of 'joining up' inevitably leads to the questioning of pre-existing jurisdictional boundaries between organizations, and of traditional lines of accountability (Fountain 2001). New linkages and new interrelationships rub up against old rules defining organizational borders. The blurring and redefining of jurisdictional borderlines may not have attracted much public attention—it is often seen as a purely technical issue—but in fact it can easily have significant implications for the practice of 'separation of powers' or federalism or bureaucratic accountability (Bekkers 2000).

3.11 Changing Technologies Change Space and Time

Finally, we arrive at the proposition that technological change actually shifts our perceptions of space and time themselves. Our perceptions of time change for a number of reasons. Most obviously, in many (but not all) cases, we become accustomed to much *faster* service than in the pre-digital era. We tap in the details and expect to get a reply almost straight away—certainly for information requests, and often for more interactive contacts also. We also get used to being able to engage with government at any time of day or night—we are no longer confined to 'office hours', nine to five. This is one factor helping to blur the older dividing lines between 'working time' and 'leisure' or 'private' time. For many, but not all of us, the 'pace of life' seems to be speeding up, and the traditional divisions of the calendar are under pressure (Pollitt 2008: 59–63, 180–4). We may fill in our online tax form at home on Christmas afternoon, or sit in the office emailing our Christmas greetings with electronic cards, confident that, although we are sending them all round the world on 23 December, they will nevertheless arrive 'on time'.

As far as space is concerned, the most obvious recent change, as indicated earlier, is the reduced sense that the government is to be found in certain specific public buildings— the town hall for local government and White-hall for central government. More and more the government is to be found in cyberspace rather than material space. Beyond this, a number of other types of spatial shift are noticeable. There is the periodic concern with deconcentration—in the English case taking the form of getting govern-ment offices away from London and the south-east. The technological angle here is that such exercises have in principle been made much less difficult with the appearance of new communications technologies—first telephones, then high-speed trains and motorways, and, more recently, conference videophones and the Internet. Then there is a different kind of 'spreading out'—the allocation of public functions to contracted-out agen-cies, which may be wholly or partly publically owned, or private but non-profit, or private and for-profit, with a headquarters anywhere in the world (the case of Educational Testing Services, mentioned earlier). Again this has an important technological dimension—computerization and the Internet have made it far easier to package up and farm out blocks of work and data.

Such changes in basic perceptions of space and time may seem to be of primarily sociological or even philosophical interest. Yet there is a good deal of research to show that they also have consequences for the making, implementation, and evaluation of public programmes (Pollitt 2008).

3.12 Concluding Reflections

The foregoing framework suggests that the effects of changing technologies may usefully be analysed under a number of headings, where each heading concerns a particular set of relationships (see Table 3.1). The important point is that most technological change generates effects in most or all these 'compartments', and therefore to focus on only one or two of them may be to miss something important about the 'big picture'.

Such a framework is adaptable for several purposes. To begin with, its multi-relational focus promotes rounded, inclusive descriptions and discourages the dominance of any single perspective or single set of relationships. Beyond that, it may be deployed within a variety of theoretical approaches, and to

Table 3.1 A conceptual framework for analysing the effects of technological change on the public services

DIMENSION	COMMENT
Shifts in citizen's perspective	How do citizens look *at* new technologies?
Shifts in service provider's perspective	How do public-service staff look *at* new technologies?
Changes in tasks	New technologies = new kinds of work
Changes in public officials	New technologies often require new kinds of people
Changes in service users	New technologies may require new kinds of user
Changes in location of activities	Activities can be carried out in new places
Technological change and profit	Public-sector technological change is big business—some governments have poor records in managing this business
Technological change and savings	Often a primary motive—sometimes fulfilled, sometimes disappointed
Impacts on rules	New technologies put old rules under pressure
Shifts in perceptions of space and time	Deep changes in social perceptions may have widespread effects

address a range of theoretical questions. For example, if a researcher is interested in questions of power, the framework can be used to ask who (if anyone) is in the driving seat in relation to specific types of technological change—who shapes the nature of change and who benefits from it? Alternatively, if the researcher is more interested in organizational issues, the framework can be used to track what organizational changes are needed in order to implement a particular technological change, what new staff training may be required, how relations with service users may be affected, and so on. The framework can accommodate both cyberoptimist and cybersceptic theoretical orientations. It is also suitable for the consideration of how new technologies influence both the speed at which activities can be carried out and their locations. A third case would be a more sociological or philosophical enquiry into the ways in which technological changes gradually—or swiftly—altered our perceptions of our daily lives, by redefining our 'normal' boundaries of space and time. Again, it would be important for such a study to capture the variety of perspectives and relationships that are built into the proposed framework.

In sum, technological change is a pervasive influence on public management, and, within that, on the question of where things take place. It deserves a more central position in public policy and management scholarship. In the next chapter we will develop a more general model of governments as placemakers, incorporating many of the relationships identified above.

4

Governments as Placemakers: Modalities and Effects

4.1 Eight Modalities

Making government, for the moment at least, our central actor and focus, we can now bring together a considerable number of the theoretical and practical issues that have been identified in previous chapters. Most of these issues can be synthesized into a single perspective, which will henceforth be termed government as placemaker (GAP). GAP will be the perspective taken throughout the rest of this book, and will, *inter alia*, serve as a framework for the analysis and discussion of the four empirical chapters that follow this one.

Using GAP, one might envisage the role of the political executive and its administrative apparatus as follows. In historical terms the first move comes when a would-be government turns a space into a proto-place by setting boundaries to it and claiming the area within, above, and below those boundaries as its territory. (Even in the twenty-first century, only governments in exile lack an actual territory, and they always *claim* one.) Within those outer boundaries it usually sets internal boundaries between different subnational authorities of various kinds. Then, within these territories, it begins to shape particular places, using a wide range of modalities (policies, procedures, and actions). These range from symbolic designations (a national capital, a monument to war dead) through highly regulated spaces (a national or municipal park) to concrete constructions (a road here, a new town there) down to micro-scale pieces of 'public furniture' such as postboxes or road signs. It can also play an important role in creating or giving access to *virtual* spaces, both through its own websites and educational provision, and by directly providing or subsidizing the provision of broadband Internet connections in areas where, without government facilitation, the 'digital divide' would be likely to manifest itself

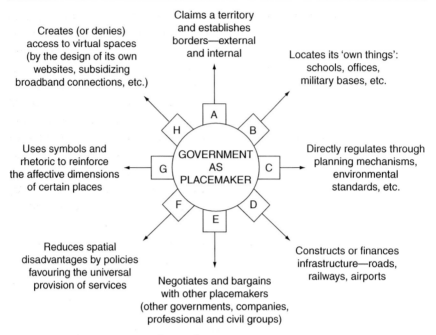

Figure 4.1 Government as placemaker

most severely. Some of the more obvious and frequent of these modalities are shown in Figure 4.1.

It is worth pausing for a few moments to review these modalities, beginning with the most direct and obvious, and moving towards the somewhat less concrete (though by no means necessarily less influential). We therefore begin with four very direct actions, A, B, C, and D.

A.   Government establishes a state by claiming jurisdiction within a bordered territory. This in itself usually entails the creation of specialist territorial public services—customs, border police, immigration, etc. These can vary greatly in mix and effectiveness, and much apparently depends on their degree of cooperation with their counterpart services on the other side of the border. Borders, in fact, 'are institutional zones, not lines of separation between states' (Gavrilis 2008: 5). Furthermore, the variability of 'grip' that states have on their borders is paralleled by uncertainties in their more central territories. In practice, as we have noted, government's actual, operational effectiveness within 'their' main territories is itself variable. In a European medieval state, it was usually low. In some contemporary states, such as Somalia, Colombia, or Mexico, it is also low. Furthermore, within their territories, governments usually divide up both policy-making and administration between subnational units of various kinds—units that are almost invariably defined by territorial boundaries (Paddison 1983: ch. 7; Harloe et al. 1990; Pickvance and Preteceille 1991). These subdivisions are almost always matters of some political contention, as any given configuration will offer advantage to some groups and disadvantage to others. A final point is that, outside the state altogether, governments may have quite an effective grip on certain territories that are *not* officially 'theirs'. Small ocean islands may host superpower military bases; one government may control a neighbouring power's only access to the sea; an economic giant may effectively dictate economic and trade policy to a small adjacent country, and so on.

B. Governments shape places by putting their own 'things' into them. They build town halls, air bases, government offices, social housing projects. Roosevelt's 'New Deal' in the USA was one of the most spectacular examples of this. Two New Deal agencies, the Public Works Administration (PWA) and the Works Progress Administration (WPA), created a huge slice of American physical infrastructure, much of which survives today. The PWA financed constructions in all but three of the 3,071 American counties. The WPA built more than 480 airports, 78,000 bridges, and nearly 40,000 public buildings, including town halls, concert halls, and schools (Smith 2006). Chapters 5 and 6 will be concerned with empirical examples of this modality. The range of effects produced by such investments can be rather wide (from direct economic impacts to symbolic effects). Furthermore, the placeshaping achieved by direct investments may not all be foreseen by the governments concerned and, even where foreseen, may not have been at all the primary objectives of the original policy. Thus the threatened rundown of a hospital may lead directly to the formation of new political coalitions within a locality, and to discomfiture for government policy-makers (see Chapter 6).

C. Governments shape places by directly regulating what others can and cannot put into them. In the UK after the Second World War this regulatory activity centred on 'town and country planning'. Public authorities were empowered to decide, *inter alia*, what kinds of physical developments could be approved in a given locality (see Cullingworth and Nadin 1994: ch. 4). One might consider this the most self-conscious, direct, and intentional form of placemaking. It is the subject of an extensive literature, but is not the main focus of this book. Nevertheless, it appears in a number of our empirical examples, and certainly needs to be included in any overall approach.

D. Governments also shape places by infrastructural investments, which, though they may not be *within* a particular place, significantly affect its further development. Thus a new motorway, or the modernization of a railway line so that it will accept high-speed trains, or the construction of a new airport—all these things and more can affect the 'life chances' of cities, towns, and villages. The building of a high-speed rail link from London to the Channel Tunnel may have been undertaken primarily for strategic and commercial purposes, with an icing of national pride and symbolism. Yet some of the unintended local effects (demolishing buildings, separating local residents from what was formerly their local church or village shop) may have quite drastically reshaped particular localities.

We now turn to less direct government actions, which nonetheless help to shape places and alter spatial relationships:

E. Governments negotiate and bargain with other placemakers. In the UK and other West European and North American states, much of this bargaining takes place within the regulatory framework of planning laws (as in C above) but much also takes place outside this framework, and sometimes under very ad hoc conditions. As with C above, this is a self-conscious, direct, and usually quite intentional form of placemaking.

F. Governments indirectly affect places by a wide array of policies that are not overtly spatial in character, but that nevertheless have important spatial effects. The setting-up or running-down of public services—especially those that are notionally supposed to be 'universal' in character—are one main type, and are a central focus of this book. The money-driven closure of thousands of post offices referred to in Chapter 2 would be one example. The introduction of EU fishing quotas, aimed principally at environmental and conservationist goals, would be another in so far as it may have highly concentrated effects on small coastal villages that were hitherto dependent on fishing as their principal economic activity. The placeshaping effects of such moves are usually secondary factors in the minds of the relevant policy-makers, and sometimes actually unintentional or even unconscious/unnoticed.

G. In less material, more symbolic ways, governments endow, or attempt to endow, particular places with affect. Most contemporary European and North American states have these 'sacred' places—often the sites of battles or catastrophes. The French have Verdun, the Americans the Alamo, the Flemish nationalists Dijksmude. Sometimes these places can even be outside the national territory—British politicians like to invoke the 'Dunkirk spirit', and in 2007/8 the Russian government became highly exercised by the Estonians' 2007 relocation of the Soviet era 'Bronze Soldier' to a nearby Tallin military cemetery (Wikipedia, 'The Bronze Soldier' (accessed 17 Jan. 2011)). At a less heroic level, many local governments attempt to boost development by marketing a particular symbol for their area. Cowen (1990) gives a detailed account of how the Cheltenham Council in England successfully focused on the Regency architectural style that had survived in some parts of the town and used it to create an image of elegance and historical significance. Public services can also have a role here: as we shall see in later chapters, hospitals and schools may carry significant symbolic import.

Last, but not least, we have the influences governments may exert over the formation of virtual spaces:

H. Governments may have considerable influence both over their citizens' access to the Internet/'cyberspace', and over the rules and procedures governing such spaces. The Chinese government, for example, has taken vigorous steps to try to prevent its citizens from being able to see Web material of which it disapproves (Jacobs et al. 2010). And in many countries, as we shall see in Chapter 6, the police are involved in attempting to control Internet crimes of various types, including identity theft, money laundering, and paedophilia.

Four salient points about this list of GAP modalities should be noted. First, the total impact of *all* these activities on places is likely to be both substantial and complex—far more than that achieved simply by the direct and explicit use of formal planning (C alone). Second, to coordinate all these different streams of governmental activity, so as to achieve a single, coherent set of place-related purposes would appear, at first sight, to be quite a formidable task. A codicil here would be that putting together an integrated calculus for measuring all these multiple effects is also dauntingly difficult. Third, although placemaking may be one of the *effects* of each and all of these activities, it is by no means necessarily uppermost in policy-makers' minds; it is not by any means necessarily always the prime objective. Indeed, in some cases, the placeshaping effects may not be noticed or thought about at all. Fourth, public services can feature in most of the different modalities: A, B, C, D, F, G, and H. Yet, as the earlier chapters have argued, large tracts of the geographical, urban studies and planning literatures say very little about the placeshaping role of public services, while the public-management literature itself says almost nothing. Modalities A, B, F, and G are perhaps the most understudied or least acknowledged, and it is particularly upon these that much of our empirical material will focus.

4.2 The Modalities in More Detail

Let us pause for a moment to consider the first of these modalities—that of establishing jurisdictions within bordered territories. While national territories are frequently the residue of wars and/or treaties, subnational entities are more likely to be the product of conscious, politically directed reform. A huge academic literature exists concerning the best principles on which to 'size' such entities. (For earlier but still illuminating reviews, see Paddison 1983: 215–37 and Pickvance and Preteceille 1991; many of the underlying arguments still apply. For a more recent treatment, see Baldersheim and Rose 2010.) Economies of scale in service provision, for example, may point towards quite large units for some services, but not for others. On the other hand, many commentators who advocate more citizen participation in local government have seen small, neighbourhood, or 'community'-sized units as attractive (although their assumption that 'localness' fosters healthy participation has long been the subject of theoretical and empirical challenge). Or, again, a coordinated approach to, say, public transport may point towards the need for larger, regional-sized authorities (to cover the commuting zone for large cities such as Frankfurt, Glasgow, Manchester, or New York). Yet the residents of the surrounding countryside—in the English case often the leafy 'shires'—may strongly object to being governed by an urban-centred authority, seeing themselves as different in lifestyle and preferences from those inhabiting the inner cities. So perhaps one could allocate transport to larger authorities and more local issues such as primary schools or planning decisions to quite small jurisdictions? Yes, except that that would tend to produce a plethora of specialized, different-sized authorities, which would be both hard to coordinate and hard for citizens to understand. Neither would such a functionally defined solution be particularly stable, since changing technologies constantly change the 'optimum' size for particular activities.

Overall, decentralization has a long and chequered history, with some evidence of patterns of alternation or cycling, where governments pursue the benefits of decentralization and localism for a while and are then distracted by the appeal of larger local government units, or central control, standardization, and economies of scale (Pollitt 2005; 2008: 51–9). Furthermore, and even more fundamentally, 'all territorial reform, because it alters the pattern of access to decision-making, is a game of "winners" and "losers" and in this sense is inevitably an issue that is highly charged politically' (Paddison 1983: 216).

Thus we can already see that the state's first line of 'placeshaping' is bound to entail conflict and is unlikely to be wholly amenable to any kind of technocratic solution. Baldersheim and Rose (2010) offer a useful overview of recent European developments. They note that, overall, most countries have attempted to upscale (Baldersheim and Rose 2010: 6), but that, while some have carried this out on a radical scale (Denmark, the UK), other countries have done little or nothing (France, Italy). They conclude that the (quite divergent) experiences of different countries in subdividing their territories have been driven by 'three sets of policy problems: a quest for competitive regions, better governance of fragmented urban areas, and more distributional efficiency in local service delivery' (Baldersheim and Rose 2010: 255). The third of these is, of course, a central concern of this book.

Moving on, it is important to note (modalities B, C, and H) that, while all governments (central and local) are inevitably placemakers (and virtual placemakers as well as 'real' ones), they are never the *only* placemakers. Other important placemakers, at least in contemporary Europe and North America, are business companies (very much including multinationals), professional groups (architects, civil engineers, planners, and so on), civil society associations (such as those concerned with civic aesthetics, or aircraft noise, or environmental protection) and, not least, supranational and intergovernmental authorities (EU environmental standards, UN World Heritage Site designations, the actions of the governments of the authorities on the other side of your national or subnational borders). Needless to say, the balance of power between these various placemakers is never fixed, and there is certainly no guarantee that the national or local government is going to be the most influential player in the game. (Incidentally, it is quite common for national and local governments to find themselves opposed to each other's placemaking activities, as when the UK central government calls in planning decisions and overrules the local authority's views (Cullingworth and Nadin 1994: 87–8).) Massey's 'power geometry' of places is a variable geometry.

While it is conventional to think of governments as placemakers in respect of land-use plans and planning regulations, it is less common to think of the provision of public services as constituting a placemaking activity. Yet the location of such services frequently has a powerful shaping influence on communities. It is the realization of this that leads local residents so often to campaign hard to save 'their' local school or hospital or park or library or swimming pool. Similarly, the many government deconcentration exercises (some of which we will examine in the next chapter) are undertaken with ideas of economy and efficiency to the fore, but without exception they cannot fail also to have a placemaking component (intended or not) both in the location from which the agency or unit in question has been removed and in the site at which it is newly received. Earlier in the chapter we mentioned the success of Cheltenham Council in selling the town as a desirable Regency 'heritage centre'. There were, however, other components in the economic success of the town, especially the movement there, in the early 1950s, of the Government Communications Headquarters (GCHQ) (Cowen 1990). One might say that the world's misfortune, in the shape of the growth of Islamic fundamentalist terrorism from the 1990s, turned out to be Cheltenham's good fortune, since it increased the importance of GCHQ as the UK's premium intelligence-gathering centre.

Or again, Allard's study of social services in Chicago, Los Angeles, and Washington DC showed both that low-income individuals frequently had great difficulty travelling more than short distances and that, in terms of service provision, areas of high poverty were heavily underprovided for. Why were the providing organizations (many of them non-profit organizations working as contractors to the public authorities) seemingly in the wrong places? Allard's analysis (2009: 36) revealed the complexity of location decisions:

Some agencies may choose to be closer to concentrations of low-income individuals in order to achieve economies of scale for service delivery. Others may locate to be proximate to potential private donors, clients who generate fees revenue, or partnering service organizations. Agencies may choose to locate in a particular community because of staffing concerns and the need to access trained professionals. Programs that address sensitive needs or serve at-risk populations may choose locations that prioritize protecting anonymity and confidentiality over shorter commutes. Office space or facility concerns also may dictate location. Service providers may be bound to particular neighbourhoods due to a lack of adequate facilities in more preferred areas, insufficient funds to relocate, or ownership of property and facilities that limits mobility.

Before moving on from the eight modalities, we should just mention the usually unsung matter of sewers, water pipes, and power lines (modality D-type infrastructures). Some or all of these have usually involved public investment, and their maintenance (or the regulation thereof) also often rests with public authorities. In the developed world, provision of such things is frequently taken for granted. They are below ground, out of sight, and seldom go badly wrong. They are, however, fundamental to civilized life as we have come to know it. When severe earthquakes struck New Zealand and Japan in 2010 and 2011, damage to these systems posed one of the hardest problems to tackle. Rescue teams can search the collapsed buildings for survivors, fires can be put out, and emergency food and shelter can be provided. These are commonly the images delivered to the public via the TV news. But broken sewer or water pipes (which normally take weeks and months rather than days to repair) mean that disease is an early threat, and that life in even still-habitable dwellings becomes extremely difficult. If power lines are down or gas pipes are fractured or the public roads that give access are blocked, then these difficulties are compounded. So, while this book concentrates mainly on the classic face-to-face public services such as health care, education, and the police, we should not underestimate the capacity of basic public infrastructural utilities to *unmake* places when they fail.

Overall, then, a government seems to have a wide range of policy instruments that could be brought to bear on placeshaping tasks. Obviously, though, it is never starting with an empty landscape (or airspace, or below-ground space). One has to begin with what is there already, some of which may prove remarkably difficult or expensive to move (Roman sewers under twentieth-century cities; a railway network constructed in the nineteenth century; ageing nuclear power stations from the 1960s and 1970s). Other 'heritage' items may, in contrast, turn out to be very valuable, such as Cheltenham's or Brighton's Regency terraces, Scotland's mountains and castles and clear-running streams (whisky), or Barcelona's multiple manifestations of Gaudi's extraordinary architecture.

With such a wide range of potential instruments, one may wonder why governments so often appear to fail to achieve their stated objectives with regard to specified regions, cities, zones, or localities. Let us say that a government aims to shape a particular place within its territory in a particular way, but that it fails to achieve this. How could that be explained? There are at least three possibilities. First, the government did its best but was outgunned. The other, rival placemakers were, on this occasion, simply too powerful (this is a constant theme of the Marxian urban studies literature but is a commonplace observation from other theoretical perspectives as well). One thinks, for example, of the government of a small developing country struggling against the wishes of a large and powerful multinational company that already boasts one or more large plants on its territory. Second, the government might have been successful *if* it had been able to summon all its resources, but in practice it was too divided by conflicting interests. For example, if, in a case of a proposed airport expansion, the Ministry of Transport supported the aviation industry in favour of growth, while the Ministry of the Environment opposed the increased noise and pollution, and the Ministry of Local Government sat on the fence because it could not decide whether to fight the expansion because it conflicted with the regional plan or support it because it promised economic growth. The problem here is a lack of political leadership, engendered by a lack of consensus within the governing elite. A third possibility would be that the government potentially had the power and authority to get its way, was not too hamstrung by internal political splits, but nevertheless failed to get what it wanted because it did not manage to organize itself well enough to bring all its guns to bear at the right time. In other words, it was a problem of un-joined-up government—an organizational and managerial failure. These three types are not mutually exclusive. Indeed, they may well be additive. Chapter 5 will offer a pair of case studies where governments apparently possess all the powers they could need to develop new capital cities, and yet soon find themselves with mixtures of the planned, the replanned, the unplanned, and the sheer unforeseen.

Therefore, both the context and the mechanisms would need to be investigated (as suggested in Section 2.5). Examining the context would include identifying the other placemakers in the particular case, their goals, perceptions, and resources. It would also require an analysis of physical and technological constraints—perhaps the goals of some of the placemakers were simply unrealistic in relation to extant technical capacities? Examining the mechanisms would entail the identification of each policy instrument that the government could have used, and the extent to which it was used, and was used skilfully. Thus the task of analysis would be complex and detailed, and in the end it might still be difficult to be sure which of the three above possibilities was the most likely. Distinguishing between the second and third—internal political splits versus failure adequately to coordinate policy actions across a network of organizations—is often particularly awkward. It is not unusual for researchers to find that the civil servants concerned will privately blame lack of political leadership while the political leaders will blame the ineffectiveness of the civil servants.

However, even if the final answer were not devastatingly clear-cut, the process of analysis would have eliminated other possible explanations and greatly clarified the remaining areas of uncertainty.

4.3 Problems of Coordination

Visions of governments as huge, threatening monoliths have always been the stuff of fiction rather than empirical reality. Even deadly intelligence services such as the Stasi, the CIA, or the KGB are frequently revealed to be internally divided, inefficient, and prone to the left hand not knowing what the right hand is doing. At a more mundane level, Hood (1976: 18) cited the example of different public utilities digging up Main Road, Harwich, more than 700 times during the 18 months ending in January 1973. In every country there are different departments and agencies with different policy objectives, cultures, procedures, work schedules, and types of staff. But surely, with a bit of political determination and organizational skill, they can be made to 'sing from the same song sheet'? In our particular case, surely they can be encouraged, or even ordered, to act in a coordinated way within particular spaces and places? If that could be accomplished, then governments could much more easily 'punch their weight' as place-makers (and, of course, in many other respects). The answer to this question seems to be 'rarely, and then usually only temporarily'. Despite the fashion, since the late 1990s, for 'joined-up government' (JUG), 'integrated service delivery' (ISD), 'collaborative public management', or even 'holistic government' (6 et al. 2002), there are few recorded empirical cases of these ideals in fully-fledged action. Certainly there are a number of examples of relatively successful integration of several services (see, e.g., Kernaghan 2007; HM Treasury 2010: 33–5), but several of the more detached scholarly treatments identify a number of significant problems and limitations with the concept itself (Pollitt 2003b; 6 2004, 2005; Bogdanor 2005; Davies 2009). One experienced 'joiner-upper' put it like this: 'Any advocacy of "joined-up" government must start from the recognition that cross-cutting work is an unnatural activity' (Klein and Plowden 2005: 108). Since 'joining up' therefore appears, prima facie, to be an important prerequisite for governments to act as successful placemakers, it is important to understand why, in practice, the ideal is so difficult to realize.

A first step towards this understanding is the realization that 'the challenge to improving coordination horizontally within government is an eternal one' (6 2004: 103; Hood 2005). 'All democratic and totalitarian regimes attempt to coordinate governmental and non-governmental activity in pursuit of putatively common goods, often with little success' (Davies 2009: 80). So, while the acronym 'JUG' may be relatively new, the aspiration to get everyone singing from the same song sheet is anything but.

A second step is to remind oneself that the unified political will that seems a prima facie requirement for at least the more ambitious forms of joining up is actually a rare commodity. Far more common is the situation of muted, or even strident, political competition, with this minister wanting this and that minister wanting something different, and the minister of finance wanting to avoid novel or unusual expenditure. These differences are not just matters of temperament or doctrine (though these may play their part). They are also ways in which different interests in society are mobilized and institutionalized within different sections of the government machine. So the public-sector organizations that are subordinate to these politicians will pull in somewhat different directions. A powerful and determined president or prime minister may be able to moderate this and 'bang heads together' to get a single approach, but the exercise of doing this tends to be costly in terms of both time and political capital, and is unlikely to be sustained over a long period. Thus, for example, JUG was a priority of the Blair administration in the UK from 1999 onwards, but by 2005 Page (2005: 139) was already writing that, as far as the UK government was concerned, '"joined-up" has passed into the language of administrative change and reform as a *good* thing, but it is not the *big* thing that it was . . . '. Halligan (2010: 253) records how in the early 2000s ambitious attempts by the Australian federal government to achieve improved horizontal collaboration benefited from the personal commitment of the then head of the Australian Public Service, but that this was, inevitably perhaps, 'transient'.

Third, quite apart from divisions of political interest, strong forms of coordination are often just difficult to organize. 'Organizations and professions have their own routines, cultures and languages—all of which are integral to their operations. Cross-cutting work requires people to learn new routines, new cultures and new languages. In short it imposes heavy costs on both organizations and individuals' (Klein and Plowden 2005: 108). The development of organizational divisions and subdivisions is not an accident. On the contrary, specialization and differentiation were already identified as leading characteristics of modern societies by 'fathers of sociology' such as Durkheim and Weber (6 2005). Far from being merely a perversion or pathology, it represents a constant drive towards greater expertise and therefore, hopefully, efficiency and effectiveness. Yes, coordination of this advancing specialization is a perennial problem, but, for the most part, it is regarded as a price worth paying for the benefits of institutionalized expertise. We would rather our surgeons were no longer also barbers, even if the super-specialized surgeons of today develop their own organizations, cultures, routines, and so on. Or, if we are looking at the organization of governments, we should remember that, as Page (2005) reminds us, the much abused bureaucratic 'silos' were created for a good reason— or rather for a number of good reasons—and most of those reasons (expertise, accountability, clear political control) still apply. Halligan (2010: 252) expresses the matter thus:

The principle of 'function' is the universal basis for most central government organization. The key issue with whole-of-government is about re-focusing agencies constituted around functional hierarchies into ones that routinely incorporate horizontal collaboration into their modes of operating. However, the question remains of 'how far vertical accountabilities can be sacrificed'.

Fourth, while the development of modern ICTs has in principle made 'joining up' much easier, the practice has proved to be more difficult. In a number of countries, large-scale government ICT projects have taken longer than planned, cost far more than estimated, and even just failed to function (see, e.g., Dunleavy et al. 2006; 6 2007). In the UK, in particular, there is now a long and quite dismal history of problems, apparently produced by a complex web of factors, including a predilection for huge, over-ambitious projects, repeated political interference in technical details, government over-reliance on a few multinational companies and a lack of strong internal expertise in either systems or contract management—not to mention the usual ebbing and flowing of party politics and the tightness of fiscal constraints. (The national identity card system, for example, became a political target for the Conservative Party while in opposition, and they duly killed off the scheme when they came to power in 2010.)

None of this is to argue that coordination cannot be improved. Very often, it can, and sometimes it is. Furthermore, new technologies definitely do ease the problems of coordination in some respects. To take an obvious example, it is noticeably easier to organize public demonstrations, election campaigns, and public-service networks now there are mobile phones and the Internet than it was before these technologies existed. But any form of coordination has its price, and JUG is a matter of balancing costs and benefits, a calculus in which we should not assume that more coordination is always desirable, or that its benefits will always outweigh its costs (Pollitt 2003). Kernaghan offers a balanced and useful account of attempts at

Integrated Service Delivery in Canada—a country with an international reputation for being advanced in this field. He describes a number of large-scale projects that seem to have achieved a measure of success. Most of his observations ring true for the experience of other OECD countries. However, while overall he sees ISD as both achievable and very popular with citizens, he also discusses a considerable list of 'challenges' (Kernaghan, 2007: 111–19). These include:

- *political/legal challenges*: meeting ministers' frequent, but 'silo-istic' desire to be able to control and take credit for the activities of 'their' ministry; addressing legal constraints such as privacy laws, or the different legal powers of different agencies involved in an ISD partnership;

- *structural challenges*: reducing departmentalism, and even administrative walls within departments (such as the tensions between technical experts and policy analysts, or personnel and finance); minimizing rivalry and suspicion between different jurisdictions (especially salient in a federal state such as Canada, where the provinces have frequently clashed with the federal government); finding sufficient resources to fund both the (often considerable) start-up costs and the ongoing running costs

- *organizational and managerial challenges*: ensuring interoperability of technical and administrative systems (we will see examples of this in Chapter 8, which deals with the police); satisfying staff in a new situation where staff from different agencies may find themselves doing similar, or highly cooperative work yet working under significantly different terms and conditions; balancing the representation of the different partners in key decision-making processes; ensuring privacy and security for users of the systems (again, this issue will recur at various points in the later, empirical chapters).

- *cultural challenges*: blending the cultures represented by the different partner organizations, which can be hard work over a considerable time period, as can defining and establishing a set of values appropriate to the newly integrated service.

Despite these challenges, the attractions of ICT-facilitated service integration are very great. They often appear to be highly popular with citizen users (Kernaghan 2007: 102) and they hold out the possibility of significant savings. Canadian data from 2004 showed the per-citizen-transaction cost of the Internet as $0.84, telephone agents at $2.99, regular (snail) mail at $18.86, and in-person, face-to-face service at $38.24 (all figures in Canadian dollars (Treasury Board Secretariat 2004)). Significantly, Canadian citizens appeared to be asking for a choice of channel—the Internet would do for many things, but on other occasions they wanted to be able to use the phone or see a service provider face-to-face. This (understandable) desire for flexibility, if it is to be satisfied, brings with it additional challenges. Most obviously, keeping open all channels can easily reduce or even reverse the financial savings made by the move to a more Internet-based service. Less obviously, perhaps, it requires service providers in all the different channels to deal with issues in a similar way—citizens are not likely to be satisfied with a second class or differently branded or harder-to-understand service in one channel than in another.

The above considerations apply to the generality of public services. Their relevance to our specific focus on placeshaping is direct. The degree to which governments try to and are able to coordinate their activities affect their effectiveness in most of the eight modalities identified in Section 4.1. Effective external border control (modality A) frequently depends on achieving a harmonious approach among the several agencies involved (police, customs, immigration, and so on). Effective internal border management may involve different regional or local authorities with different parties in power and different priorities coming to working agreements about what is to be done. In the next chapter we will see the example of the Australian Capital Territory (ACT/Canberra) and its surrounding state of New South Wales. In Chapter 8 we will chronicle how both structural reforms and new communications technologies have been used to try to improve coordination between neighbouring police forces. For modality B the need for coordination is obvious. If large government offices are deconcentrated from the capital to dispersed locations, then those locations need to have the requisite schools and transport links (Chapter 5 will look at some of these schemes). Furthermore, the physical dispersal of offices must not lead to organizational fragmentation and loss of coordination in policy-making and/or implementation. For modality C, the influence of planning officials, perhaps seeking balanced, sustainable, and environmentally benign development, will be lessened if the ministry of industry is at the same time championing the siting of a new plant that will attract skilled staff away from existing local firms and that will significantly add to the local burden of pollution—a problem of local/central policy coordination. For modality D, occasional tales of underused bridges or motorways or stadia or high-speed train lines remind one of the possibility of 'vanity' projects that are not founded on realistic estimates of public demand for certain kinds of facility. London still struggles from the nineteenth-century heritage of five major rail terminals, sited close to each other in the central city but without adequate interconnections. For modality E, the same lesson applies as was mentioned for modality C above—if governments speak with more than one voice, their overall influence will be weakened, and other placemakers will be able to divide and rule. Similarly for modality G, the effectiveness of governments' attempts to establish a distinct symbolic identity for a particular place will depend partly on the different arms of government all singing from the same song sheet.

4.4 Cooperation and Competition with Other Placemakers

Since roughly the turn of the century, the term 'governance' has become extremely fashionable in studies of public policy and management. Although it admits a wide range of definitions, if it does have a stable core meaning, then that is probably to do with the idea that governments do not usually govern alone: they are obliged to share the business of 'running the country' with a range of other organizations, from big corporations through international standard-setting and regulative bodies (Brunsson and Jacobsson 2002) to local civil associations such as residents' committees or charitable service providers (Pollitt and Hupe 2011). (As we have discussed above, governments are also divided among and within themselves, but here we put that issue temporarily on one side.) Although sometimes presented as a new insight, this is in fact the latest version of a very old insight. For a century or more political scientists have theorized how governments must to some extent share power with interest groups, while practising politicians have presumably recognized this from the start (taking the world of liberal democracies as our frame). There are intricate arguments about how far, and under what conditions, the state can act autonomously (see, e.g., Nordlinger 1981), and we will not settle that debate here, but the important point for us is that it has long been recognized that, in placemaking as in its other activities, sharing power is the norm rather than the exception, even for the most powerful states.

If we focus for a moment on the concrete business of planning and developing a site or place, it is relatively easy to identify some of the other placemaking roles that governments typically have either to deal with or to take over themselves. Thus we can think of landowners, investors, financiers, builders, architects, designers, and residents—both existing and prospective. At one extreme, governments can undertake all or most of these roles themselves; they can take ownership of the land, provide the investment, use their own building and construction staff and architects, and so on. One of the fascinations of the study of greenfield site capital cities is that sometimes governments seem to hold all these cards—at least for a while—so one has a rather 'pure' test of government placemaking at its least constrained (see the comparison of Canberra and Brasília in Chapter 5). More commonly, however, governments turn to the private sector to play most of these roles, and confine themselves mainly to regulation (Carmona et al. 2010: ch. 10). In this regard, one of the main findings of many of the academic commentators on planning and urban development is that, in North America and Western Europe, the period since 1980 has seen a shift in the way many governments discharge this regulatory function. As early as 1990, writing about economic development in the UK, Harloe et al. (1990: 29) observed that 'inner city policy since 1979 has been marked by three main trends: a decline in the role of local authorities, a greater involvement of industrial and financial groups and an increased dependence on private funds'. However, the nature of the industrial and financial groups has itself been changing. Processes of globalization have meant that more and more of these groups are not local or even regional groups, but multinational actors, able to move their new investments to particular locations that currently 'offer the best deal':

as development companies have grown in size and complexity, small locally based companies with links to local decision-makers have increasingly given way to companies whose centre of operations typically reside outside the locale...The result is a growing disconnect between those responsible for development and the locality.

(Carmona et al. 2010: 277)

In response to this, according to Brenner and others, governments have become less concerned with issues of social and regional equity and 'balanced development', and more concerned to meet the very particular needs of mobile capital:

National, regional and local governments have attempted to channel urban (re) development into particular locations by introducing new jurisdiction—and area-specific institutional forms. Prominent examples of this trend have included enterprise zones, urban development corporations, airport development agencies, and development planning boards, all of which have been designed, in some manner, to intensify and accelerate economic growth within strategic, clearly delineated urban zones. Such institutions are autonomous from local state control and dominated by unaccountable political and economic elites. They have also frequently entailed the suspension of existing planning regulations in favour of 'exceptional' (but increasingly normalized) tools and modes of intervention within strategic areas or infrastructural configurations.

(Brenner 2004: 216)

This is, then, a picture of a trend in which spatial developments become more uneven, more concentrated, and less subject to any planning dictates concerned with wider socio-demographic criteria. Not everywhere, and certainly not always in precisely the same way, but nevertheless very frequently, governments are backing away from earlier planning ideals, and are less and less willing (or possibly able) to resist or confront the imperatives of business and profit in the name of the wider social good. In GAP terms, Brenner and like-minded urban studies scholars are essentially saying that the autonomy of governments as placemakers has shrunk and the placemaking power and influence of big business have grown.

As indicated earlier, we cannot here go very far into the academic debate about neoliberalism and the changing 'global and supranational circuits of capital' (Brenner 2004: 3). We can, however, draw one lesson from this analysis that Brenner himself does not pick up. It is that, *if* this picture is tolerably accurate, then responsibility for the earlier Keynesian-style planning objectives of 'national territorial equalization and sociospatial redistribution' (Brenner 2004: 3) will now fall even more heavily than they did before upon our central focus—GAP modality B. That is to say, if the planning of economic development is no longer much influenced by the goals of social equity and integration, then the planning and positioning of public services will play a proportionately even greater role in these respects.

4.5 Temporal Dynamics

Up to this point, our model of governments as placemakers has had a somewhat static quality. Governments do this or that, or they fail to do this or that. It is clear, however, that many of the 'moves' made to shape places engender counter-moves, path-firming amplificatory positive feedback, or direction-changing negative feedback, or other kinds of consequence for the longer term. So public authorities, while they *do* try to fix specific, identified problems, frequently find that what has actually happened is that their (partial) solution has displaced other elements, and led to the formation of new problems, which, in turn, require attention. Take the example of the planned capital city of Canberra, which will feature as one of the cases examined in Chapter 5. For nearly fifty years the government struggled with minimal success to persuade organizations and people to come to the designated site. Then, for a while, internal political difficulties were overcome, and a strong leader, combined with a strong central development organization, ushered in a phase of extremely rapid growth. Within a couple of decades, however, new problems began to appear, as the development agency could see itself running out of land, and as the surrounding state of New South Wales, itself suffering land price inflation in the areas adjacent to Canberra, refused to cooperate in solving the problems of 'overheating' (Sparke 1988: 231–44). Soon after this, another 'sequencing' problem emerged, as the suburbs, which had absorbed the first wave of Canberra 'boomers'—often young families—began to age. Demand for local schools then declined, and the education authority wanted to close some of them, but this triggered organized resistance from some residents (Halligan et al. 2002: 56).

These Canberra examples are no more than particular instances of a very common—one might almost say universal—phenomenon. Each choice of policy option advantages certain further options and disadvantages others. In placemaking there are frequently strong elements of path dependency: that is, the further one goes in one direction (growth/decline, high tech/ low wage), the harder it is to go back and take another route (Pollitt 2008: 40–51, 91–104; Pollitt and Bouckaert 2009: 143–58). There are also many examples of slow, incremental adaptation of buildings and organizations over time (Mahoney and Thelen 2010). Places are defined by their land forms, their buildings, and their resident populations. While all these elements can and do change (see Chapter 2), they hardly ever change overnight. People are perhaps the least difficult to move, although most West European countries can show examples of settlements from which most of the employment has disappeared but where resident populations stubbornly cling on. Solutions have to be found for them—the 'old problem' if you like—at the same time as, elsewhere, solutions are being sought for the 'new problems' of overheating or congestion. Clever planners and politicians often seem to find courses of action that link the old and the new, and attempt to solve both simultaneously. Consider, for example, the location of the headquarters of the UK General Register Office (GRO). In the late 1980s and early 1990s, the 'new' policy was to disperse public agencies from expensive, overcrowded London and place them elsewhere (Chapter 5 deals with this at some length). The GRO had for long been sited right in the heart of London, close by Waterloo Bridge. Meanwhile, however, an 'old problem' was manifesting itself far away, at genteel Southport on the Lancashire coast. The National Health Service Records Centre, located in Southport, had finally come to terms with the technological shifts in record-keeping, and was downsizing and needing to lay off significant numbers of staff in an area where new jobs would not easily be found, and where political sensitivities were high. The solution to both problems came in the form of the 1991 move of the GRO to occupy the building previously used by the NHS Records Centre (TPT interviews 8 and 12; for more on changes in the civil registration service, see Chapter 7).

It may be useful to illustrate and systematize this issue of temporal dynamics diagrammatically. It is possible to draw separate diagrams of the knock-on effects over time of government actions under each of the eight modalities set out in Figure 4.1. In fact it is possible to draw dozens of diagrams for each of the modalities, because the dynamics of, say, building a new hospital in a particular part of a particular city will be quite different from the dynamics of closing a post office in a country village. Clearly it would be impractical to attempt any such comprehensive treatment within the confines of this chapter—there is no room for the hundreds of diagrams that would result. Instead we will adopt a much more modest approach. We will simply take the first two modalities (A and B) and set up *one* example for each. Hopefully even these two limited examples will have the value of summarizing and somewhat systematizing much of the foregoing discussion.

Figure 4.2 deals with one specific type of modality A boundary-drawing: the changing of local-authority boundaries. There has been a great deal of this type of change within Western Europe over the past half century, and reform schemes continue to flow down the pipeline (as this book was being written my wife and I had to suffer the renaming of the little track to our Finnish farmhouse, because a merger of municipalities meant that suddenly there were two roads with the same name within the new enlarged jurisdiction, and this was deemed too confusing for the authorities).

Let us assume that this was a case where it was decided that traditional local government units were too small, and the decision was taken to enlarge them. If local authorities were to be able to gain the economies of scale in operations in certain services (such as further education or secondary health care) or if they were to be able to plan roads and public transport on the same scale that contemporary commuting seemed to require, then they needed to be bigger. Being bigger would also enable the new authorities to recruit and retain suitable specialists to deal with some of the problems of contemporary government, such as, say, environmental protection or local systems for e-government. (These are actually typical arguments, which have been heard in many countries over the past several decades (see, e.g., John 2010).)

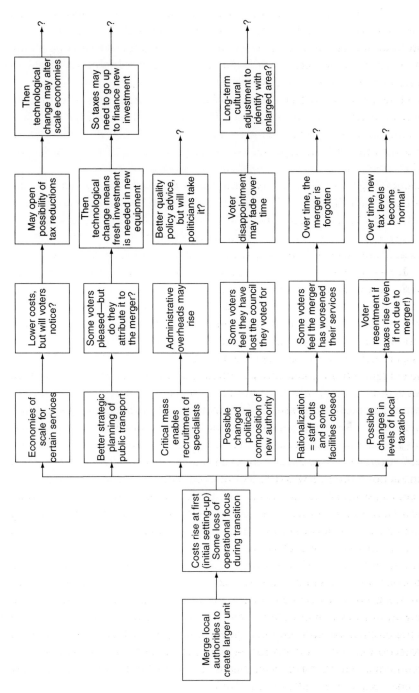

Figure 4.2 The dynamics of changing local-authority boundaries

Yet, even if all these aspects of the pre-decision analysis were accurate, and all these benefits did indeed accrue to the new, larger authorities (see top three boxes in the third column of Figure 4.2), other, less beneficial effects may also follow. For example, when major restructurings like this take place, it is common that the first stage of the reorganization is accompanied by extra transitional expenses (to set up new systems and recruit new staff) and by some temporary loss of focus on policy-making and service delivery (because staff are worried about their new jobs and are getting to know each other and attending to the task of creating new ways of working). However, these 'hiccups' should be temporary.

More importantly, perhaps, the party political complexion of the enlarged authority may be different from that of at least one of the previous authorities. So the voters of previous authority X may in the past have usually elected a social democratic council but now find that, after the merger with a larger neighbour, Y, the new, merged council is predominantly conservative. Therefore, policies may change (for example, more money to be spent on security and less on social housing). What is more, new boundaries may include, or exclude, or divide, particularly strong communities, based on language or religion or ethnicity or some combination of these. At the time of writing this book, I am living and working in Belgium, where there is and long has been a major divide between the Dutch-speaking Flemish and the Francophone Walloons. Bitter political disputes between these two groups (each of which has its own set of political parties) have led to long periods where a federal government could not be formed at all (the current interlude has already lasted a year and a half, after an earlier one beginning in 2008 and itself lasting many months). Many issues divide the warring parties, but probably the most intractable recently has been what to do about the Brussels–Hal–Vilvoorde voting district, which is constitutionally part of Flanders but which contains large numbers of Francophones. The Flemish parties want to split it in a particular way and the Francophones find this wholly unacceptable. This is a struggle over places and borders.

Furthermore, a merger is highly likely to lead to some rationalization of the council's facilities. Some local offices may be closed. What used to be the head office/'town hall' in X now becomes only a secondary office because the headquarters has moved to Y (this is exactly what happened in our local Finnish example). There may also be longer-term cultural adjustments. Perhaps X was always the 'poor relative' of more prosperous Y. It is possible that this perception of separateness and difference will lessen over the years, now that the whole area is one political and administrative entity. On the other hand, X may become an embittered 'ghetto', believing that the dominant political elite in the new authority favours Y. Much may depend on how responsibly and visibly the elected representatives act to heal previous rivalries and divisions.

Furthermore, after a few years the technological and organizational circumstances that prompted the original merger may begin to change once more. For example, emerging transport technologies or health-care technologies or communications technologies may favour either yet bigger authorities or a return to smaller-scale 'localism'.

Figure 4.3 offers an example of the modality that is central to this book: the location of public-service facilities (modality B). In this case we set out some of the consequences of opening a new school in a particular neighbourhood.

As with Figure 4.2, this diagram (a) represents only one example of the modality and (b) illustrates a much-less-than-comprehensive set of interactions and effects. Indeed, the figure is suffused with further assumptions and unknowns. For example, it assumes that parents have some degree of choice as to which school they send their children—which is not so in every part of Europe or North America. It also assumes that schools gain a reputation and that that reputation is widely known and shared among local parents. In practice we may find that certain groups of parents are concerned and very well informed, others are concerned but not well informed, and some are not concerned at all, so the effect of, say, better-than-average exam results will not influence the whole of the community in the same way. The figure also leaves out important environmental factors such as the state of the teacher job market. If a school has, say, a slightly but not dramatically weak reputation, it matters a lot whether the teacher job market is tight or slack. If there is a shortage of teachers and they are not very well paid, and other jobs are easily come by, then such a school would struggle to recruit its teaching force. If, on the other hand, teachers are relatively well paid, and the supply of graduates coming from the teacher training courses is plentiful, then the school would be more likely to be able to staff itself well. In short, a full critical realist-type analysis of the situation would produce a much more complicated diagram than Figure 4.3 (see Pawson 2006). Nevertheless, the figure carries a basic message: that just putting a public facility in a particular location sends out all sorts of ripples that affect many aspects of that place.

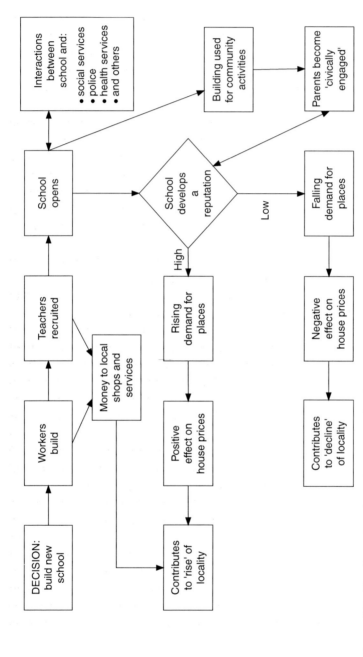

Figure 4.3 The dynamics of opening a new school

4.6 Places Fight back: Location, History, Materiality

A final set of observations concerns not the ways in which governments can make places but, working in the other direction, the *ways in which the material aspects of places can prompt and then shape government actions*. Almost unmentioned in the general public-management literature, and little discussed by radical geographers (who apparently prefer to focus on political and economic forces), such effects are actually quite common. Consider, for example, the immediate issues posed for government when oil, or uranium, or diamonds are found in some particular part of its territory. It immediately comes under pressure from companies, taxpayers, environmentalists, and so on—both from its own country and internationally. A regime will have to be established, or adapted, to govern the exploitation of the find, and, again, it will need to be one that is consonant with the government's international obligations as well as purely domestic concerns. Of course, to say that such material aspects have effects is not to say that the causation is deterministic. It is mediated by a number of factors—so that one would expect, for example, that a liberal democracy would not set up exactly the same regulatory framework for an oil or uranium discovery as would a kleptomaniac authoritarian regime.

To take a different example, consider the implications for government of the concentration of one or more ethnic minorities or immigrant groups in particular localities: implications for housing, education, policing, and many other public services. Or, finally, think of the organizational and political challenges that stem from something as simple as having remote, lightly populated regions of a national territory. How can basic public services be organized for dealing with small, dispersed populations in remote areas—postal services, schools, health care, policing, and so on? Even in urban areas, population density and concentration matter a good deal. Allard, in his study of American social services, found provision was less poorly matched to need in Washington DC than in Los Angeles. He reasoned that 'it is easier to make services more accessible in a compact or densely populated community, all things being equal...Also, public transportation systems help poor persons access providers more easily in compact cities than in cities that have emerged in the post-automobile era' (Allard 2009: 84). Again, how far such effects are actually observed depends on intermediate factors, including the type of political regime and the extent to which it actively pursues polices in favour of universal provision of public services.

The landscape itself can also intrude itself into what might otherwise, on a flat earth, seem a neat set of bureaucratic rules. In Chapter 2 we discussed the closure of UK post offices. In an attempt to allay public anxieties about the closure programme, the relevant ministry announced in 2007 that it would not allow closures to go so far as to breach certain criteria, for example: 'Nationally, 99% of the UK population to be within three miles and 90% of the population to be within 1 mile of their nearest post office outlet' (National Audit Office 2009: 16). However, this rule had to be qualified as follows: 'In applying these criteria, Post Office Ltd will be required to take into account obstacles such as rivers, mountains and valleys, motorways and sea crossings to islands to avoid undue hardship' (National Audit Office 2009: 16). Just as weeds are frequently defined as plants in the wrong place, the rugged and beautiful mountains and lakes of, say, a national park are, from the Post Office's perspective, 'obstacles'.

4.7 Placing Public Services: The Range of Effects

Figure 4.1 set out a range of modalities by which governments could potentially shape places. Figures 4.2 and 4.3 illustrated some possible dynamics resulting from use of the first two modalities—drawing borders (A) and locating public-service facilities (B). These two examples indicated some particular effects that could flow from defining boundaries and locating a school. In this section we will take that a little further by attempting to construct a broader, more generic typology of effects. We will, however, restrict ourselves to modality B—the placing of public facilities and activities—since this is the prime focus of the book. Table 4.1 is the result.

Naturally there are also effects at the place that has 'exported' the public-service facility. These are not an exact mirror image of the effects at the 'importing' location, but slightly more complicated. Some of the more obvious ones are depicted in Table 4.2.

As Tables 4.1 and 4.2 indicate, changing the place of a public-service organization can and does lead to a very wide range of effects. To begin with, it is usually supposed to have functional impacts—that is, the service itself is supposed to improve along one or more dimensions: speed, accuracy, understandability, standards, convenience, cost. Then it has financial and economic impacts—most basically the price of the land and buildings used for a particular activity may change, as may the costs of the staff necessary to carry out that function. It has economic but also social impacts on the surrounding area—infusing money, people, ideas, and possibly

Table 4.1 Placeshifts: Typical effects on locations to which public-service organizations are transferred

GROUP AFFECTED	TYPICAL EFFECTS			
	Functional	Financial and economic	Social	Political
Service users	Service is usually supposed to improve. The move is taken as an opportunity to modernize. If the service has a face-to-face component (e.g. school, post office), then closer proximity is itself an improvement	Not clear. Some services may lower unit costs, but will this be passed on to service users?	Little effect?	If the service really does improve, this may marginally effect perceived legitimacy of service *and* government
Service staff	Likely to have to learn new skills and working arrangements as such moves are frequently taken as opportunities to modernize	Not clear. Sometimes new staff are hired at lower wages. On the other hand, the relative purchasing power of national salaries may be higher in a new location	Mixed effects. Typically some disruption to social networks (schools, friends) but also possible a higher quality of life	Little effect, except in so far as they represent new voters in local elections
Residents (of new location)	Little effect, except possible increased pressure on local services if the incoming organization is large	Additional incomes will be (partly) injected into the local economy	New arrivals are likely to enhance local social activities	May make residents more optimistic about the locality, but will that influence voting?
Politicians	Ministers may find it harder to steer the service 'at a distance'	Little effect?	Little effect?	Local politicians gain kudos by claiming 'we brought it here'. Ministers may claim they are decentralizing and modernizing

Table 4.2 Placeshifts: Typical effects on locations from which public-service organizations are taken away

GROUP AFFECTED	TYPICAL EFFECTS			
	Functional	**Financial and economic**	**Social**	**Political**
Service users	May benefit *if* the service improves with the move. But, if the service has a face-to-face component (e.g. school, post office), then the move will appear as a loss	Not clear. Some services may lower unit costs, but will this be passed on to service users?	Little effect?	There may be some resentment from local user—'they took our service'.
Service staff	See Figure 4.4. Some staff may be left behind and will have to find new posts and possibly retrain	Those who move may be able to afford better accommodation (e.g. if the move is out of a capital city)	Social networks are likely to be disrupted both for those who move and for those who stay— but less so for the latter	Little effect, other than that the staff who have moved will now be voting in a different constituency
Residents (of old location)	Little effect, except possible reduced pressure on local services, if departed organization was large	Some incomes will be removed from the local economy	Possible damage to local social and community networks	There may be some resentment from residents, which could affect voting
Politicians	Little effect?	Little effect?	Little effect?	Local politicians appear to have 'lost business'. Ministers, however, may claim they are decentralizing and modernizing

status. Last but not least, it is likely to have political effects—on local residents and politicians and possibly even on the wider electorate (particularly if the move appears to trigger a significant change in the quality of the service). These various effects impact on a range of individuals and groups. Thus, for example, it may well have impacts on the people who use the service in question, which in some cases (schools) will be mainly local people, but in others will be people across the country, or even internationally (tax offices, population registries). Usually moves are said to be opportunities to improve the quality of service. This may very well entail the adoption of new technologies (these were central themes, for example, in the Lyons Review 2004). Such technological shifts will themselves require staff to acquire new skills and working habits (see Table 3.1 on the impacts of changing technologies). And so on: as we noted in Chapter 2, the modern theoretical stance is often to view 'place' as a shorthand for a range of relationships. Hence, when place changes, so will many of these relationships.

4.8 Using GAP as a Heuristic Tool

The GAP perspective set out in Figures 4.1–4.3, and Tables 4.1 and 4.2 is not a theory, and neither does it advance a specific set of hypotheses about what works and what does not. Rather it is a kind of checklist combined with a suggestive but not exhaustive set of summaries of some typical dynamic processes and effects. As such, it can be used to evaluate some—but not all—aspects of particular theories and interpretations. It claims, in effect, that 'governments, wittingly and unwittingly, can do or fail to do all these things, each of which shapes places'. It further suggests that some processes are usually self-reinforcing, while others tend to decay over time, and that the speed with which these shifts take place is both highly variable and frequently significant for analysis. So this perspective can be employed as a way of checking what has been put into, and left out of, specific theories and interpretations—and, for that matter, specific government programmes and initiatives (see Section 4.9 below). Why, for example, do some books and articles on planning and urban studies focus almost exclusively on modalities C and E (using planning regulations and negotiating with other placemakers) while ignoring modality B (locating public services and government facilities, even though, as was shown in

Chapter 1, public services actually represent a substantial slice of most OECD economies)? Why is the organization of borders (both external and internal) frequently left out? How much attention is paid to temporal dynamics and sequencing—the way in which one thing follows another (which means that a static snapshot can be particularly misleading)? Are the creation and management of virtual spaces treated as an entirely separate topic, by its own group of scholars, or are they integrated with an analysis of the parallel—and often complementary—management of traditional forms of citizen access to public services?

There is a great temptation at this point to introduce a 'model place'. After all, we have identified a range of factors that influence government's ability to act as a placemaker, so can we not also put together a 'model place', on which the model placemaker can act? It is a temptation that I have decided to resist. Certainly there are factors that are commonly important in the set of geographically specific relationships that we regard as a place. It is not hard to identify some of them: terrain, climate, distance from other major settlements, transport links, socio-demographic make-up, employment structure, system of governance, and so on. A list could be made. Then it could be arranged into a diagram with boxes and arrows. The problem, however, is that these elements combine in an almost infinite number of ways. Climate will be very important in one case and not at all in another, and the same goes for almost anything on the list. In one place the link between transport and the employment structure will be crucial (for example, in a commuter suburb) but in another it will be of little consequence (for example, a retirement community in Florida). The whole point about *a* place is that it comprises a unique ensemble of these and other elements, and, further, that asking a specific question about a specific place raises a different subset of these factors to attention. So, while we will certainly be discussing the particular features of particular places (especially in the next chapter), we will not attempt to build a single, generic, model place. Neither, though this is even more tempting, will we be putting forward a typology of different types of place. Geographers have tried to do this, with varying degrees of success, and have certainly succeeded in showing how complex the task turns out to be (see, e.g., Brenner 2004: 185; Carmona et al. 2010: 23–34). While we may admire some of these efforts, the principal focus here remains on how governments, by providing (or withdrawing) public services, help to shape places. Our concern is more with what is done (or not done) rather than with what patterns of settlements may eventually emerge.

4.9 An Illustrative Example: *Total Place*

In March 2010 the UK Treasury and the Department of Communities and Local Government published a report entitled *Total Place: A Whole Area Approach to Public Services*. In the foreword, the two sponsoring ministers wrote that, by 'putting citizens at the heart of service design', the government could 'deliver true transformation in public services across the country' (HM Treasury 2010: 3). 'It offers a means of reshaping resources based on the needs of people and places rather than through the funding streams of individual organizations, putting citizens at the centre of service redesign' (Humphries and Gregory 2010: 3). In slightly less visionary language, one could say that the document reported on thirteen pilot projects, each of which had involved some 'joining up' of services, combined with an examination of multiple flows of public expenditure into specific geographical areas. Thus, to take just one example, it was found that within the single London suburb of Lewisham there were 210 projects or programmes offering support for unemployed and workless people, and that these were financed by 15 separate funding streams channelled through more than 50 provider organizations (HM Treasury 2010: 19). Surely, a more citizen-centred approach to programme design and budgeting could produce a system that was simpler for both citizens and service providers to understand, and that at the same time delivered more 'bang per buck'? (*Total Place* had been born out of the 2009 budget, as one element in the Operational Efficiency Programme (OEP), an early government effort to tackle the evident need for public expenditure savings in the aftermath of the global economic crisis.) One final quotation should give an impression of the spirit (and the sometimes desperate wordiness) of the main document:

The findings of many pilots point to the same future: an agreement between place and government on shared outcomes at less resource, in return for responsibilities for the specific means of outcome delivery, and associated spending decisions, being held by the place, with the focus always being on better outcomes for customers.

(HM Treasury 2010: 61)

This report evidently generated quite a lot of enthusiasm (see, e.g., Leadership Centre for Local Government 2010). The pilot projects developed some innovative ideas for local service integration and for saving money by eliminating duplication. They also found some potentially reformable features of current service provision that had a high 'place component':

Our objective was to inverse the triangle of care—to shift the focus of investment towards activity in or near people's homes rather than in hospital. We knew that at least 30% of older people admitted to hospital in an unplanned way were avoidably admitted and need not be there . . . We calculated that if we could divert 15% of those avoidably admitted and had their needs treated either in their homes or closer to home, the annual saving would be around £18 million.

> (Project Director, *Total Place*, Bournemouth, Dorset and Poole, in
> Humphries and Gregory 2010: 20)

The sponsoring ministers urged the pilot areas to keep up the momentum, and other 'place leaders across England to consider how they too can develop their own whole area approach to services' (HM Treasury 2010: 3). However, three months after the publication of *Total Place* the general election saw the expulsion of Labour from government and its replacement by a coalition of the Conservative and Liberal Democrat parties. As so often happens, the new government did not want reminders of the reforms of its predecessor, so the first thing to change was the name; 'Total Place' was henceforth officially dead. However, the new government was committed to 'localism', to 'returning power to communities', to promoting 'the Big Society', and was also quite attracted by the idea of more joined-up budgeting at local level. Thus, many of the previous ideas lived on under new labels. 'Community budgets' was one of these, with the idea that groups of local service providers could apply to central government to have much more of their funding channelled through a single budget, which would give them more flexibility in how they applied it. However, the atmosphere in which these possible reforms were being discussed and developed had changed significantly, as the new coalition government swiftly announced deep spending cuts, which hit local authorities particularly hard—many of them faced the loss of more than one-fifth of their budgets within just a few years. Ideas of service integration were still there, but now they were mainly a means to make savings. As a number of participants noted from the outset, there is a potential tension between, on the one hand, radical service redesign based on the needs of citizens and, on the other, radical efficiency savings (Humphries and Gregory 2010; Leadership Centre for Local Government 2010; TPT interview 32). Sometimes the two goals will coincide, but at other times they will clash.

Applying the GAP perspective to *Total Place* helps point up some of its features. First, and most obviously, this was a programme that was far more strongly concerned with some modalities than others. Its main focus was on the financing of public services and the extent to which they could be joined up. It said very little about modalities A, C, or D. It did, however, do its best to adopt the symbolism (G) of localism and innovation, though the exercise of this rhetoric was largely confined to the relatively small group of directly interested civil servants and local government officers, plus a few politicians. So redrawing local-authority boundaries (A), for example, lay outside its scope. For the most part, so did town and country planning (C), and infrastructural investment (D). And, although the symbolism of local choice and freedom to innovate was deployed, the various reports and documents say very little about the symbolic and affective dimensions of *places*. Once the coalition government was in power, other measures were announced that seemed to cut right across the spirit of *Total Place*. For example, health authorities, which had often shared boundaries with local authorities, were abolished, and most of their powers for purchasing secondary and tertiary health care were given to groups of primary-care doctors (general practitioners). These group catchment areas for the most part did not coincide with those of any other public services, and general practitioners' track record of cooperating with other public services was modest (most of these doctor groups had previously operated like small businesses, and the doctors themselves were actually independent contractors, not salaried public servants) (Humphries and Gregory 2010: 5).

One could take this further. To put it provocatively (and contrary to its title), *Total Place* was not much about specific *places* at all. There is very little discussion of the specificities of place in the main document (although there is more in some of the individual pilot documentation). For example, there is no attempt to classify different types of place and their associated needs and trajectories. There is no analysis of how differences in the nature of local networks and cultures might influence what is selected as the most appropriate management strategy. The main elements in the analysis are individual 'customers', organizational networks, and budgetary flows—not places. There is plenty of discussion of partnering and joining up, but most of it is on a functional rather than a geographical basis. Curiously, there is not all that much about the placeshaping potential of new information technologies either. It is true that some geographical items are mentioned, but they are mainly drawn in as evidence of inefficiency. A number of the examples cited are worded in such a way as to suggest that the main aim is to save money by rationalizing and cutting down on the number of points of contact available to citizens. Thus, for example, it is stated that Leicester and Leicestershire have almost 450 face-to-face service points, with the clear implication that this number is far too large (HM Treasury 2010: 19). Despite the claims to citizen-centredness, there does not seem to have been much research on what density and geographic pattern of service points the residents themselves might want.

The temporal dynamics of *Total Place* were treated in a fairly limited way. The picture drawn in the original document was basically that there was a lot of duplication and waste, and that, as the programme unfolded, duplication would be eliminated, services better integrated, budgets pooled, and money saved. There was only modest recognition of the possibility that such rationalizations might themselves have interactive and knock-on effects, not all of which would point towards better and cheaper provision. For example: 'Looking at service provision through the eyes of the service user' (HM Treasury 2010: 20) by no means necessarily leads to the most efficient or economical solutions. What suits the user may be rather an expensive set of arrangements. Further, improving citizens' access to service information and advice can easily *increase* the demand for services (and therefore costs). Structural reorganizations (for example, to achieve shared management between adjacent local authorities, or to simplify multiple inspection and reporting regimes) frequently lead to loss of key staff and experience, to a temporary loss of focus by management, and to increased initial costs as the new systems are being set up (Pollitt 2009b). Pooling budgets may well require consequent changes to the arrangements for accountability and audit, and that is likely to concern national organizations far beyond a particular set of local authorities. Sharing data is recommended, but this often raises privacy and data-protection concerns, especially where partnerships with commercial companies and third sector non-profits are involved. Sharing chief executives or senior management teams between different local authorities (as has been implemented in some pilots) is fine while the respective local authorities are in broad agreement, but what does a chief executive do when his or her two employing authorities are in conflict over policy? Partnership working (the need for more of which is constantly stressed) is likewise fine while the going is good, but which partner is going to be accountable for what when something goes seriously wrong? Some of these problematic issues are recognized, but few solutions are offered for these barriers and trade-offs. Such problems are not necessarily insoluble, but they are not convincingly addressed in the original *Total Place* documentation, and their solutions seem highly likely to take both resources and quite a long time.

This has been no more than an empirical snack before the main meal. In Chapter 5 we begin to apply the GAP perspective at greater length and in more depth. Then we will continue to focus on modality B: what happens when government places 'its own things' into particular places.

5

Capital Flight: Moving out from the Big City

In the past, the geography of government has received intermittent bursts of attention, but never been subject to sustained challenge. A different approach is likely to be needed in future.

(Lyons Review 2004: 4)

5.1 A Practitioner's Theory of Deconcentration

Moving a set of government offices and the civil service inhabitants from one location to another is perhaps the most obviously 'spatial' thing a government can do. It is the most direct expression of GAP modality B, as discussed in the previous chapter. The practitioner's theory of moving civil servants out from the capital to the regions beyond can be simply stated. ('Capital flight' by the way, is a pun—perhaps not a very good one, because a reviewer of the first proposal for this book expressed disappointment that this chapter did not deal with international movements of finance capital.) Moving out will save money, because, away from the capital, both buildings and staff are cheaper. This straightforward motivation seems to have been at the root of many of the deconcentration proposals and actions in the UK and other advanced liberal democratic states since about 1960 (see, e.g., Jefferson and Trainor 1996; we will look at some of these in more detail in a moment). Against this, however, it needs to be recognized that such cost savings usually accrue only in the medium or long term. The short-term operating costs may increase, because of the one-off costs of relocation—for example 'the initial provision of new accommodation at the dispersed locations will mean at first that there is an increased burden on the exchequer' (Hardman Report

1973: 6–7; see also Lyons Review 2004: 3; Association of Higher Civil and Public Servants 2007: 15–16).

Our model of governments as placemakers (GAP) immediately suggests that deconcentration should not be thought of only in these simple terms of a trade-off between increased short-term costs and more substantially decreased long-term costs. There is much more to it. To begin with, even if for the moment we stay within the narrow confines of an analysis of costs, we have to recognize that the straight counting of the direct operational expenditures and savings arising from an act of deconcentration is an inadequate *economic* analysis. This is because operational costs are unlikely accurately to represent opportunity costs. For the accounts of (a fictional) agency X, moving from London to Llandudno may mean it can rent cheaper office accommodation and hire cheaper staff (at least at the lower grades, so long as national wage agreements no longer apply and/or London weightings are lost with the move). But for the economy as a whole the benefit is greater than this, because the 'disemployed' staff who stay in London will mainly find other jobs without too much difficulty, whereas many of those taken on in Llandudno would otherwise have remained unemployed (and therefore drawing state benefits). Similarly, the London offices will be rented out to another organization, whereas, without Agency X, the office block in Llandudno may well have remained empty. This has long been recognized by those charged with considering deconcentration—for example, Sir Henry Hardman, in his 1973 report on dispersing civil servants from London, noted:

It is the value of new net output which represents the gain to the nation as a whole, whereas the Exchequer effects are relevant mainly to the distribution of income, not to its total size ... the economic element of the case for dispersal does not rest on changes in the pattern of Government spending; it rests on the resource gain to the nation as a whole.

(Hardman Report 1973: 37)

There is also the technical point about mobility noted in Chapter 3—that cost–benefit analyses conventionally value travelling time negatively (as unproductive time), but the technological environment is now such that many kinds of travel can be highly productive, in terms of both work and social contacts (Lyons and Urry 2005). Logically, therefore, the 'losses' resulting from larger numbers of public servants regularly having to travel to the capital in order to have face-to-face meetings with ministers and senior officials should now appear much smaller than they would have been before the days of mobile phones, Blackberries, and wi-fi laptops. Even in the 'old days', a decent train compartment allowed one to catch up on reading the files.

If, however, we move beyond a narrow concern with costs, many other aspects present themselves. The deconcentration reduces the spatial disadvantages of Llandudno. It diversifies its employment base. It strengthens virtual communications links between the town and the capital (modality H) and it may also lead to some improvement in real communications links—the maintenance of a local post office, improved roads, more or better trains, the upgrading of a regional airport, or whatever (modality D). It improves the 'quality of life' of the agency's staff (shorter, cheaper journeys to work, better accommodation per pound spent, beautiful, uncrowded countryside within easy reach). At the same time, it will inconveniently disrupt the lives of other members of the agency staff, who had their children at good London schools, while their partners occupied good jobs there, or who had simply built up rich social networks in London that would have to be left behind if they moved to Llandudno. The move also makes a symbolic statement about the government being a government of the whole of the United Kingdom, one that is concerned not only with London and the south-east (modality G). It may help the local Member of Parliament at the next election, by enabling him or her to point to Agency X and claim that he or she was instrumental in 'getting these jobs into our town'. (One study suggested that changes in the regional distribution of civil servants between 1980 and 1995 were quite strongly correlated with parliamentary constituencies that were key marginals for the Conservative governments of that period (Cole and Talbot 1997).) It may persuade other employers (shopkeepers, solicitors, general practitioners, plumbers, video rental stores, office supply firms) either to stay in town or even to move to Llandudno. It will probably please local estate agents and property developers. Meanwhile, back in London, the departure of Agency X will not only save the government money. It will also (theoretically) marginally ease rush-hour congestion, the inflation of office rents, and the overheated spiral of house prices. Some of these elements are no doubt difficult to calculate, but many of them can at least be nominally identified and included in decision-making around specific proposals for deconcentration. Some may also change in magnitude—or even direction—quite quickly (if, for example, a general economic crisis leads to a collapse in London property prices and office rentals, as happened in 1991 and 2008). This is the complex, unceasing dynamism of place already noted (Chapter 2) in the work of contemporary geographers such as Massey and Thrift.

5.2 The Practice: The UK, 1960–2010

Now we will examine two actual trajectories of deconcentration, one for the UK and the other, more recently, for Ireland (in Section 5.3).

There has been a long history of deconcentration-from-London initiatives affecting civil servants. Most notably, there was the Flemming Report in 1962, the Hardman Report in 1973, a series of deconcentrations accompanying the 'Next Steps' agencies programme in the late 1980s and early 1990s, and the Lyons Review in 2004. Note, however, that the 'average' civil servant was never in central London in the first place. As Hardman recorded, of a national total of 500,200 non-industrial civil servants in 1973, 70 per cent were already more than 25 kilometres from Charing Cross (Hardman Report 1973: 5). Flemming had sought to move out blocks of routine clerical and executive work, but by the time Hardman was reporting in 1973 the focus was genuine 'headquarters' staff.

Flemming recommended that 57,000 jobs should be deconcentrated. In the ten years following his 1963 report, about 22,500 were actually moved, with 70 per cent of these going to the 'assisted areas' (regions that had high unemployment and weak economic growth). In 1973 Hardman focused on 78,000 London HQ staff, and ended up recommending that about 31,000 of them should be deconcentrated. However, although the report was broadly accepted by the government, few of the moves had been completed by the time that Mrs Thatcher's administration came to power in 1979. The new government was not very enthusiastic about regional policy in general, and in any case its declared priority was to reduce the size of the civil service rather than spread it out. Furthermore, the phenomenon of having to pay more in the short term in order to gain savings in the long term (noted above) was not at all to ministers' taste:

The present programme would cost over £250 million during the remainder of the present public expenditure survey period to 1983–84, and we should be well into the 1990s before the benefits from dispersal began to offset the costs . . .

(House of Commons Debates, 26 July 1979, column 902)

In the end fewer than 12,000 of Hardman's projected 31,000 jobs had actually been dispersed between 1973 and 1988 (Jefferson and Trainor 1996). Thus fewer than half the dispersals recommended, respectively, by Flemming and Hardman ever came to fruition. And, despite the brave talk about the importance of economic costs, the main calculations in Hardman were actually based on operating cost savings.

From the late 1980s, Mrs Thatcher's government finally began to warm to the idea of deconcentration. This time, however, it was seen as part of a wider structural reform involving the shift of large blocks of operational work out of ministries and into semi-autonomous agencies that would be professionally managed at arm's length from ministers. This was the 'Next Steps' programme (Pollitt et al. 2004: 105–14) and 'there was a lot of pressure from ministers to apply it to the NHS [National Health Service]' (TPT interview 15). Regional considerations were present, but less prominent than in the Flemming and Hardman exercises. It was decided to extract the NHS Executive from the ministerial department and move it up to Quarry House in Leeds (where, at the time of writing, some remnants of the long-since restructured and renamed Executive still remain). Four or five alternative sites had been considered, and some quite detailed comparative costings and analyses were carried out. The then NHS Chief Executive hoped that the geographical distance 'would cement the separateness of the Executive from the Department' (TPT interview 15).

One participant described it as follows: 'Of course the reasons for the move were only partially financial; it was seen as part of the Government regional employment policy to move civil servants outside London, and I think also it was seen as symbolically advantageous for the NHS Executive to be physically separate from Whitehall.' Then there were wider effects on staff: 'And few people complained about the higher quality of the countryside or of the lower housing prices in the North (although that did make it hard to afford moving back South should that be desired or needed.' Technology also played its part: 'A key mitigating factor was the excellent DH [Department of Health] computer network and video conferencing links. I frequently had to remind new PAs in London that an hour's meeting in London meant a day's travelling for me, but by VC it took an hour' (all from TPT interview 14).

In this case all staff had been asked whether they wanted to go, and votes had been organized. From the staff's viewpoint 'Leeds improved massively in the 1990s', but nevertheless 'we had to put a lot of pressure on some people to go there' (TPT interview 15). Some of the most senior staff did in fact stay in London and commute to Leeds on a weekly basis. The view of my two (participant) interviewees was that overall the move had gone reasonably smoothly, and that most staff had, at least after a while, appreciated the higher quality of life available away from the metropolis. Subsequently, however, the NHS Executive was reabsorbed into the Department and, in 2002, it ceased to exist.

After the Next Steps moves of the early 1990s, the next major wave of deconcentrations arrived in the shape of the Lyons Review of 2004. Lyons had persuaded government departments to identify 27,000 jobs that could be moved out of London and south-east England, including 20,000 that 'should be taken forward urgently as part of the Government's forthcoming spending review' (Lyons Review 2004: 3). Promisingly titled *Well Placed to Deliver? Shaping the Pattern of Government Service*, this was an independent review by Sir Michael Lyons, tasked to report to the then Deputy Prime Minister and Chancellor of the Exchequer. Lyons claimed to have developed 'a radical new approach' (Lyons Review 2004: 1), asserting that the Hardman exercise of the 1970s had 'helped to promote a rather narrow view of "relocation" as the transfer of self-standing clerical functions from one part of the country to another—a kind of bureaucratic chess game' (Lyons Review 2004: 18). In a rather 'New Labourish' effort at 'rebranding', Lyons criticized the term 'relocation' itself, recommending that it should be replaced by the (strikingly ungainly) phrase 'locational dimension to business planning' (Lyons Review 2004: 5).

So what was radical and new about the Lyons Review? The report itself contains various hints, including the following:

- The assumption that 'the principal basis of any decision to disperse must be the business case of the relevant organization. Centrally imposed moves, as characterized by the 1973 relocation review by Sir Henry Hardman, did not strike me as realistic in modern circumstances' (Lyons Review 2004: 10). There was no explanation of *why* such an approach was now unrealistic and, in practice, although departments were left to manage their own moves, the Lyons Review and its targets were endorsed by the Deputy Prime Minister and the Chancellor of the Exchequer, and backed up by several central procedures, including a steering team in the Office of Government Commerce (OGC). The relocations could therefore hardly be regarded as entirely voluntary.

- Continuing stress on the fact that relocation was an opportunity for— indeed, should normally be accompanied by—major reorganization of the work done. Tasks should be re-engineered as they were moved, using modern management techniques and the latest ICTs. In particular, the Review stressed the scope for slimming down HQ functions, and directly criticized departments for their conservative stance in this respect (Lyons Review 2004: 7).

- Insistence that many of the potential benefits of dispersal would be achieved only if there was 'local pay flexibility'—that is, if the relocated staff were paid less than they would have been if they had remained in London. Standard national pay rates were now to be regarded as old-fashioned and retrogressive.

- A more sophisticated economic analysis (carried out by a consultancy in the usual New Labour way) than Hardman had managed. This pointed to greater economic benefits for receiving locations than Hardman's figures.

- An emphasis on the need for dispersals to be 'clustered in a limited number of locations rather than very widely spread' (Lyons Review 2004: 6; the Review did acknowledge that this conclusion had also been reached by Hardman).

Lyons recommended 'an approach which emphasizes moving posts rather than people, and to seek to redeploy staff who do not move with the post, rather than make them redundant' (Lyons Review 2004: 8).

The Lyons Review does seem to have got much closer to its headline targets than either Flemming or Hardman (this may have been helped by a combination of New Labour's more general commitment to targetry, and its long, unbroken period in office). The Chancellor's Pre-Budget Report in 2009 stated that well over 20,000 posts had been relocated. Lyons was on target and slightly ahead of schedule. The largest groups came from the Departments of Work and Pensions (4,000) and Defence (3,900), with the Home Office in third place (2,200). The biggest receiving regions were the north-west (4,461), Yorkshire and the Humber (4,243) and Wales (3,601). Roughly 135,000 civil servants remained in Greater London (www.ogc.gov.uk/government_relocationrelocation_programme_progress_81 (accessed 20 January 2010)). Senior officials responsible for the roll-out of the programme stressed the stability of the government and the lack of political interference. However, they also emphasized the need for strong central steering (from a unit in the OGC, based in the Treasury) and the leverage that derived from creating a powerful central database, which allowed them to keep up with, and sometimes even outguess, departments. The database told them when individual leases expired and breakpoints came up, and they could match possible moves with underused space elsewhere in the country. Departments had to get clearance from the Treasury if they wanted to renew a lease in central London. 'The consistency of the OGC's role has been pivotal' (TPT interview 26). OGC staff contrasted this stability and lack of politicking with the parallel experiences of Denmark, Ireland, and Scotland (for the Irish story, see the next section). Further, by 2010 the fiscal context had become so desperate that departments were focusing on relocation as a way of achieving their savings targets. 'The economic climate is a burning platform' (TPT interview 26).

While targets for numbers of posts were achieved, other aspects of the original Lyons vision fared less well. The government had never really managed to put together a 'strategic view of government'. 'This has been largely missing'—there had perhaps been some gains in integration within particular departments, but very little inter-agency integration (TPT interview 26). Departmental cooperation with regional bodies was an aspiration honoured more in the breech than in the observance. Departmental questioning of what was really policy work had been less radical than Lyons would have wished—and there were even instances of corporate services units (for example, procurement) trying to rebrand themselves as policy units (TPT interview 26). Finally the shift to regional pay flexibility, which had been much emphasized as a necessary element in savings in the original report, had proceeded far more slowly than some had hoped.

5.3 The Practice: Ireland, 1960–2010

Up until December 2003 the Irish government had never had an explicit, strategic policy for deconcentration. A number of individual acts of deconcentration had certainly been carried through, but not as part of a headline policy or programme. All that changed when the then Minister of Finance announced that 10,300 posts were to be decentralized from Dublin to over fifty locations, including no less than eight departmental headquarters. These included Agriculture, Community, Marine and Natural Resources, Defence, Education and Science, Environment, and Social and Family Affairs. This project was dramatic, significantly disturbing what had been 'a previously consensual and gradualist policy environment' (Humphreys and O'Donnell 2006: p. x). In the following paragraphs we will trace the trajectory of this project, before offering our own analysis of it.

First, some background. Ireland is a small country, but one in which central government is dominant and local government relatively weak. Further, 'centralisation is strongly imbued within Irish administrative culture' (Callanan 2003: 477). A recent OECD report on public management in Ireland notes that local government has limited autonomy, and that local taxation represents one of the smallest shares of total taxation of any OECD member state (OECD 2008: 68–9).

An interesting early example of Irish deconcentration was the 1967 announcement that two whole departments would be moved out of

Dublin—Education to Castlebar and Lands to Athlone. In the event this never happened. Opposition from staff led to a major scaling-down of the proposal, so that only selected units within the two departments, mainly consisting of younger, junior staff, were moved. In 1974 a plan to decon-centrate the whole of the Department of the Gaeltacht (Irish language community) to Furubo was similarly deflated (Humphreys and O'Donnell 2006: 44).

In October 1980 a new programme was announced, relocating 3,200 civil servants from Dublin to twelve provincial towns. Yet, following a 1981 review, the government deferred further action, mainly on grounds of cost (shades of the fate of the Hardman Report). Then in 1987 came an announce-ment that 2,380 staff would be relocated to eight regional centres, followed later by a second wave of 2,500 (Humphreys and O'Donnell 2006: 45). Most of these shifts were actually carried through, amounting in all to the dispersal of about 10 per cent of the then civil service.

Then came the surprise 2003 announcement. It was a startling set of decisions in several respects, not merely in its scale. First, procedurally, it seems to have been hatched in a very small circle, with little or no consul-tation. Even the then Taoiseach (prime minister) appears not to have known much about it. Second, despite ministerial claims to the contrary, most independent observers assessed it as bearing no relation to a 'National Spatial Strategy' that had been published just over twelve months previ-ously. Third, the plan was to spread the deconcentration out over 53 differ-ent locations, most of them quite small towns (or, in one case, a remote airfield, where 140 staff were to be placed in underused aircraft hangers and administrative buildings). This scatter-gun tactic flew in the face of both the National Spatial Strategy and the received wisdom of the development planning profession, which usually emphasized the desirability of co-locating a range of functions and firms so that a particular city could achieve 'critical mass'. As Lyons put it in the UK context: 'The economic benefit is likely to be maximized where functions are clustered in a limited number of locations, rather than widely dispersed' (Lyons Review 2004: 31–5). The new policy therefore did little to honour the long-standing objective of Irish planners to create some kind of urban counterweight to all-dominating Dublin (curiously, nothing at all was to be deconcentrated to Ireland's second city, Cork). Fourth, at a time when the Irish government was one of several to be concerned about achieving 'joined-up govern-ment', this radical dispersal did not seem likely to help, particularly since, apart from a few vague references to the wonders of modern ICTs, there was little detail about how existing coordination could be preserved, let alone improved (see, e.g., Walsh 2004; OECD 2008: 86). Finally, the 'business case' for the plan was conspicuous by its absence (OECD 2008: 85). The levels of rhetoric ran high, but, unlike Hardman or Lyons in the UK, the cost–benefit analyses, if they existed, were not available for public consumption. Indeed, two and half years after the announcement, a detailed report from the top civil servants association commented that, apart from one or two vague and unsubstantiated cost estimates, the Decentralization Implementation Group had completely failed to address the issue of the costs of the moves: 'The plain truth is that neither the DIG [Decentralization Implementation Group] nor any other body—Oireachtas [parliament] and Government included—has any idea of what the bottom-line costs of the decentralization programme will amount to' (Association of Higher Civil and Public Servants 2007: 16).

What could explain this approach? Most Irish observers seem to have concluded that the best (and most obvious) explanation was politics. The Environment Editor of the *Irish Times* put it vividly:

Mary Coughlan, then Minister for Family and Social Affairs, let the cat out of the bag. The Government's aim was to decentralize to locations where an influx of civil servants would have the greatest impact—smaller towns such as Ballina and Ballyshannon, rather than Galway where they would hardly be noticed. But this argument could not conceal the fact that clientilism was at the root of the locational choices made by ministers . . . And for what? To bring joy to the business community of every town—the publicans, shopkeepers, auctioneers, estate agents, car dealers and fellows with land to sell at a premium price for a new government office block.

(McDonald 2005: 9)

Whatever the true motives may have been, it is instructive to track the subsequent attempts to implement this bold policy. It turned out to be quite a rocky road. An early bump was the relocation of the minister responsible—Charlie McCreevy—who less than two years after his dramatic announcement was taken out of the Minister of Finance role and sent off to be a European Commissioner in Brussels. The Decentralization Implementation Group that McCreevy had set up after his speech had so many details to fill in that it began to look more like a policy-*making* group than a policy-implementation group. Resistance—not least from the civil service itself—was strong and often well informed. It became clear that many civil servants, particularly the more senior ones, were determined not to move (Association of Higher Civil and Public Servants 2007). So what had originally been announced as a voluntary programme (as far as individual civil servants were concerned) gradually became a 'coerced voluntarism'. Even so, by mid-2006, against a schedule of 7,215 relocated jobs, only 3,863 applications had been received from Dublin-based staff, while another 3,352 eligible, Dublin-based staff had declined the invitations and incentives to move (Association of Higher Civil and Public Servants 2007: 3). At that stage only about 500 staff were actually moved and in their new places. Nevertheless, the Decentralization Implementation Group was still insisting that the full 10,300 would be in place by the end of 2009. But this was not to be.

Furthermore, 'making the numbers' was only part of the change agenda. On the basis of an extensive programme of interviews with senior staff directly concerned, Humphreys and O'Donnell concluded that most of the planning for the big 2003 decentralization had focused on logistical and operational issues, and that wider questions of change leadership, sustaining collegiality despite dispersion, and preserving corporate experience and memories still needed attention. They had no doubt, however, that the 2003 programme was a fundamental shift: 'Overall, respondents felt, without exception, that the direct and indirect changes resulting from the current decentralization programme were of such a scale and character as to be the most radical introduced into the Irish system of public administration within living memory' (Humphreys and O'Donnell, 2006: 31).

By the autumn of 2008 the programme was fairly bogged down. Some of the original basic questions about the wisdom of the dispersal had still not been answered, the composition of the government had changed, and Ireland was taking a particularly harsh beating from the global economic crisis. On 14 October the government announced that it had reviewed the decentralization programme and identified certain 'priority elements' that were to proceed, while other elements would be effectively frozen until a later review. The number of posts that were still part of the programme that was to be 'progressed' was not 10,300 but just over 6,000. The announcement was widely seen as a smokescreened retreat by an embarrassed administration. Yet the political fiction that the programme was not dead lingered on, and even in late 2010, at a time when the post-banking crisis Irish economy was in a disastrous state, and newspapers were full of the photos of its uncompleted building projects, the government was not entirely willing to abandon it—at least in public. At the last look, the government's website reporting progress contains a long list of moves deferred for later reconsideration (www.decentralisation.gov.ie/ProgressJune2010.html (accessed 28 March 2011)).

5.4 The UK and Irish Histories Compared: Applying the GAP Model

One crude conclusion might be that, on both sides of the Irish Sea, large-scale deconcentration attempts often come unstuck, at least in the sense that they fail to move anything like their target numbers of posts. This would be true for Flemming, Hardman, the Irish 1967 attempt to move two departments, the Irish 1984 attempt to move the Department of the Gaeltacht, the 1980 relocation programme, and, of course, the great McCreevy decentralization from 2003. In the UK the 2004 Lyons Review seems to have been much more successful in hitting timetables and targets, though only by dint of constant pushing from a central unit that was in possession of very detailed information about leases and building availabilities, and that was backed by a powerful Treasury minister.

A second finding would be that hopes that deconcentration exercises will facilitate wider gains in coordination and joined-up services have yet to meet with much fulfilment. Even in the relatively successful Lyons exercise, departments still seem to have worked away at deconcentration in fairly silo-ed ways. The idea expressed in the original report that governments could take a strategic approach to positioning themselves (in our terms a rational–comprehensive treatment of modality B) was not carried through into implementation (TPT interview 26). The persistent barriers to co-ordination enumerated in Section 4.3 seem to apply to deconcentrations as to other kinds of organizational change.

A third observation is that many (but not all) moves attract a good deal of politicking. This is not particularly surprising—relocations mean moving money and jobs, and they also have obvious symbolic potential. If one could generalize across the various UK and Irish cases reviewed above, one might say that *too much political intervention* (McCreevy) leads to incoherent, pork-barrelled outcomes, while *no political intervention at all* leads to feeble results, as the reforming forces lack the firepower to overcome silo-ed departmental and professional resistance to change—particularly at senior levels. The Lyons Review represents a middle case, where there was a mechanism for invoking the authority of a minister from within the core executive, but at the same time there were enough data and enough transparency and enough calculation of gains and losses to ward off the worst excesses of pork-barrel political 'solutions'. We will find another middling case later in this chapter, when we consider the burst of growth that Canberra experienced between 1958 and 1988.

Clearly, deconcentration is a prime example of GAP modality B—the government putting its own things into particular localities. Equally clearly, however, it does not stop there. Its symbolic value (modality G) is particularly high—governments deconcentrate partly to show that they care about the whole country, and to combat the (seemingly almost universal) perception outside capital cities that these places are favoured by the governments that inhabit them. As far as direct planning mechanisms (modality C) are concerned, in both countries these are mainly the responsibility of subnational authorities. The latter, however, far from acting as any constraint on centrally driven deconcentrations, tend to compete for central government favours. Both the Lyons Review and the earlier 'Next Steps' deconcentration of the 1990s were accompanied by individual local authorities putting their own cases forward: 'come to us—we can offer you X and Y'. In Ireland, the McCreevy programme has been widely regarded as having been shaped by a political rationale: it would have rewarded each of a large number of fairly small local authorities with the gift of new jobs and additional sources of income. Further, some infrastructural investment (modality D) usually follows deconcentration, even if this is not necessarily large scale or automatic. Thus, for example, the deconcentration of the Meteorological Office to Exeter led to the upgrading of certain aspects of the local airport, while the move of the NHS Executive to Leeds required the wholesale modernization of the huge Quarry House building. In this study we have not focused on modality E (negotiations with other placemakers), but it is nevertheless clear that a certain amount of interaction has taken place. Irish developers and estate agents were certainly quick to start putting up new housing for the expected influx of ex-Dublin civil servants. Staff associations have been active in both English and Irish relocation exercises—either to oppose them outright or to negotiate better rights and terms for their members. Finally, deconcentration has also involved the virtual (modality H). As we saw in the NHS Executive example, good computer and video-conferencing links with the ministry in London played an important part in easing the problems of separation.

To conclude this half of the chapter, it should be acknowledged that, from a critical realist perspective, these cases—and those that follow later in this chapter and subsequently—only scratch the surface. They identify the different modalities involved and focus on some of the key drivers—saving money for the Lyons Review or building provincial political support for the McCreevy programme. But they do not, and cannot, penetrate very far into the detailed operations and interactions of the relevant mechanisms. Thus we do not, for example, ask precisely why Quarry House, rather than any other building in Leeds, was chosen for the NHS Executive, or what the precise party political coloration of the designated receiving locations were in the Irish case, and how these might have related to the electoral map at the time. We do not examine the basis of the estimated costings and how these may have shifted over time. All these and more would certainly be worthwhile things to investigate, but they would also require so much space that the book could not possibly accommodate the range of cases that it needs to probe and illuminate the larger issues that constitute its main agenda. As we have from the book's outset, we therefore remain mainly on the middle level, reaching down occasionally into local detail and sometimes connecting upwards to larger national and international trends and events.

5.5 Canberra

Instead of selecting and moving certain administrative tasks, why not move the whole of the government out of its existing city or cities, and put it onto a greenfield site? As indicated by Table 5.1, a number of countries have chosen this option, and here we will examine two: the movement of the Australian seat of government in the early twentieth century and the movement of the Brazilian capital in the late 1950s.

First, then, Canberra:

I grew up in Canberra, and I love the place. That's not difficult, whatever stupid outsiders say, blaming the city for the decisions of the politicians they elect. I love the high country light, its ancient hills at the end of new streets, its clean air. Its hot unhumid summers and frosty winters. Yet it's not a simple place.

(M. Halligan 2008: 158)

Table 5.1 The creation of new administrative capitals

Year of inauguration	Country	New administrative capital
1800	USA	Washington DC
1927	Australia	Canberra
1960	Brazil	Brasília
1966	Pakistan	Islamabad
2010	Malaysia	Putrajaya
2015?	Japan	Nasu or Abukuma
2020?	Korea	Chungcheong

Canberra was a greenfield site capital for the Australian Commonwealth (federal) government, chosen as a compromise location between the two pre-eminent (and deeply rivalrous) cities: Sydney and Melbourne: 'The sooner the Commonwealth can be administered from a neutral center, the sooner will Commonwealth politics lose the provincial bias which, up to the present, has militated against the healthy development of federal sentiments' (*Sydney Morning Herald*, 27 Nov. 1909, quoted in Pegrum 1983: 149). The notion of a 'neutral' location is an interesting one, but, given the theoretical perspectives developed in Chapter 2, it should come as no surprise to learn that such neutrality proved elusive. Rather, the struggle between the different Australian states continued, but now with a new player, who was seen, by the others, as anything but neutral (and rather greedy). This new player also took a very long time to get onto the pitch.

Indeed, the history of Canberra's development was a tortuous, long-drawn-out saga, with multiple delays and frustrations punctuated by sudden bursts of intense activity. Forty-five years after its designation, the population of the 2,359 square kilometres of the Australian Commonwealth Territory (ACT) had risen from the original 1,712 to only 28,000. The current state of the capital (at the time of writing in early 2011) is one that inspires deep loyalty among most residents, and admiration from many of its international visitors, yet still attracts jibes about its allegedly *petit bourgeois*, suburban character ('bungalow bliss') from some critics (for a particularly dyspeptic recent version of this, see Wanna and Craik 2010). Curiously, for such a much-criticized place, it currently faces the problems of success—in particular the fact that it has expanded so much that it is running out of land. ACT was created a century ago with the expectation that its capital city would eventually grow to a population of 50,000. The current population (2011) is about 350,000.

Canberra was a true twentieth-century city, conceived in 1912 and built mainly between 1958 and 1988. Its basic chronology is summarized in Table 5.2. During the early comparison of possible sites by Alexander Oliver, 1899–1900, forty-five sites were proposed and twenty-three visited, with great stress being placed on the proximity of railway lines, the adequacy of the water supply, and the moderation of the local climate (Pegrum 1983: 46–54). Then in 1902 a group of senators made a tour of the competing sites, only to find most of them uninspiringly dry and dusty—New South Wales was in the third year of a drought. Of the red dust in Yass one member of the visiting group said that 'he did not want to eat the site, but to see it' (quoted in Pegrum 1983: 78). At the end of 1902 a four-member

Table 5.2 A chronology of Canberra

Date	Development
1899–1909	Various commissions and committees conducted investigations to try to establish the best site for a capital. An astonishing variety of arguments (and special pleading) were advanced by interested groups (Pegrum 1983).
1901	The Australian Commonwealth (a federation of states) came into being (having been proclaimed in 1900). One provision in the agreement between the states was that there would be a new capital, somewhere between the two most populous states: Victoria (capital = Melbourne) and New South Wales (capital = Sydney). The new capital was to be located somewhere within NSW, but at least 100 miles from Sydney (Pegrum 1983: 27–37). Meanwhile the parliament building was chosen to be in Melbourne.
1908	The plains between the Murrumbidgee River and the Brindabella Ranges were chosen as the site for the new capital. (Canberra later became known as 'The Bush Capital' (Pegrum 1983), and there were several jokes along the lines of 'a good sheep paddock spoiled' (Greig 2006b). Canberra is about 250 kilometres south-west of Sydney and 650 kilometres north-east of Melbourne.
1912	Design competition for the capital (anonymized) was won by an American couple—Walter Burley Griffin and Marion Mahoney—who had never been to Australia.
1913	Griffin came to Canberra as Federal Capital Director of Design and Construction, but was continually frustrated by political and bureaucratic delays and obstructions. He left in 1920, having accomplished very little.
1924	First auctions of Capital Territory leasehold land.
1925	Griffin plan is gazetted—confirmed in the parliamentary gazette.
1927	A provisional Parliament House was opened, and the federal Parliament was transferred from Melbourne.
1930	Canberra's population reached 9,000, but the world economic depression put an end to the considerable construction of the mid- and late 1920s. Development halted.
1945	Population 13,000. For the next decade development was slow, and housing construction, in particular, constantly fell well behind the official plans (Greig 2006; Sparke 1988). Melbourne civil servants were most reluctant to be relocated to Canberra.
1955	Pivotal Senate Select Committee report on the development of Canberra; recommended a powerful and independent authority to accelerate construction.
1956	Population reached 30,000.
1958	Creation of the National Capital Development Commission (NCDC), which, over the next thirty years, was to oversee Canberra's rapid transformation into a city of 270,000 (1988). 'The planners were dedicated to a low-density, decentralized city of interlocking suburbs separated by parkland' (Greig 2006b: 49).
1975	Electoral victory of Liberal Country Part (Fraser) ushered in a new phase of financial restraint and public-service cuts. Rapid growth of Canberra ended.
1978	Offered two alternative types of self-government in a referendum, Canberrans voted decisively against both (Sparke 1988: 285–90).
1988	The Commonwealth Parliament legislated self-government for Canberra, despite continuing lack of any great enthusiasm from residents.
Early 1990s	A national economic downturn led to heavy cuts in public services and infrastructural spending; Canberra's growth was halted.
From late 1990s	Economy picked up and entered a long boom. Canberra's growth resumed.

Capital Sites Enquiry Board was set up to undertake a more detailed analysis. They ranked eight sites in seven categories: accessibility, water supply, land costs, building costs, climate, soil productiveness, and 'general suitability'. In the accessibility category they concluded that proximity to a railway line was essential (there was already a line between Sydney and Melbourne, and various smaller lines in the hinterland of Sydney). Seven of the eight sites were on or near the railway (Pegrum 1983: 86). In their report of July 1903, the Capital Sites Enquiry Board came to a totally different set of recommendations from the Oliver inquiry of just a few years earlier. Oliver himself condemned their methods. Their recommendations immediately led to further politicking, with Sydney politicians and newspapers aghast that sites that they believed favoured Melbourne had been ranked highly. The parliament (now in Melbourne) was to vote on a bill, but furious subsidiary arguments took place about the voting methods that should be used to rank the sites (a far cry this from anything in the early stages of Brasília!). One leading politician argued for his favoured site (the coldest one, Bombala) by claiming: 'The history of the world shows that cold climates have produced the greatest geniuses . . . Look where we like, it will be found that wherever a hot climate prevails, the country is revolutionary' (quoted in Pegrum 1983: 95–6). After six rounds of balloting, however, the House of Representatives chose a somewhat warmer location, Tumut. This decision was rapidly overturned by the Senate, who chose the genius-favouring Bombala. But this decision did not stick either; it was swiftly followed by a general election, after which the debates on the site were renewed. In August 1904 a Seat of Government Act was passed naming Dalgety as the site (a place even further from Sydney than Bombala, and therefore deeply unpopular with the Sydney faction). But that decision proved no more durable than the earlier ones. Finally, in October 2008, after nine further Senate ballots, Canberra was chosen (Pegrum 1983: 138). In October 1909 the Senate further approved a federal territory to enclose the new city.

But this was not by any means yet 'the end of the beginning'. Now the new capital had a site, but it did not have a design, or a name. In 1911–12 competitions were held for both. The three best designs were to be selected from anonymized bids. The Griffin and Mahoney design was chosen from 137 submissions. Yet this 'decision' did not last long either. The minister referred the winning designs to a departmental board of experts, who promptly came up with a hotchpotch hybrid of the three highest-scoring bids. It was on the basis of this hybrid that the first peg of a survey line was driven into the ground in March 1913 (Pegrum 1983: 166–7). On that great day Lady Denman, the wife of the British Governor General of Australia, announced that the winning name (from the 750 entries) was Canberra, with 'the accent on the Can' (quoted in Pegrum 1983: 75). Before much could be done, however, the First World War intervened, and a decade later there was still scant sign of a capital city.

'Start as you mean to go on' goes the popular saying, and in Canberra's case the capital's somewhat elongated labour pains gave way to four decades of fitful, frequently interrupted growth. Little happened between 1913 and 1925, then there was a little spurt of building (notably including the opening of the 'provisional' Parliament house in 1927) and then again little happened during the 1930s. The Second World War provided another interruption, and afterwards growth remained weak even from 1945 up to 1957.

Whereas Brasília emerged with eyewatering speed between the turning of the first sod in 1956 and its formal inauguration in 1960, Canberra took almost fifty years really to get going; its take-off came during the National Capital Development Commission (NCDC) period after 1958. Thus the winning Walter Burley Griffin design of 1912 remained largely unbuilt

Figure 5.1   One of the few Canberra houses built during the 1930s

Note: This capital federation-style house was built in 1937 in the inner Canberra suburb of Ainslie. My thanks to Alastair Greig, who provided me with the photo, and once lived in the house. Even quite small government-built houses in inner Canberra districts such as Ainslie or Braddon are today coveted and expensive (and frequently almost invisible behind the lush garden foliage that has become one of Canberra's trade marks). From the beginning, Canberra was low rise.

until well into the 1950s. The centrepiece was a triangle of major routes crossing a set of artificial lakes. Forty years after the design had been accepted, there were no lakes, and the bridges to carry two of the three sides of the triangle were not started. Even the parliament building (erected in 1927) was expressly 'provisional'. But then, in 1958, exactly half a century after the Canberra site had been chosen, the government set up a powerful planning and development body, the NCDC, and this commission (which at first enjoyed the support of an exceptionally dominant prime minister) galvanized the situation on the ground. By 1964 the lakes had been dug and filled with water, and two elegant bridges had been built to carry the main roads forming two sides of the triangle (Sparke 1988: 131–44). A 1945 population of 13,000 became 93,000 in 1966.

The year 1958 was clearly a good one for new cities. It marked the take-off of rapid development for Canberra. It was halfway through the super-fast, five-year construction of Brasília. And in the Siberian wastes it witnessed the launch of Kruschev's academic utopia of Akademgorodok, which by 1965 housed 40,000 scientists and 15 new research academies. (However, while at the time of writing both Canberra and Brasília are expanding and popular with their inhabitants, Akademgorodok features in traveller's tales as a wholly derelict symbol of the lost dreams of the Soviet period (Thubron 1998). All three cities offer ample confirmation of the theoretical postulate from Chapter 2 that places are *made* (and unmade).)

By 1970 the NCDC was obliged to publish plans for long-term growth up to a city of 500,000: *Tomorrow's Canberra* (National Capital Development Commission 1970). This was based on something called the 'Y-Plan', which had been developed secretly a few years previously. The Y-Plan envisaged the further development of Canberra following three corridors (in a Y-shape) from the city centre (Sparke 1988: 153–8). The corridors followed the main valleys to the north and south, and in each corridor a series of lesser, satellite cities would be built (Belconnen was the first of these (see Figures 5.2 and 5.3)). This projection already envisaged the politically sensitive possibility that Canberra would overflow the boundaries of the Australian Commonwealth Territory (ACT), and would therefore 'invade' the surrounding state of New South Wales. Relations here were complex and sensitive. In a federal state, ACT certainly could not tell the State of New South Wales what to do with its land. Yet NSW was already experiencing land speculation and price inflation near the ACT border. On the other hand, NSW farmers relied on Canberra for a large part of the demand for their produce, and NSW residents made plentiful use of the excellent ACT schools, hospitals, shops, and cultural facilities. In 1973–5 it briefly seemed

Figure 5.2 Canberra: main built areas in the mid-1970s

Note: In Belconnen—the first satellite city to be developed within Canberra—neighbourhoods were designed around high schools and neighbourhood centres (see Figure 5.3). The basic principle was that every able-bodied person should be able to walk to the local school and neighbourhood centre. Thus the pattern of local public services played a pivotal role in the emergence of local political formations.

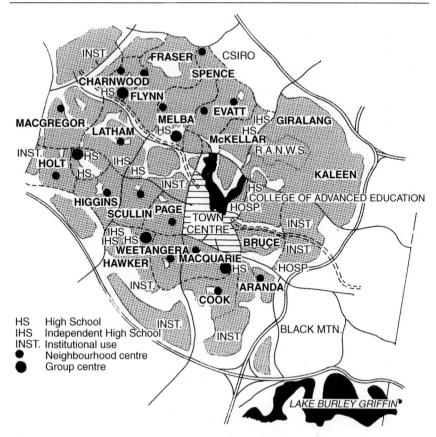

Figure 5.3 Belconnen: layout of a town within Canberra

as though some kind of deal might be possible in which, in return for compensation, NSW would cede land for an enlargement of ACT (Sparke 1988: 232–44). Political shifts destroyed that (possibly always faint) chance, and border tensions continue up to the time of writing (Halligan and Wettenhall 2002: Wanna and Craik 2010). As noted in Section 4.1, almost any line-drawing offers advantages to some groups and disadvantages to others.

In Canberra threats to the existing urban layout and density, and the closure of local schools, later became rallying points for the creation of a variety of community groups (Halligan et al. 2002). This was, in a sense, an echo of the civic activism that had existed in the early days of rapid growth, when local 'progress associations' had lobbied for more services as soon as possible. It is significant that, both in early growth and at the later stage, it was local public services that seemed to trigger the greatest activity:

It [participation] was actually quite high in the early days with each suburb having its own progress association. They are basically gone now, except for some new suburbs (especially Gunghalin) looking for services. That was the nature of the early ones too... There have been local planning consultative groups established by ACTPLA [the planning authority] but most Canberrans are rather cynical of anything that the government promotes with the word 'consultation' in it. My impression is that the government is more frightened of not consulting than residents are committed to participation.

(personal communication, dated 7 January 2011, from interviewee TPT 39)

Canberrans seemed considerably more interested in demanding and then defending such local facilities than they were in self-government *per se*. During the 1970s and 1980s, for example, there is evidence for civic activism of the kinds described above, but it is also clear that the majority were distinctly cool about acquiring self-government. In a 1978 referendum offering them two alternative types of self-government, Canberrans voted 36 per cent for one or other of the self-government options and 63 per cent for continuing the existing arrangements under which Canberra was administered by the Commonwealth (federal) government (Sparke 1988: 269–90). When self-government arrived a decade later, it was fairly much imposed on still-reluctant Canberrans by a Commonwealth parliament that contained many members who thought that Canberra had been financially privileged and should be made to pay more for itself. Why such reluctance to become self-governing? 'A simple answer, infuriating to the advocates of self-government, was enlightened self-interest—Canberrans knew when they were well off... If they were living under an oligarchy, at least it was generally benevolent, accessible, easily stung by criticism, responsive, and rarely short of funds' (Sparke 1988: 272).

The reign of the benevolent oligarchy—the NCDC—came to an end in 1988, at which time ACT acquired its own 'local' government, instead of being administered by NCDC and the federal ministries. The Australian Capital Territory (Self-Government) Act 1988 provided for a small unicameral legislature elected by proportional representation, with an executive of four or five ministers. Within an Australian system, which is usually three tier (federal/state/local), the ACT government and administration represents a unique fusion of the second and third tier (Halligan and Wettenhall 2002).

Soon after this, the rapid growth of Canberra came to an end. During the 1990s the Commonwealth (federal) government embarked on a programme of 5,000 job reductions in public service and cuts of about 70 per cent in its infrastructural spending in ACT. This was part of a severe economic recession, which Australia (and most other OECD countries) experienced from 1990. If governments feel obliged to make major expenditure cuts, the impacts on 'government places' such as Canberra or Brasília are almost bound to be significant. However, the dip in Canberra's fortunes was a pause rather than a permanent condition, and, as the Australian economy emerged from the recession (and entered a decade or more of low inflation growth), so the growth of Canberra revived.

5.6 Brasília

5.6.1 Beauty and the beast

Brazil's astonishing, high modernist capital, positioned on the vast interior plateau (*altoplano*), 1,000 kilometres from the Atlantic coast, has from its origins simultaneously played the roles of the beauty *and* the beast. To its founders, and still to some commentators, it partakes of the quality of a miracle—a prime symbol of the opening-up of the huge Brazilian interior, of modernization, of technological and design prowess, of the national pride of a developing country, and even of the fulfilment of the religious visions of a nineteenth-century Italian cleric who foresaw a 'promised land' between the fifteenth and twentieth parallels (Story 2006: 26–30). By 1970 most of the upper echelons of the Brazilan federal government had moved from their coastal cities to work and live in the new capital. In 1989 the central *Plano Piloto* (Pilot Plan) was designated by UNESCO as a World Cultural Heritage site.

Yet to its critics (and this has now become the left-of-centre critical orthodoxy) Brasília embodies the rigid, elitist, geometries of high modernism. It displays the linear rationalism of a bygone age and fails to engage with the 'real' culture and economic problems of contemporary Brazil (Holston 1989; Scott 1998). 'The once-celebrated architecture has become decidedly unfashionable' (Story 2006: p. xiv). If it symbolizes anything in the twenty-first century, it is the arrogance and inhumanity of the planners, the way they managed to produce, from what was 'in theory, an entirely public city', a place that eliminated 'the outdoor public life' that elsewhere is so central to Brazilian culture (Holston 1989: 136, 162). The satellite cities that have grown up around the planned capital are said to demonstrate the planners' failure to provide for the workers who actually built the city and subsequently serviced its privileged residents (Scott 1998: 129–30). In 2007 the *Plano Pilato* and its closest neighbourhoods represented just three of the thirty administrative districts making up the capital conurbation. These three (RA I, RA XVI, and RA XVIII) housed only 12 per cent of the total population (Holanda 2010; see also Table 5.3). Once one realizes that Brasília is not just the *Plano Pilato* but a multi-centre metropolis of 2.5 million inhabitants, new aspects become visible. For example, most of the 'planned city' turns out to have been unplanned, and demographically and morphologically the centre now lies well *outside* the World Heritage *Plano Pilato* (Holanda et al. 2008).

Thus 'myths abound in the apologia and the critique of the capital: the "love it or leave it" approach' (Holanda 2010: prologue). Perhaps the history of Brasília should lead us to expect such paradoxes and contradictions. After all: 'Brasília was planned by a Left-center liberal, designed by a Communist, constructed by a developmentalist regime, and consolidated by a bureaucratic-authoritarian dictatorship, each claiming elective affinity with the city' (Holston 1989: 40).

It is first necessary to summarize the oft-told story of Brasília's genesis. Its immediate origin was an election campaign. Kubitschek, the successful candidate in the 1955 campaign for the Presidency, had stood on a platform of developmental nationalism. He promised '50 years of progress' in a five-year term. Driven by heavy rain into the garage of a Goiás Studebaker dealership in April 1955, he was questioned by a local man about whether he would carry out the constitutional provision that envisaged the construction of a new capital in central Brazil. Kubitschek responded that he would, and henceforth the new city became the 'metasynthesis' of his

Table 5.3 Development of population balance between the planned city (*Plano Pilato*) and outlying settlements in the federal district of Brasília, 1960–1998 (%)

Year	Plano Pilato	Other cities within the federal district of Brasília
1960	44.4	55.6
1970	25.4	74.6
1980	21.5	78.5
1991	13.3	86.7
1998	10.6	89.4

Note: All figures are percentages of the total population of the Federal District of Brasília.
Source: adapted from Holanda et al. (2001: 10, table 1).

thirty-point 'target plan' (Story 2006: 1). This was new, in the sense that, until that point, there had been no clear commitment to fulfil the constitutional provision that had existed in the constitutions of 1891, 1934, and 1946, but had never been implemented. A 'federal district' had been drawn on maps for more than half a century, but there were no paved roads and only a few ranches within its borders. Nor is there any evidence that Kubitschek had carried out feasibility studies or, indeed, any studies at all, prior to the 1955 commitment.

Kubitschek won the election, and served as president from 1956 to 1961. An intense programme of construction began straight away. Between 1956 and April 1960 roughly 150,000 workers came to what was a huge building site, including about 40 per cent from the distant and impoverished northeast. A powerful new agency, Novacap, was created in September 1956 to oversee both planning and construction. The new city was inaugurated on 20 April 1960, almost exactly five years after the question-and-answer session in the garage. It already had a population of 100,000, but was far from being complete. Its construction is estimated to have accounted for between 2 and 3 per cent of national GNP during those years, and to have represented roughly 20 per cent of the total federal budget (Story 2006: 40–1).

5.6.2 Brasília's trajectory of development, 1960–2010

The paradoxes were there from the start. Satellite towns for poorer families (such as Tagatuinga—see Figure 5.4 for a map of the administrative subdivisions of the Federal District) were springing up even before the official inauguration of the city in 1960. As Table 5.2 illustrated, the *demographic* centre of gravity was never Luis Costa's SuperQuadra apartment blocks in the *Plano Pilato*. (The *Plano Pilato* is a small part of the Brasília administrative region shown in Figure 5.4. A SuperQuadra apartment block is shown in Figure 5.6.) The demographic centre was always outside the central district (Figure 5.7). During the intervening half century many of these settlements have been transformed out of all recognition. Shacks have become tower blocks. Sandy red tracks have become paved roads. Modern shopping centres have been constructed. The legal basis of many such settlements has been regularized and they have acquired mechanisms of government. The satellite cities cannot be municipalities with elected mayors and councils because the federal district cannot be divided into municipalities. It is, however, divided into administrative regions, each of which is ruled by a Regional Administrator, appointed by the Governor of the District. Yet as

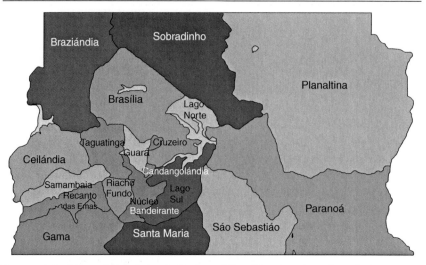

Figure 5.4 Map of the federal district of Brasília, showing the administrative regions with satellite cities

Figure 5.5 The National Library of Brasília

Note: At the time this photograph was taken in 2010 the National Library building had been complete for several years, but it was still not functioning as a library. Ventilation problems and software problems had prevented the library from either safely storing books or from managing the stock.

Figure 5.6   One of the original SuperQuadra (large apartment blocks) in Brasília's *Plano Pilato*.

one settlement is regularized another shanty town springs up, as the magnet of the Brasílian job market draws in more poor people from other parts of Brasil (Figure 5.8). Land use planning policies have usually been ineffective, and private—especially entrepreneurial—interests have been able to get their way (Holanda et al. 2009, pp. 10–11).

Figure 5.4 shows the outline of the Federal District and the boundaries of the administrative regions. The central *Plano Pilato* lies within the district of Brasília, just west of the lake. In 2010 the population of this district was just under 200,000. Compare this with other districts that contain large satellite cities, such as Taguatinga (244,000) or Samambaia (164,000). Figures 5.5–5.8 show the different character of three of the different types of settlement in Brasília (all photographs were taken by the author in March 2010). The first two images were taken within the *Plano Pilato*.

Figure 5.7 shows Aguas Claras, a forest of high-rise apartment buildings, which appeared at dizzying speed in an area 20 kilometres from the *Plano Pilato* but now connected by metro and major road. The extension of the metro system beyond the *Plano Pilato* has naturally proved to be a magnet for development. Figure 5.8 shows the main shops in a still-emerging shanty town, one that has just acquired its first school (three shifts of 600-plus children per day) and health centre. This settlement began near a municipal rubbish tip, where poor people came to pick through the waste. We should note that the arrival of permanently housed public services is a highly significant marker on the trajectory from shanty town to legitimate township. Indeed, politics plays a vital role here—although this is certainly not formal 'participation and consultation' on the Canberra model. The poor may be poor, but they have votes, and politicians attempt to secure those votes by providing material improvements:

the fact that the federal district has statehood status has promoted the recognition of the social demands of the 'cidades satélites'. After all, the governors need the votes from the city dwellers. The voters in the *Plano Piloto* are mostly public servants and

Figure 5.7 High-rise development at Aguas Claras, a satellite city 20 kilometres from Brasília's *Plano Pilato*.

Figure 5.8 The main shops in Strutural, originally an illegal settlement of poor people that developed in what was supposed to be the 'green belt' between Brasília's *Plano Pilato* and the satellite city of Taguatinga.

tend to vote for the PT [Partido dos Trabalhadores (Workers' Party)], due to the party's connections to public services unions. Thus only the votes in the satellite cities are 'up for grabs', so to speak.

(C. Andrews, personal correspondence, 13 Jan. 2011)

The existence of these different types of settlement should not be reified into a belief that everything fits exactly into three mutually exclusive categories: *Plano Pilato*, established satellite towns, and slums. Some of the most interesting features of the metropolis are 'mixed' localities, where different socio-economic groups are co-located. Holanda et al. (2008) describe Vila Planalto, close to the heart of the *Plano Pilato*, where wealthy and much less wealthy have lived together since construction of the city began. Increasingly, there are also instances where wealthier people are drawn out to the satellite cities, where their money will buy a big villa with land (Holanda 2007). Nevertheless, the overall picture remains one of a wealthy *Plano Pilato* with high employment and low crime, and a string of outlying cities where, to differing degrees, average wealth is considerably lower, jobs are fewer, and crime is higher (Brasilmar and Costa 2007).

As with Canberra, transport plays a crucial role in Brasília's existence. Brazil is a huge country, and the building of Brasília provided the stimulus for an orgy of road construction, with large national highways connecting the capital to different parts of the country, north, south, east, and west. Indeed, some studies have suggested that it has been the consequent road-building, rather than the mere existence of government buildings and jobs, that has provided the biggest boost to the regional economy. This is a controversial issue among academics, but it does seem that the road-building has been an important factor in stimulating the growth of agri-business, a sector in which Brazil has had considerable economic success. Locally, bus transport is crucial for the many thousands of workers who come into the *Plano Pilato* area every day, and the central bus station is the true hub of the capital. It is common for the lower-paid workers to have to travel long distances. Although London and Paris are much bigger than Brasília, the average distance their citizens have to travel to get to the centre is much less (Brasília = 24.3 kilometres; London = 12.6 kilometres; Paris = 10.0 kilometres (see Holanda et al. 2008: 6)). The construction of a metro that reaches out beyond the *Plano Pilato* has stimulated a wave of new construction, Aguas Claras being a particularly spectacular example (see Figure 5.7).

Brasília was definitively *not* the product of the kind of study groups or public reports that have festooned the earlier parts of this chapter. The buildings and roads themselves were planned—yes—but the project as a whole was more visionary and symbolic than the product of any cost–benefit analysis. Neither was it halting, long-drawn-out result of an elongated process of party political and regional bargaining, as was Canberra.

Measured against some of the more millennial visions of its founders and foretellers, the new city must be accounted a failure. More specifically, the idea that the city alone would prove a national catalyst transforming the whole of a huge country onto a new growth path and into a new mindset has, unsurprisingly, proved unsustainable. More specifically still—and this is a point of repeated criticism from social scientists—any notion that Brasília would be able to insulate itself against the unplanned growth of outlying, low-income settlements was clearly wishful thinking.

Yet all this does not even come close to making Kubitschek's achievement a flop. Consider that, first, a large city *was* built and occupied, very quickly. That virtually the whole of the Brazilian federal government has moved there, even if the completion took a decade or more. That the project boosted the economic growth of the interior—at least regionally—and that at the time of writing the regional growth rates are among the highest in the huge and fast-growing Brazilian economy. That life in the city is popular with many of its residents, who 'are generally wealthier, better educated, and healthier than their compatriots in other regions' (Story 2006: p. xv; Holanda et al. 2008). And finally that, in so far as we can assess symbolic effects, Brasília was for at least a generation a worldwide icon for modernity, and a source of considerable national pride. 'Today, the year 1958 figures in the Brazilian popular imagination as a golden age, their Camelot' (Story 2006: 73). It was a year of democracy (before the military dictatorship that arrived in 1965), of rapid industrial growth, of the burgeoning international popularity of Bossa Nova, of the country's first victory in the football World Cup, and—of Brasília.

5.7 Canberra and Brasília Compared: Applying the GAP Model

> Brasília started with a fanfare of trumpets and continues now, after seven years, as if to a never ending roll of kettledrums. Canberra started with a squabble, then stopped, and went and hesitated, and went on again in a painful exhibition of democratic indecisiveness and bureaucratic stodginess.
>
> (Boyd 1964, quoted in Denton 2007: 1)

Canberra and Brasília share one important set of features. They were both projects where governments themselves seemed to hold all the cards. They had defined the borders of a territory (respectively, ACT and the Brasília Federal District). They owned all the land. There was very little there to hinder them—both were almost 'greenfield' sites. They did not even have to cope with the problems of multi-level government, because both were special arrangements, with no inferior tier of local government to articulate its own views. In both cases the governments had a lot of activities directly to put into their new capitals—ministries, parliaments, officials by the thousand. Furthermore, both projects were high on symbolic and rhetorical importance. National parliaments and libraries and all manner of museums, galleries, and statues were to be erected. In Canberra, many of these became the focus for strong public controversies—usually on grounds of aesthetics, location, and cost—but paradoxically the vehemence of these debates signalled a deeper level of agreement that these symbolic constructions were indeed both public and important. In GAP terms, both governments were very high on modality B (they had lots of 'things' to put

135

into their designated territories), they were very high on modality C (their planning controls were as complete as could be), they rated equally high on modality D (they had entire city infrastructures to construct), they were in an unusually strong position with relation to modality E (other place-makers, initially at least, were relatively weak), and they were engaged in projects of huge symbolic significance (modality G). Surely, if ever spatial plans could be vigorously and faithfully implemented by government, it was in circumstances such as these?

Another common feature in the stories of both Canberra and Brasília has been the importance of the location of basic public services (modality B). The shanty towns of Brasília and the ordered leafy suburbs of Canberra may be—are—worlds apart, but in both cases the positioning of schools and primary health facilities were crucial to the formation of places. In Strutural (see Figure 5.8) the breakthrough from illegal shanty town to the beginnings of an ordered, recognized settlement came with the construction of a large primary school and a local clinic. In Belconnen—the first town-within-a-city to be developed in Canberra—neighbourhoods were designed around high schools and neighbourhood centres (see Figure 5.3).

Yet, despite the strong hand of government, things have not turned out at all as they were originally intended—in either city. In the case of Canberra, the city had a stop–start existence spread out over almost a century, and the authorities fell out with their principal designer almost immediately. In the case of Brasília, development certainly proceeded much more quickly, and the designer became a venerated national hero, but most of the growth was unplanned, and the majority of the population live in places and circumstances that were not foreseen by the original designers and planners. These divergences require explanation.

Canberra's development offers many examples of the types of constraint on government action that were discussed in Chapter 4. Between 1945 and the establishment of the NCDC in 1958 coordination of development was handicapped by an internal coordination problem—the division of responsibilities between the Ministry of Interior and the Ministry of Works. It was also handicapped by the reluctance of the private building sector to get involved on a large scale, given better opportunities elsewhere (Greig 2006a). A further drag on development was the formal and informal resistance to relocation from Melbourne offered by civil servants based there (Sparke 1988). All these constraints were eventually overcome, but the Canberra boom of 1958–78 brought its own constraints. Success meant that the city was soon pushing against the borders of ACT, and that inter-governmental tensions with NSW began to rise. Public services featured significantly in these political exchanges, which were by no means always decorous. At various times, ACT commentators accused NSW of being badly governed, of not providing high-quality services in the areas adjacent to Canberra, and of failing to plan those areas in a responsible and professional manner. On the other side, NSW commentators portrayed Canberrans as 'feather-bedded' and heavily subsidized, living in a luxurious, low-density environment with first-class cultural, health-care and other facilities paid for by the Australian tax-payer. And, even after the NCDC was well established, the actual day-to-day administration of Canberra was highly fragmented. The NCDC and the Ministry of the Interior were the main players, but there were at least nine further departments with significant responsibilities. The function of rubbish disposal alone involved six different departments (Sparke 1988: 274–6).

Next we should refer to significant differences in political systems and cultures. If Canberra and Brasília were similar in terms of the (seeming) high degree of control governments had over their development, they were startlingly different in how that development took place. To begin with, the choice of Canberra over other locations was a hard-fought matter, the result of a process that included a mixture of rather sophisticated comparative analyses of different sites with overtly self-interested political manœuvring and voting. Such democratic to-ing and fro-ing did not detain Brasília at all. The site, it seemed, was ordained by a combination of a nineteenth-century divine vision and a newly elected president in a hurry. It was not to be the subject of Canberran bickering and irresolution: on the contrary, it was to be the focus for immediate action on the ground. Brasília must be declared open during the term of the presidency.

So political differences and organizational fragmentation were of great importance. Yet there were still other factors. As argued in the preceding chapters, places 'fight back'—they set their own constraints, some of which can be either technologically or economically impossible to surmount (or both). The easing of such constraints is intimately bound up with whatever are the prevailing technologies of transport and communication at a particular point in time. Thus, in Canberra's case, water and railways were of considerable importance in the original siting decision, and later air travel became crucial to its growth. Material constraints of labour and materials were also significant influences at certain times. For Brasília, labour constraints were less important, but the huge distances did make for heroic struggles to transport necessary materials. The relative flatness of the surrounding terrain meant both that a high-rise city centre looked imposing, and that the satellites could spread quickly, with few natural barriers. In Canberra, by contrast, the surrounding hills and mountains were so impressive that the developers opted for low rise, safeguarded the upper slopes from building, and placed the burgeoning suburbs into valleys.

Some of the divergences represent the impact of larger, 'outside' events coming and knocking plans off course. In the Canberra case, the two world wars and the global economic depression of the 1930s all qualify for this category. Thus the influence of wider relationships reach down into many particular places and produce effects. Brasília was exposed to fewer of these, partly because it was thrown up in such a short period. Other divergences represent the influence of the private sector as a co-placemaker—one that exercises influence even where the government appears to hold all the cards (but actually does not). In Canberra, even the powerful NCDC made most rapid progress when it contrived to create favourable conditions for private builders. When Canberra looked risky, or when there were shortages of materials on the market, or when there were easier profits to make elsewhere, the growth of Canberra slowed. Meanwhile in Brasília the importance of the private sector took a somewhat different form. Unplanned, private initiative growth took place in the satellite cities and, as we have seen, actually outpaced that achieved in the *Plano Pilato*.

Finally, we can also see how *sequential* development *over time* is crucial to understanding many episodes in the history of both capitals. In both cases, pioneers suffered privations and fought for better conditions. In both cases, once they had those better conditions, they wanted to defend them from further incursions or depredations. It is an old piece of political wisdom that it is much harder to take something away that citizens already have than it is to resist their demands for something new. Writing of Canberra in the 1970s and 1980s, Sparke (1988: 247) makes the point nicely: 'Citizen participation appealed to nearly everybody as an idea. Making it work was another thing. It often happened that early arrivals in a new area came to admire their view and appreciate their rural surroundings so much that they resisted any further urban growth.'

In Brasília the sequence is well recognized. Constructing the new city offered many jobs. Poor labourers came from other parts of Brazil to take that work. They lived in tents or shanty towns, with minimal facilities. They also, however, represented a political resource. Governors of the federal district wanted their votes. So they provided public facilities to win favour, as well, perhaps, as for higher motives. As the satellite cities developed, the more successful ones, despite minimal planning, now began to support a range of urban facilities, and the newest, poorest arrivals found it difficult to find places downtown. So they erected new shanties, somewhere else, and the cycle began again.

Grandiose plans to move entire administrative capitals, or construct global cities in the desert, are by no means extinct. They are, as Hirst (2005) and Sudjic (2006) have suggested, almost invariably intimately linked to concentrated political power. Yet, before we decry such projects as authoritarian or undemocratic and not the way we would wish matters to proceed, we should take note of an inconvenient truth. In our two case studies, concentrated authority backed by the highest political power (in the shape of the NCDC at its zenith, or Novacap in Brasília) is precisely what achieved many of the things we most admire about these cities—including well-planned public roads, public spaces, schools, hospitals, and government buildings. True, these powerful organizations were both spawned by democratically elected governments, but their largest achievements were nonetheless made during periods in which other placemakers were effectively excluded or at least only ancilliary to the line from the top. Similarly, the most successful of the deconcentration projects examined earlier in the chapter was the one with the strongest and best-informed central driver (the OGC for the Lyons exercise). If large-scale placemaking is to achieve its aims, it does, it seems, require not only a plan, but also some concentration of authority.

6

Save our Hospital!

Total Place has shown the benefit of a citizen centred approach to address complex public service challenges. The majority of pilot proposals, and the most exciting, start with the citizen.

(HM Treasury 2010: 20)

A lack of formal guidance on conducting public consultations, coupled with the sensitivity and parochialism that often permeate any proposed changes to the NHS, means that public consultations are often prolonged.

(Royal College of Surgeons 2006: 42)

6.1 Introduction

Are they different citizens or the same ones—the exciting innovators of the UK government's 'Total Place' programme, and the parochial, hypersensitive stick-in-the muds who are patronized in the Royal College of Surgeons' report on reconfiguring surgical services in the British National Health Service (NHS)? We will argue that there is no reason why they should not be one and the same.

In this chapter we will examine the changing locations of hospitals— where they are, and why hospital services are often on the move. We will also pay particular attention to citizen reactions to (some of) these shifts. Changes to the local hospital seems to be one of the few issues that frequently rouse citizens to active political intervention—to meetings, campaigns, petitions, marches, and even the putting forward of political candidates at elections. When Kidderminster Hospital (England) was threatened with closure in 1997, a local doctor, Richard Taylor, stood at the 2001 general election as an independent candidate, opposed to the proposed 'reconfiguration'. He was duly elected, defeating the government candidate and fuelling what the Royal College of Surgeons described as 'reluctance within central government to make decisions about locally-delivered healthcare, even when professional logic on the grounds of patient safety and cost has been clearly demonstrated' (Royal College of Surgeons 2006: 8). Nor was this an entirely isolated or freakish episode. Hospital closure or 'reconfiguration' threats have generated a whole series of public demonstrations, such as two successive marches of more than 20,000 in a modest-sized rural town when proposals were published for twenty-four-hour medical-led emergency services to cease at the local hospital, and subsequently when documents were leaked suggesting that a small elective surgery unit might close (National Institute for Health Research 2010: 134–5).

The rest of this chapter is organized into four sections. The first (6.2) takes a broad look at the topic, introducing some of the key factors that prompt hospital 'reconfiguration' (the current UK management speak). The second (6.3) presents some information about general trends in Europe and the USA. The third (6.4) offers a detailed case study of one particular area in the UK, examining the pattern of change since the mid-1960s. The fourth (6.5) reviews the earlier material through the lens of the GAP model introduced in Chapter 4.

6.2 Forces for Change

Since around 1980 hospitals have been closing all over Europe—though considerably more rapidly in some countries (for example, the UK) than in others (for example, Germany). Many of them have been small hospitals: local hospitals, 'cottage' hospitals—'our hospital' to those who live in the neighbourhood. The reasons for these closures have been multiple (see McKee et al. 2003 for a summary discussion, and for some reasons why the demand for hospital care may also expand). Local hospitals may find themselves undermined for a number of reasons—some of the key ones having to do with technological change:

- Changing medical technologies. Some of the most advanced medical technologies (such as advanced imaging machines) either are too expensive for small hospitals to buy and run, or require too wide a range of specialist support staff to make it practicable for a small hospital to find and pay for the necessary staff, or to achieve the optimal patient throughput. The logic of this kind of technology is therefore to central-ize. But some changes in medical technologies may also have the oppo-site effect. Some new technologies have made it easier and cheaper to perform certain procedures, so that they no longer have to be performed in a general hospital and can now be carried out in a primary-care doctor's office, or in a local health centre, or even at the patient's home (National Institute for Health Research 2010: 44, 53). For exam-ple, 'the advent of stenting and interventional radiology for routine [cardiothoracic surgery] cases has resulted in surgery being reserved for the more complex cases' (Royal College of Surgeons 2006: 10). Other, routine operations may be assigned to Independent Sector Treat-ment Centres, which are often rather like specialist assembly lines for treating a limited number of common and not too complicated proce-dures (for example, joint replacement). 'ISTCs have adopted the "focused factory" model of service provision—high volume, less techni-cal and less complex cases that guarantee an agreed level of throughput and income' (Royal College of Surgeons 2006: 21). A third example would be HIV, where the development of anti-viral drug therapies has helped to reduce the amount of time that sufferers have to spend in hospitals. All these kinds of change can reduce the flow of patients into a local general hospital and eventually call its financial stability into question.

- Changing numbers of patients. A variety of digital on-body and in-body monitoring devices, and diagnostic technologies are likely to mean that patients—especially those with long-term chronic conditions—will need fewer visits to primary-care doctors and/or hospital outpatients depart-ments (NHS Confederation 2010). Telecommunications devices will allow not only monitoring but also discussions and advice-giving to take place between patients and nurses or doctors (May et al. 2005). It is now well over a decade since the UK National Health Service Executive claimed that 'opportunities in the field of telemedicine will be seized to remove distance from healthcare' (National Health Service Executive 1998). These devel-opments can reduce the flow of patients into a local general hospital.

- Changing professional requirements. One feature of the medical profes-sion is its continuing ability to lay down the standards necessary for each type of medical procedure. Thus, procedure X is decreed to require doctors qualified to this level in these particular specialisms, plus nurses of this type, and perhaps also paramedics and equipment of specified types. Over the years the practice of medicine has tended (often for good reasons) to become more and more formalized in this respect. One of the consequences is that, for a hospital to be able to carry out procedure X, the professional protocol will now say that it needs a minimum 'package' of people and equipment, in a way that, thirty or forty years previously, it would not have done. 'The importance of protocol-driven work cannot be underestimated' (May et al. 2005: 1489). This can lead to some types of condition being effectively excluded from direct, traditional service provision by being 'bracketed off' to nurses and call centres (May et al. 2005: 1493). It can also lead to hospitals having to abandon certain lines of activity as unaffordable or unstaffable (or because professional accreditation is withdrawn), and such activities then gravitate to bigger, wealthier hospitals, which can sustain the necessary backup. Consider the following statement from a UK health-care manager who was considering the survival of a modest-sized hospital in a rural town (coded 'Yellow Town' in the original research): 'if anybody is saying to you think you're going to create another district general hospital in Yellow Town, it's pie in the sky. When you talk about a full DGH you're talking about a full blown accident and emergency department that requires an intensive care unit, orthopaedics on site, it requires on-site CTs, MRIs' (quoted in National Institute for Health Research 2010: 135). In this quotation we see a (typically) close intermixture of professional and technological considerations.

- Changing distribution of populations, meaning that hospitals are no longer 'in the right place'. So the health-care planners want to relocate services (or entire hospitals) so that they are closer to the new population 'centres of gravity'.

- Rationalization in the name of 'economies of scale'. Hospitals usually account for 40–60 per cent of all health-care spending in OECD states, and the health budget line itself is frequently the second largest item on the government's bill, after social security expenditures. As pressure on health-care expenditure grows, public authorities are obliged to seek ways of reducing costs. One such way can be to centralize or co-locate various services on a single site, but that may mean closing a number of pre-existing, smaller sites. In the case of Kidderminster General Hospital, it was one of three general hospitals in the jurisdiction of Worcestershire Health Authority.

- Changing patterns of disease. Some types of illness that used to require substantial hospitalization have been in retreat (for example, tuberculosis).

Indeed, it is often easy to demonstrate that a particular pattern of hospitals, perhaps originally constructed in the nineteenth and early twentieth centuries, makes little technological, professional, financial, or demographic sense in the twenty-first century. Yet popular resistance to changes is frequently vigorous. What is going on here?

A first step is to understand that a hospital is far more than just a building in which sick people receive medical attention. Hospitals are places that simultaneously serve a variety of purposes. For example,

- They can symbolize a caring state, which looks after the health of its citizens (if it is a hospital that is paid for and/or operated by the state).

- They can signal a particular political ideology (for example, in countries where one political party or parties believe(s) that most hospitals should be run by the state and another party or parties believe(s) that they should be privately owned and operated). Note that the ideological meaning of, say, creating a new hospital is not fixed. In the UK NHS, it may reaffirm the government's commitment to a nationalized service free at the point of access. In Belgium, it may represent a more paternalistic, corporatist position, where a new hospital will be run by a non-profit charitable organization representing a tradition of charitable, often religiously inspired care. In the USA, the construction of a for-profit, private hospital may symbolize popular beliefs in the dynamism of competitive markets and the power of high technology.

- They can be perceived as a civic asset for a particular place. 'In the same way that a cathedral once defined a city, the presence of a hospital helps define how a community perceives itself... Hospitals are important in attracting residents and industry, and in this way serve an economic development function. The closure of a hospital in an area in economic decline can symbolize a loss of confidence in a region...' (McKee et al. 2003: 71). 'The role of hospitals in symbolizing public entitlement to public services and maintaining trust in the NHS has been underplayed or even misunderstood' (Fulop et al. 2008: 30).

- They can function as a social and communal focus as well as a place where medical care is dispensed. Various kinds of voluntary support groups frequently form themselves around a particular hospital ('Friends of...', and so on). Community-based charitable and fund-raising events connected to particular hospitals are very common in many European countries and in North America.

- They can symbolize the power of the medical estate. Big high-tech hospitals are in a sense the fortress of scientific medicine—the home of dramatic and heroic interventions by doctors; witness the endless series of TV hospital dramas.

- They can provide a major source of employment. In Western Europe the hospital sector may employ 3 or 4 per cent of the entire workforce. A big hospital may easily be the biggest employer in a city.

- They can give individual residents an increased sense of personal security—a belief that, if there is an accident or they or their loved ones fall suddenly ill, professional help will be immediately at hand.

(This list is considerably extended and adapted from McKee et al. 2003: 69–72.)

Given this substantial list of potential attributes, it is not surprising that hospital reconfigurations arouse strong debate. Neither is it surprising that some of the new organizational forms proffered by the health authorities do not engender immediate enthusiasm from citizens:

Most members of the public understand the GP and they understand the acute hospital. Asking them to put all their faith into an intermediate care team, or a rapid response service is difficult, as we haven't yet got the alternative health services that feel solid and owned by the public.

(Humphries and Gregory 2010: 11)

It would therefore be an incompetent and insensitive manager who tried to deal with reconfiguration as though it were *only* a matter of securing the most efficient and effective distribution of acute health care, and it would be a narrow-minded and politically naive doctor who tackled the same issue as though it could be determined *solely* on grounds of the optimal arrangements for clinical practice. An extensive UK study came to the conclusions that:

There is evidence that the drivers of change are not always those stated at the outset, that proponents of change tend to exaggerate the likely benefits and understate the costs, and that the process of change itself can be a constraint to service improvement.

(National Institute for Health Research 2010: 13)

Further:

This research project has largely experienced configuration as a political issue. Frequently technical criteria are rehearsed but the prevailing view is that the strength of the political perspective is, in the end, greater.

(National Institute for Health Research 2010: 17)

And there is another point about the technical criteria:

The Department of Health and local health policy makers have often presented it as a technical matter of optimizing bed to population ratios, or co-locating services which require close connections and achieving 'rational' resource allocation... However, the evidence base for these optimal ratios is slender, and much of it relies largely on rules of thumb endorsed by established professional clinical institutes, rather than on careful evaluations.

(Fulop et al. 2008: 20)

In short, the 'power geometry' of hospital reconfigurations is complex. Many different groups with different interests and different styles of discourse are usually involved (see Figure 6.1).

The classification of interests in Figure 6.1 is useful in a number of ways, but it also has its limitations. It is not clear how far the categories are mutually exclusive, and the distinction between the 'voter' category and the 'consumer' and 'taxpayer' categories appears particularly problematic. Voters may vote locally or nationally, may vote the same way or differently at different levels, and may cast their votes for a wide variety of reasons—some related to local issues, some to national, some to taxes, and some to services, or to personalities, and so on. Ethnicity may play a role in some cases but not at all in others; social class is often important, but in

	Informal/popular goals	Technical/expert goals
Less institutionalized imperative	**Consumer public-interest type** Prioritizes ease of access, cheap access for relatives, convenience in moving along pathways of care	**Patient public-interest type** Prioritizes absolute and relative health gains, health melioration, improved treatment outcomes, survival rates, hygiene
More institutionalized imperative	**Voter public-interest type** Prioritizes community base, loyalty to an institution of status quo, local political accountability	**Taxpayer public-interest type** Prioritizes cost effectiveness, cost–benefit efficiency, crude productivity, cheap administration, auditability, controllability

Figure 6.1 Types of argument about hospital reconfiguration
Source: Farrington-Douglas and Brooks (2007: 11), adapted from 6 et al. (2005: 22).

complicated ways; there can be rural versus urban issues; the accident of whether the local member of parliament is or is not an important minister may be crucial—all these and other factors can contribute to the outcome of reconfiguration struggles (TPT interview 48). One in-depth study of three English reconfiguration schemes came to the conclusion that 'it seems that both class and geography may play an important part in the process. Smaller towns, with a large middle class population, are more likely to produce conflict between the public and the hospital on reconfiguration' (Fulop et al. 2008: 29). One may hear, in this study of the reconfiguration of public goods, an echo of the findings of Aldrich's international study of the distribution of 'public bads' (see Section 2.6).

So as a rough signpost to types of interest that may be in play in a particular instance, Figure 6.1 is a decent starting point, but deeper analysis may soon call for a more refined set of categories. Indeed, hospital reconfiguration is a good example of the kind of issue where 'power geometries' may be highly nuanced and subject to change over time (see Section 2.1), and where the complexity of 'place' may make it almost impossible to develop 'cookbook' or 'seven-step' type processes that will yield the desired results: 'The potential for variables to acquire different status or value in specific local contexts makes it most unlikely that a reconfiguration in one context will offer a generalisable model elsewhere' (National Institute for Health Research 2010: 7; see also TPT interview 48).

This makes things difficult even for well-meaning governments:

It seems that government policy in respect of reconfigurations sees enhanced public involvement and consultation as a solution. The assumption seems to be that the involvement will be educative in such a way as to lead to a smooth acceptance of service change. All the evidence gathered here from a wealth of stakeholder interviews suggests that this is very optimistic.

(National Institute for Health Research 2010: 18)

At a more local level, 'managers and clinicians alike believe that the data will convert the users—but it doesn't mean that they [the service users] accept reconfiguration' (TPT interview 48). It is perhaps an awareness of the prickly complexities of shifting hospital services around that leads to the plans for these moves becoming somewhat vague and plastic:

The degree to which reconfiguration plans have precise, measurable milestones or clear monitoring systems is quite limited. This is compounded by high levels of movement in the key actors such that there is a fading memory of the commitments, and newcomers have little personal allegiance to previous agreements.

(National Institute for Health Research 2010: 18)

The observation here about the rapid 'churn' of key actors is accurate for English hospitals during the period since the mid-1990s, but much more stability is visible in other systems that are less subject to the constant stream of politico-managerial initiatives that have characterized the English NHS since the 1980s (for a comparison showing much greater continuity in Belgium, see Pollitt and Bouckaert 2009: chs 3, 6). This is another example, therefore, of significant differences in power geometries between different places; a similar issue plays out in very different ways in Brighton and Leuven (Pollitt and Bouckaert 2009: ch. 6).

6.3 International Trends

The forces for change identified in the previous section have wrought considerable shifts in the pattern of hospitals, both in Europe and North America (we will not extend our discussion beyond these two regions). Some of the main consequences have been:

- the numbers of hospitals per capita have declined in the EU;
- the number of beds *per capita* have declined across the EU—more rapidly than the number of hospitals;
- the number of *acute* beds *per capita* have also declined;
- the average length of stay in acute hospitals has fallen quite fast across the EU for many common conditions;
- hospitals have remained expenditure 'hot spots' within the health-care system, representing more than half the total health-care expenditure in most EU countries.

Although the broad picture is reasonably clear, the details vary considerably from country to country, and the processes underlying these trends are complex (Healy and McKee 2003). In general one might say that more rapid treatment and changing clinical policies have meant that the average inpatient stays for a shorter time than in the past, but is probably more severely ill than he or she was 30 thirty or forty years ago (because more minor conditions are treated in outpatients' departments, in doctors' offices, or health centres, or by drugs that can be taken at home). However, average costs per case have not fallen by anything like as much as average lengths of stay, partly because the days now spent in hospital are more intensive, with more things being done and therefore more expenditure on staff, drugs, and equipment. The 'cheaper' days of resting or observation are nowadays more likely to be taken outside hospital.

Although our focus here is on acute hospitals, we should notice that one other major shift has been the policy-inspired run-down and closure of long-stay psychiatric and mental illness hospitals. The number of patients in such institutions more than halved in most countries between the 1950s and the 1990s (Healy and McKee 2003: 26). This partly (but only partly) accounts for the second bullet point above—the decline in beds *per capita*. There has also been a large growth in nursing home beds, but, again, these do not concern us here, except in so far as they may take some of the pressure off acute hospitals by allowing patients who would otherwise be stuck in geriatric wards (because they were not well enough to go home) to be transferred out of acute hospitals.

It is hard to document the reduction in the *number* of acute hospitals in any detail. While most experts agree that such a reduction has taken place, in several countries it is difficult to prove it—for a variety of reasons. In the UK, after 1991 individual hospitals no longer existed as separate administrative entities. The NHS organizations supplying acute care became 'NHS trusts', and trusts could (and frequently did) cover more than one hospital. So the number of trusts was not a guide to the number of hospitals. Many mergers took place—both of trusts and of hospitals within trusts—so the ability to count hospitals as distinct buildings positioned on particular sites disappeared. Interestingly, something of the earlier history of the hospitals has also disappeared, because the archived tapes holding the annual SH3 statistical returns (which were completed for each hospital) have been disposed of (personal email from J. Mohan, 16 Apr. 2010).

Despite these complications and limitations, available official statistics show the big picture fairly clearly. Table 6.1 gives the figures for the

Table 6.1 Beds in English hospitals, 1987–2006

Year	All specialities	General and acute
1987/8	297,364	180,889
1992/3	232,201	153,208
1997/8	193,625	138,047
2002/3	183,826	136,679
2005/6	175,646	133,033

Note: These figures represent the average daily number of available beds.

Source: Department of Health form KH03, www.performance.doh.gov.uk/hospitalactivity/data_requests/beds_open_overnight (accessed 1 Sept. 2007).

Table 6.2 Numbers of general hospitals in Belgium, 1988–2010

Year	Number of general hospitals
1988	260
1990	254
1995	224
2000	160
2005	147
2010	131

Source: personal correspondence with the Belgian federal Ministry of Health, 27 July 2010.

numbers of beds in English NHS hospitals between 1987 and 2006. This shows that in less than two decades the number of beds in all specialities declined by 40.1 per cent and in general and acute by 26.4 per cent. Meanwhile, in Belgium, there is evidence of a broadly similar process. There a growth in beds in the 1960s and early 1970s turned into a significant shrinkage after 1980. In just ten years (to 1990) the total number of beds fell from 37,564 to 32,596 (13 per cent) and the beds per inhabitant from 6.67 to 5.65 (Peers 1994: 22).

Table 6.2 shows the reduction in the number of general hospitals (rather than beds) in Belgium over a longer period. This table indicates a 48 per cent reduction in the number of general hospitals over the two decades 1990–2010. This number may be deceptive, however, because in many cases institutions have merged, so the number of beds may not have fallen anything like the same percentage. For example, many new hospital groups were formed during the 1990s.

Table 6.3 shows the picture for curative (acute) beds. The reduction is indeed less than that for the number of hospitals. Nevertheless,

Table 6.3 Trends in curative (acute) hospital beds in Belgium, 1985–2010

Year	Number of curative beds
1985	57,693
1990	51,857
1995	50,984
2000	48,395
2005	46,073
2010	44,895

Source: Belgian federal statistics submitted to *Eurostat*.

it shows an unremitting shrinkage, with 22 per cent of the 1985 beds gone by 2010.

6.4 Local Case Study: Brighton, Hove, and Lewes, 1965–2005

In this section we will examine the history of hospital reconfiguration in the Brighton and Hove urban area and its surrounds from 1965 to 2005. The analysis is based on the Brighton–Leuven Project, which was a pilot for the TPT research. The Brighton–Leuven project was reported in full in Pollitt and Bouckaert 2009 (see especially the project summary on pp. 195–7). The project involved an intensive search of primary documentation (hospital records and local press reports) plus semi-structured interviews with sixteen individuals who had occupied senior management or clinician positions in the area covering the entire period. Some of these individuals were subsequently recontacted to elaborate on some of the particular issues dealt with below.

As with other empirical cases in this book, we regard it as crucial to study hospital development over quite long time periods. Evolutionary patterns—if there are any—become much clearer in the medium and long term, when short-term fluctuations (hospitals are always having expenditure crises or staff shortages) can be ironed out.

Back in 1967, the Brighton and Lewes Hospital Group (Lewes is a county town about 19 kilometres north-east of Brighton) boasted three general hospitals. These were Brighton General, the Royal Sussex County Hospital (RSCH) (also in Brighton), and Hove General (Hove is a town immediately to the west of Brighton and sharing an unbroken urban area along the Channel coast). Then there were a string of smaller ones, as follows:

1. Bevendean Hospital (close to Brighton General)
2. Brighton Chest Clinic
3. Sussex Eye Hospital
4. Sussex Nose and Throat Hospital
5. Royal Alexandria Hospital (for children)
6. Sussex Maternity Hospital
7. New Sussex Maternity Hospital
8. Foredown Hospital
9. Hove Chest Clinic
10. Victoria Hospital (in Lewes)
11. Lewes Chest Clinic

151

12. Newhaven Downs Hospital [Newhaven is a small port 24 kilometres east of Brighton]
13. Newhaven Valley Hospital

(Brighton Hospitals Health Bulletin 1967a)

By 2010 Brighton General (one of the two general hospitals in Brighton) had ceased to function in that capacity, Hove General had also been closed, and almost all the smaller hospitals had closed. The other Brighton general hospital—the RSCH—had become the sole major centre for 'hot' surgery and for accident and emergency cases (Gaston 2008; Pollitt and Bouckaert 2009: 85–92). The Brighton area thus exemplifies the 'big picture' drawn in the previous sections of this chapter, in so far as it shows considerable and ongoing concentration of acute hospital facilities since the 1970s.

In parallel with these changes in the hospitals themselves there was also an accelerating series of politically driven reorganizations of the administrative authorities that governed the hospitals. While no major restructurings of this kind took place between the foundation of the UK National Health Service in 1948 and the reorganization of 1974, further reorganizations affecting Brighton followed in 1982, 1985, 1993, 2001, and 2006 (Pollitt and Bouckaert 2009: 38–43, 86–7). However, these redrawings of administrative boundaries are not our main concern here, so we will refer to them only occasionally. Some of them did, however, carry a territorial significance, because they altered the geographical boundaries of the authority responsible for hospitals—and thereby opened up the possibility that residents' perceptions of what was 'theirs' and 'local' would diverge from the scope of the authority's formal responsibilities.

If we ask why so many smaller hospitals closed, we can hear reprised most of the factors identified in Section 6.2. In many cases, both finance and technological change were spurs to change. In April 1991, Tim Sainsbury, a Member of Parliament for Hove, wrote a letter to the *Brighton Health Bulletin* advocating the construction of a small new district general hospital in Hove. He thus stood against the dominant view among local consultants, who wanted a big new single-site hospital near the University of Sussex. The new greenfield-site hospital would, he argued, be vastly expensive, and more difficult and costly for local people to get to. It would be 'remote and frightening' rather than 'friendly and accessible' (*Brighton Health Bulletin* 1991a). In the next issue, however, a Brighton consultant physician, chairman of the district medical committees, responded vigorously:

Tim Sainsbury's vision of a small friendly local hospital is superficially attractive, but 30 years out of date. Health-care personnel and technology are now so expensive that large hospitals are the only way the service can work cost-effectively. Large hospitals do not have to be unfriendly if they are well-designed and maintain smaller units within them.

(Brighton Health Bulletin 1999b)

New technologies and financial issues are intertwined in many ways. New technology may make existing procedures cheaper, but only if the hospital can find the up-front capital cost to buy the new equipment. New technology may make it possible to do existing procedures much more quickly, so that, even if each individual procedure is cheaper, the hospital's expenditure still goes up, because it is now able to do so many more procedures than formerly. Or new technology may enable clinicians to do things they could never do at all before—thus expanding the hospital's field of operations, and probably increasing its costs. If we go back to 1976, we find a Brighton businessman donating money so that the RSCH could buy one of the brand new EMI whole-body X-ray scanners *(Brighton Health Bulletin* 1976). This system was 'hailed as the most significant advance in radiology since the discovery of X-rays in 1895', and provided TV-type pictures of 'slices' through the whole of a human body. However, even if the gift was generous, that was far from the end of the story, financially speaking. To begin with, an extension to the existing building had to be built to accommodate the equipment. Then, once it was in place, extra funds had to be sought from the Regional Health Authority to cover its annual, recurrent, running costs.

The architectural fabric itself was also important. Old buildings were not simply unnecessarily expensive to maintain; they were also in an increasing number of ways unsuitable for the practice of modern medicine. The minutes and documents of the relevant authorities are full of complaints about leaking roofs and cramped quarters. In 1987, for example, the chairperson of the health authority referred to 'the enormous obstacles presented by our obsolete buildings. A new hospital is essential...' (Cumberledge 1985: 3). Yet they did not get a new hospital, and part of the reason for that was indeed a change in the geographical boundaries of the health authority. One senior Brighton manager from that time comments:

Following the introduction of the East Sussex Area Health Authority [AHA] [a considerably bigger administrative unit than the Brighton and Lewes Group had been back in the 1960s], by the mid 1980s the AHA had deemed both Eastbourne and Hastings districts [two other substantial towns in the area] as more needy of new hospitals than Brighton, largely because their hospital stocks were very poor, whereas at least Brighton had a relatively new tower block! Hence, frustratingly, Brighton took third place in the pecking order.

(personal communication from TPT interviewee 42, 17 Aug. 2006)

In a number of cases, closure of smaller facilities was synchronized with the modernized reprovision of that service at the Royal Sussex site. Thus in 1970 the Sussex Maternity Hospital was closed, but a 28-bed ante-natal ward, a labour ward, a 24-bed post-natal ward, and various other facilities were opened at the Royal Sussex. Births are, perhaps, a local operation *par excellence*, because mothers-to-be do not want to be far from home and neither do their families want to miss the occasion. Then in 1986 the Sussex Throat and Ear Hospital closed in one part of the town, but a parallel department opened at the Royal Sussex. In 2007, the Royal Alexandra Hospital for Sick Children left its seriously outdated 1881 building on Dyke Road to occupy a state-of-the art new hospital located on the Royal Sussex site. A veteran clinician summarized his experience as follows:

So, for example, there was little objection to the closure of Bevendean (a former fevers hospital unfortunately sited between the cemetery and the crematorium and used for slow track medicine), which went in 1987. Neither was any grief experienced over the slow run-down of Brighton General Hospital, which was the old workhouse, and has only just stopped daily services. But there was quite a campaign and much sadness about the closure of Hove General Hospital in 1997, which had served very much as a community general hospital and was popular and indeed loved. The Trust tried to explain the needs in terms of the difficulty of duplicating infrastructure and maintaining on-call rotas for very small hospitals, but that is quite a sophisticated message to get across.

(personal correspondence from TPT interviewee 41, a long-serving
senior clinician in Brighton who had been personally
heavily involved in planning, 20 Apr. 2010)

In this testimony we hear some important clues as to what differentiates hospitals in the eyes of the citizens who use them. First, there are factors of precise location and general appearance. Bevendean was a fairly drab hospital right next to a huge municipal cemetery and crematorium. Not far away, Brighton General was a much bigger campus, with a much wider range of services. 'The General' itself was, however, a singularly ugly and depressing set of buildings, with its nineteenth-century workhouse origins not at all hard to guess. In this case the authorities ran down services gradually, over a period of many years, so there was never really a moment when the community was likely to rise in protest at the drip, drip of services being transferred to the Royal Sussex—which was anyway just on the other side of the same small hill. Hove General, however, was different. To begin with it was a more recently built hospital, with a far less depressing aspect than Brighton General. Further, it was in Hove—a continuous urban area with Brighton to the eye of a visitor, but administratively and politically a separate town, with a concern for its 'own' public facilities. 'The local politicians were absolutely fixed on the idea that Hove is a different place from Brighton' (TPT interview 41). What is more, Hove General had, over the years, managed successfully to convert itself from a district general hospital (for which it became too small) to a community hospital. It thus occupied a place in the local affections that Brighton General had never achieved.

The picture that emerges from the Brighton case is, therefore, one in which precise *locations* and physical condition and appearance were of great importance. The story of hospital development in Sussex 1960–2010 is hardly one of the unrolling of any great strategic plan (Pollitt and Bouckaert 2009). On the contrary, it is a story of constant reorganization, of temporary fixes involving patching and altering old buildings, of local politicking based to a significant extent on *where* politicians had their constituencies and doctors had their practices and professional loyalties. There were many plans, certainly, and endless 'option appraisals', but very few of these were ever carried through to implementation. In the words of a top manager, referring to the elaborate option analyses of the 1980s: 'The harsh reality was that nobody could agree' (TPT interview 45). This was the reality that public-service managers were dealing with, and local citizens were experiencing and, occasionally, participating in. It was a politico-spatial play in many acts, with strong financial and technological subplots. It was also very much concerned with the maintenance of a decaying and increasingly unsuitable set of elderly buildings. Despite large investments in new buildings between 1995 and 2006, in that latter year the RSCH contained 277 beds in buildings constructed since 1960 but still 209 in buildings erected before 1850 (personal correspondence following TPT interview 2, 20 Nov. 2006). And that, remember, was the hospital that had 'won' the evolutionary struggle among the sixteen Brighton hospitals listed in 1967. The bricks and mortar of a place can be remarkably durable: it takes a long time and a lot of money completely to renew a big hospital.

6.5 Hospital Reconfiguration from a GAP Perspective

GAP modality B—the one we have been most interested in so far—concerns governments putting their things in places. But what is given can also usually be taken away, and hospital reconfiguration is often controversial precisely because it involves taking something (a medical speciality, an accident and emergency department, a whole hospital) *away* from somewhere. Furthermore, if what is taken away is a whole hospital, then that is a *big* thing to remove—the economic, political, and social effects are likely to be further reaching than if one was dealing with the removal of, say, a local post office or a registry office. I stress removals rather than new constructions because, given the European trends discussed in Section 6.3, there are likely, overall, to be more hospital closures (or part closures) than openings.

Hospital reconfiguration touches on several other modalities. The location of such substantial facilities may help to address spatial disadvantages (modality F)—for example, in an economically run-down locality like Hartlepool (north-east England), where the local hospital is one of the biggest employers, offering every level of job from medical consultant to cooks and cleaners. Certainly, as we have seen, hospitals develop symbolic and affective functions (modality G). Once in place they are seen as an entitlement of citizenship and an embodiment of 'our town'. They will be one of a small number of buildings that will be known to almost every resident. In the twenty-first century, the local hospital may well be more prominent and better known than the English town halls and French *mairies* mentioned at the beginning of Chapter 1. Finally, hospitals will be involved with modality C (direct regulation) but in a variety of ways. It will, most obviously, be subject to regulation by the local and national authorities. One item that was a hardy perennial at board meetings during the redevelopment of the RSCH in Brighton was the issue of car parking, where the local council argued endlessly with the hospital management about how and where visitors' cars could be parked. These disputes arose because of the specificities of the location—the RSCH is perched on a small, over-crowded and hilly site in a busy part of town where car parking is a big problem for local residents. More seriously, perhaps, hospitals are subject to a wide array of regulations concerning cleanliness, the handling of nuclear isotopes, the physical isolation of certain infectious diseases, and so on.

Technological change has certainly had a major impact on reconfiguration, but, in spatial terms, in several directions rather than just one. Some changes encourage centralization (expensive, highly specialized equipment) while others encourage decentralization (telemedicine; the possibility of patients communicating with their medical advisers from their homes, using the Internet). Both these trends tend, however, to eat away at the middle-sized general hospital that had become such a core feature of health care (and local landscapes) during the twentieth century. They have also already changed the nature of the individual patient's relationship with the hospital. Average lengths of stay for many conditions have fallen remarkably since 1980, so that patients no longer linger in hospital for days or even weeks on end. Instead they have their preliminary diagnostics done by a primary-care doctor or in an outpatients' clinic, and then they come in for a short but intensive stay ('day surgery', where there is not even one overnight stay has been much encouraged by the cost-conscious UK government). Overall one might say that technological change is one driver— interacting with others—that constantly destabilizes any given spatial configuration. It may also have some accumulative, longer-term effect on how citizens 'feel' about 'their' hospitals, but, in health care, as so often elsewhere, this aspect has as yet received only very limited research attention.

For governments, coordination problems (see Section 4.3) loom large, both in the Brighton case and more generally. When the local hospital planning authority was small, fights took place because the political interests of Brighton and Hove were perceived as diverging. When the planning authority later came to cover a much wider geographical area than Brighton, Hove, and Lewes, the tensions between Brighton and Hove continued, but were overlain by struggles for scarce capital resources against other towns elsewhere in the county—struggles that Brighton, on the whole, lost. This kind of problem of spatial coordination and conflict has been a constant in the history of the UK NHS. In 2010 the new coalition government announced that Primary Care Trusts (PCTs)—the main authorities commissioning hospital care—were to be abolished, and the function transferred to consortia of general practitioners (GPs). This was to be done in the name of returning the power to choose and book hospital treatment to patients and their own GPs. Unfortunately, however:

The abolition of PCTs potentially destabilizes the organizational ability of the NHS to contribute to place-based solutions; GP consortia are unlikely to be coterminous with local authority boundaries, and if their commissioning budgets are excluded from the total local public services spend, it is difficult to see how a place-based solution could work.

(Humphries and Gregory 2010)

In short, if the hospital care-purchasing authorities are not coterminous with the local authorities responsible for social care, then the coordination of these services (for example, organizing and paying for more home care to avoid the need for hospital admissions for the elderly) becomes significantly more difficult.

The study of hospital reconfiguration also reinforces Chapter 4's message that 'places fight back' (see Section 4.6). Material and social aspects of the geography of Brighton and, upscale, south-east England helped to shape the Brighton hospital story. On a regional scale, the proximity of London, with its surplus of teaching hospitals, restricted Brighton's opportunities to develop itself as a broad-spectrum regional centre of excellence. On a county scale, the well-heeled socio-demography of the Sussex Weald meant that the Princess Royal Hospital at Hayward's Heath was fiercely and ably defended by well-organized, articulate local groups, and could not be 'absorbed' by the RSCH to the extent that some would have wished. On the local scale, the RSCH constantly struggled with its cramped site, and old buildings, and for most of the period could not claim to have won the hearts of the residents of Hove, who had their own, well-loved hospital.

In conclusion we might remark that the recent professional and academic literature on hospital management has tended to be focused on the application of generic management techniques and broad and somewhat abstract organizational approaches: benchmarking, clinical governance, 'patient focus', business process re-engineering, payment-by-results systems, and so on. There is nothing wrong with this in itself, but this chapter has at least suggested that the daily agendas of practising managers are often equally occupied with other issues, many of which have a distinct, locally embedded component. Managers must attend to the arrangements for clinical governance, but they must also fix the car parking on a crowded site, maintain old and leaking buildings, rebuild one floor of a 1960s tower block so that it will accommodate the latest scanner, debate with doctors who want to move the whole operation to a new, greenfield-site hospital out of town, and respond to articulate groups of local residents who are opposed to moving the local accident and emergency department to a bigger hospital 23 kilometres away. These highly specific, place-based issues demand a good deal of managers' time and skills, but lack the glamour that apparently attaches to the latest management technique. Woe betide the hospital manager who does not 'know his place'.

7

Births, Marriages, Deaths, and Identities

Technology is something that just happens. There are no real strategies for managing it.

(Belgian municipal civil registration official, interviewed 8 Dec. 2009)

The perfected state holds and guards the monopoly of certifying birth. Either you are given (and carry with you) the certificate of the state, thereby acquiring an identity which during the course of your life enables the state to identify you and track you (track you down); or you do without an identity and condemn yourself to living outside the state like an animal.

(Coetzee 2008: 4)

7.1 Introduction

Coetzee, a Nobel prize-winning novelist, has got this partly right and partly wrong. His core point is absolutely right: it is states that normally confer upon us our official identities, until recently usually by giving us a piece of paper (certificate). However, the contrast with animals is not as clear-cut as he implies—more and more animals nowadays *do* need to have identity papers, which are also often issued, or at least regulated, by states. Furthermore, Coetzee does not pick up on the fact that multiple identities are quite common nowadays—facilitated by the information technology revolution. 'Identity theft' is an exceedingly frequent crime, and many self-respecting criminals (just like spies) will have several sets of official identities.

Curiously, this absolutely fundamental business of conferring identities has been one of the least glamorous, least researched aspects of the modern state. In most West European states, 'births, marriages and deaths' (or, more correctly, population registration) has been regarded as a bit of an administrative backwater, not at all a hot political topic or a desired posting for upwardly mobile young public-service managers (Pollitt and Op de Beeck 2010). Indeed, in the UK a 2003 government document asserted that 'today's system of civil registration has changed little since it was first introduced in the 1830s' (Office for National Statistics 2003: 1). On the surface, therefore, civil registration would seem to provide a clear counterpoint to the endless technological change, placeshifts and reorganizations that were portrayed in our treatment of hospitals (see Chapter 6).

Yet below the surface the picture becomes more complex. In some countries major changes have taken place (no pun intended), and, even where they have not, they are bubbling upwards and may pop out very soon. In this chapter, therefore, we will examine the evolution of civil registration in several European countries over the period since the 1960s, paying particular attention to changes in place and technology, and to the interactions between the two. The discussion is based on an extensive survey of primary source material from civil registration organizations in Belgium and the UK, plus a set of semi-structured interviews with senior staff, both at the national and local level.

7.2 Place and Technology in Civil Registration

In most European countries civil registration arrangements were created during the nineteenth, or early twentieth century, when large parts of the population were not particularly mobile, and *where* you came from was seen as of great importance. So, from the beginning, identities were tightly linked to particular places—the phrase 'date and place of birth' still rolls off the Anglophone tongue as a kind of unity. Further, this localized character of civil registration has persisted into the twenty-first century. In both Belgium and the UK, for example, citizens still generally have to visit their local registrar (the *Burgerlijke Stand* in Belgium) in order to register a new birth. The geographical pattern of local register offices in England and Wales altered very little during the period from 1970 to 2005; compare this with the extensive movements of government offices reported in Chapter 5, or the slaughter of post offices mentioned earlier in the book (TPT interviews 5, 6, 7). (When I married a Finnish woman in London in 1997, I still had to go to be personally interviewed by the registrar where I lived in Buckinghamshire, and to produce documents there and make some of the arrangements.) Wholesale attempts to modernize the system have been made, but all have failed at one point or another:

We did issue both a green paper and a white paper on how the system could be changed during my period of tenure as DRG [Deputy Registrar General] but were never able to persuade ministers that the changes warranted the allocation of parliamentary time to change the legislation. Understandably, they saw the civil registration system in E&W [England and Wales] as being effective and inexpensive to operate and of no great political profile against competing demands for oversubscribed parliamentary time.

(personal communication from John Ribbins, 24 May 2008)

What explains this impressive stability in both organizational procedure and location? Can it be the case that the waves of technological change that have transformed many aspects of hospitals (and, as we shall see in the next chapter, many aspects of police practice) have had little or no effect on civil registration?

In interview, civil registration officials in both Belgium and the UK largely shared an explanation of why the service had been so stable. To encapsulate: it was trusted, uncontroversial, cheap, and largely below the political radar. For all these reasons, individually and in combination, it seldom thrust itself onto reform agendas:

It worked well and was inexpensive to run.

(TPT interview 12)

It's like the drains—no one thinks it is important enough until it gets blocked.

(TPT interview 6)

It is dull but worthy.

(TPT interview 4)

There isn't enough political drive to really start pushing drastic changes through.

(TPT interview 17; this interviewee also mentioned the small budget)

As for the political interference with the *Burgerlijke Stand*, one can say that there is almost none.

(TPT interview 18; this interviewee also mentioned that the service did not cost much)

The first three of these quotations came from interviews with registration staff in England, the last two from the municipal level in Belgium.

The American saying 'If it ain't broke, don't fix it' comes to mind. Furthermore, 'fixing it' would carry both costs and risk. It would carry costs because, while the running costs are currently low, to computerize or recomputerize in a fundamental way would require a substantial initial investment. As with the deconcentration exercises discussed in Sections 5.1–5.4, the timeline is one where, in order to make savings later on, governments first have to invest. Radical change would also carry risks, because civil registration is a continuous, mass-processing business. Every day it deals with thousands of cases, and all of them have to be treated in exactly the same way. Furthermore, the data it generates feed into all sorts of other government agencies, which need population data in order to plan their own activities. It is vital, therefore, that this operation is not interrupted. (That is one reason why, in the UK, registrars were not allowed to strike, and, in Belgium, a law was passed forbidding municipalities to permit more than a forty-eight-hour interruption in the flow of their data into the national *rijksregister*. Indeed, in the UK, bodies could not be buried without a certificate from a registrar—a doctor's certificate alone was not enough.) If a big change was made, staff all over the country would have to learn new routines, and citizens all over the country would have to accustom themselves to new procedures. This could easily lead to accidents—as, indeed, occurred in 2004 in England, when the brand new electronic Registration Online (RON) broke down after two days and half the country had to be taken off the system. It was subsequently, gradually, restored to functioning order. Although this new system may have looked like a major punctuation, in practice it was not that dramatic. One registration district cannot access the records of another (except for marriages). To ensure accuracy the staff input the data, not the citizens. The latter still have to visit an office and sign a paper (TPT interview 29).

The picture, however, is by no means one of total stasis. What we rather see is a complex pattern of change. On the one hand, there are major 'punctuations' when underlying computer systems change—either opportunistically or because they are so seriously out of date that replacement becomes imperative. Belgium and Finland (to which we will come in a moment) have both had 'turning points' of this kind. On the other hand, there are more subtle, partly behind-the-scenes changes of types that historical institutionalists term displacement, layering, and drift (Mahoney and Thelen 2010: 14–22). Each of these will now be dealt with in turn.

7.2.1 Punctuations

Punctuations come when there is fundamental technological or institutional change (or both). In the case of Belgium, this happened in 1983, when municipal feeding of registration data to the national *Rijksregister* was made compulsory. This was computerized, at a time when many municipalities still had little to do with computers, and certainly not in the

Burgerlijke Stand (civil registration section). So the national register depends on local 'supply', but it is also widely used by municipalities to obtain data that they could not otherwise get themselves, or could get only with great effort. The municipalities, however, still retain the responsibility for collecting registration data and guarding the (paper) *aktes* that provides the basic legal record. A second major shift occurred from the late 1990s, when the *Rijksregister* developed a PIN-coded electronic chipcard that could act both as an identifier (by storing personal data) and as an authenticator (through its PIN code system). This was dubbed the eID and was given a legal basis in 2003. In 2004 pilot projects in eleven municipalities were positively evaluated (www.ibz.rrn.fgov.be (accessed 4 Oct. 2009)). The system began gradually to be rolled out to all Belgians. By 2010 every adult had an eID. The eID was developed mainly internally, following an original suggestion by a relatively junior official (TPT interview 10). As time has passed, it has become clear that its potential uses are quite wide. One's own population register entry can be checked, but also tax forms can be completed online, declarations of thefts or vandalism can be made, library cards can be obtained, and so on. The card chip contains personal identification and e-signature components. An initial limitation was that citizens required a card reader built into or linked to their computers in order to be able to use the eID on the Web, but the importance of this constraint is diminishing over time. (Interestingly, an attempt to develop an electronic identity card in the UK met with huge political and mass-media resistance, and, despite being at an advanced stage, it was scrapped by the incoming coalition government in 2010 (LSE 2005; Lips et al. 2006).)

In Finland the punctuation occurred in the period 1969–74. In 1969 the population register (*Vaestorekisterkeskus*) was set up as a national agency, and in 1974 it acquired responsibility for issuing all Finnish Personal Identity Codes (PICs). It was critical that the decision to adopt an identity code was taken at more or less the same time as the central population register was being computerized (TPT interview 13). The use of a common identifier has made it possible to collect change of circumstance data from various official sources and share this data with a multitude of users. Note that in Finland, unlike Belgium or the UK, civil registration is regarded very much as a fundamental responsibility of the central state, not local authorities. (In fact the location of this responsibility varies all over the world.) The PRC has fifty-nine service points distributed across the country. The national register was first held on an IBM 360 mainframe computer, which lasted for about fifteen years before it had to be upgraded. 'Some people say that you couldn't do what we did in the 1970s now, because of the current spirit of downsizing and localization'

(TPT interview 13). In so far as this is true it reflects an interesting paradox. A centralized, computerized state-run system was installed in the 1970s and has run for decades without major problems. It is trusted, efficient, scandal-free, and, indeed, an object of envious study by civil registration experts from some other countries. Yet changes in (*a*) public management doctrines (in favour of decentralization and contracting out) plus (*b*) public opinion (the some-times fanciful international debate about the 'big brother', 'surveillance state') have combined to produce a situation in which it would be difficult, if not impossible, to launch such a project again today.

Finally, the basic business of registering a birth—or changing one's address—has itself been radically accelerated and simplified. My stepdaugh-ter recently gave birth to a baby in Helsinki, and the hospital automatically informed the population register, which immediately sent back the unique new PIC for little Otto. The parents did not have to do anything or go anywhere. Overall, the system appears to be uncontroversial with citizens, and has suffered no significant breakdowns or scandals in recent history. This is one way, given time, that the Belgian eID could also develop.

7.2.2 More subtle changes

In 2011 Belgium was in the middle of a gradual change that may well accumulate in future so that, retrospectively, it will eventually look like a fundamental change. This is an example of the process labelled as 'layering' by Mahoney and Thelen.

Processes of layering often take place when institutional challengers lack the capac-ity to actually change the original rules...They instead work within the existing system by adding new rules on top of or alongside the old ones...Each new element may be a small change in itself, yet these small changes can accumulate, leading to a big change over the long run.

(Mahoney and Thelen 2010: 17)

For some years now a municipal system called *e-Loket* (e-office) has been under development, and is being used by a growing number of citizens. This system allows a citizen user who has a computer to access various official documents and to download forms. 'Whereas people had to come to the *Maison Communale* (town hall), they can now apply for documents from their homes...The number of visits to the *Maison Communale* is slightly declining' (TPT interview 24). There is also a new system called e-Birth, which is beginning in some localities on a pilot basis. It involves cooperation between municipalities and local hospitals. Initial registration is done electronically, but the parent still has to come to the municipality at a later date to confirm the birth (TPT interview 24). These new systems, together with the eID referred to above, have generated a situation in which, without any political drama, a large gap has opened between what Fountain (2001) termed the 'objective technology' and the 'enacted technology' (see also Section 2.5). Objectively, these technologies could be used to provide rather a wide range of services, which would cut down on the need for paper documents and office visits. Thus far, however, only a few of these possibilities have been enacted, and some of these only on a local, pilot basis. However, there is no strong reason to believe that the gap will not be gradually narrowed, as usage spreads to larger groups of citizens and as new services are added.

In England one apparently small place change proved to be very popular. From 1995 civil marriages no longer had to take place in the local registry office itself. The ceremonies could be held at any licensed premises, and (for a fee) the registrar would attend and confirm the marriage. This resulted in a large surge of 'business', a new flow of cash to local authorities and, in some cases, registrars developing the 'theatrical' side of their skills (TPT interviews 7, 16, 29). Within the Westminster District alone, for example, there are more than 130 approved premises. About half of all marriages now take place outside church, some in quite exotic locations.

Other little-publicized changes have resulted in closer connections between civil registration and other parts of the state apparatus. Governments became interested in using the local registration service to identify unmarried fathers, to check identity and marriage documents for immigrants, and to share details of deaths with the police so that the latter can better identify (no pun intended) identity thieves (TPT interviews 8, 16, 29). On the other hand, 'the registrar does not want to become an inquisitor' (TPT interview 16).

7.3 Beyond Births, Marriages, and Deaths: Towards Identity Management

It did not take long after their nineteenth-century foundation for civil registration organizations to discover that they had other uses than simply registering births, marriages, and deaths. In the UK, the 1874 Births and Deaths Registration Act made it compulsory that death certificates be accompanied by a medical certificate specifying the cause of death and signed by a medical practitioner (Nissel 1989: 32). Death certificates were already an important building block for medical and epidemiological research, and many other uses for civil registration data have been found since. Then again, in 1938, the Population (Statistics) Act required citizens to furnish additional information to the authorities (such as the mother's age and the number of her previous children), which was to be used for statistical purposes.

In Belgium, too:

The responsibility of the Registrar's office goes beyond the registration of births, deaths and marriages. It also registers other facts (e.g. address, profession, membership of the jury of courts, military drafts, elections, migration, unemployment) gives information and delivers documents (e.g. identity cards, passports, social security cards).

(Bouckaert 1993: 13)

The more recent emergence of the eID, a 'home-grown' innovation from within the Ministry, further extends and updates this tendency. 'Without knowing it, they were building an identity management system' (TPT interview 10).

Finland affords a glimpse of additional possibilities. Since its introduction in the 1970s, the personal identity code (PIC) has gradually accumulated a wider and wider range of functions. For example, it absorbed the social insurance codes and work pension codes, which had previously been separate systems. In 1980 the population register was also linked to the building register, so that now, for example, planners can ask 'how many people over 70 years of age live in apartments above the ground floor, but without a lift?' (each building also has a unique code). The buildings register contains extensive details on more than three million buildings, including year of construction, floor area, equipment and subsystems, owners, and so on. Furthermore PICs are used (under a careful licensing procedure) by some private banks and insurance companies, credit management companies, consumer surveys, and direct marketing organizations. 'It is hard to manage daily life in Finland without a PIC' (TPT interview 13). Information users pay for the privilege, and this offsets more than 50 per cent of the cost of maintaining the register.

Such individual additions and expansions may be considered as examples of 'layering' ('the attachment of new institutions or rules onto or alongside existing ones' (Mahoney and Thelen 2010: 20)). Over time, however, the whole assemblage of extensions and additions begins to look like a major shift. *De facto*, matters of identity and civil registration have to a considerable extent been merged.

So far, so good. But the new technological possibilities also bring with them new problems. Privacy and identity theft have been major talking points in

Belgium, Finland, and the UK, as well as in other countries (see Kernaghan 2007: 117 for Canada). In 2007, 84,700 cases of online identity fraud were recorded in the UK (Association of Chief Police Officers 2009: 2), and in the first six months of 2010 there were officially 6,558 instances of cybercrime in Belgium, the majority concerning identity manipulation, especially with respect to financial transactions. Interestingly, this is one of the forms of crime that (as we shall see in the next chapter) tends to draw police resources away from local, 'neighbourhood' work. That is because 'e-crime is a non-geographical problem' (Association of Chief Police Officers 2009: 5). This whole topic has begun to attract considerable academic interest (see, e.g., Bennett and Lyon 2008; Lips et al. 2009a, b). In these public debates it often seems as though there are two opposing camps:

From within a state service approach, identification and authentication procedures are viewed as a necessary precursor to high quality service-providing aimed at the individual citizen, both in on-line and off-line settings... From the surveillance state perspective, however, this incipient concern to identify the citizen in many different settings is interpreted as marking a sea-change in relationships between the citizen and the state, one that demands constant and critical appraisal.

(Lips et al. 2009b: 137)

This is by no means simply a matter of preventing identity theft, or even of protecting privacy. The debate also stems from a concern by scholars and other concerned groups that new forms of identity will be used by public authorities for 'administrative sorting'—policies and procedures that discriminate between different categories of citizen on new and possibly tendentious grounds (Lips et al. 2006; 2009a). Strenuous efforts have been made to develop sets of principles to govern the various systems under development. One of the best known is Cameron's 'Seven Laws of Identity' (2005), which is summarized below:

1. Digital identity systems must reveal information identifying a user only with the user's consent.

2. The solution that discloses the least identifying information is the most stable solution.

3. Disclosure must be limited to parties having a necessary and justifiable place in a given identity relationship.

4. A universal identity system must support both 'omni-directional' identifiers for use by public entities and 'unidirectional' identifiers for use by private entities. Thus a private citizen should be able to access a public website without his or her identifier being shared with other

entities (it will be unidirectional—related only to that particular public website).

5. A universal identity system must channel and enable the interworking of multiple identity technologies run by multiple identity providers, because there is no one way to express identity. We may have good reasons for wanting to have different identifiers in relation to, say, the government, an employer, a firm that we are buying something from, and so on.

6. A universal identity system must define the human user as a component of the system, one that is protected by unambiguous and secure human–machine communications.

7. A universal identity system must guarantee its users a simple, consistent experience while enabling separation of contexts through multiple operators and technologies.

Cameron (2005: 1) warns that, if these seven 'laws' are not met, 'we create a wake of reinforcing side-effects that eventually undermine all resulting technology'. Needless to say, few if any of the government systems that have yet emerged satisfy all these tests.

There is also a place dimension to the emergent identity management technologies. Whereas name and place of residence (plus, more recently, photographs) long constituted the basic elements of traditional identity systems, newer technologies include biometric elements such as fingerprints, iris scans, or DNA. In effect, as these grow in importance, they may downgrade place-based identifiers, or even facial recognition, as they provide unchanging, unique identification of individual bodies, wherever they may have been.

7.4 Civil Registration from a GAP Perspective

Civil registration is not a service that, by itself, has made or will make the kind of obvious physical, economic, and social impacts on localities that we have seen in the case of moving government agencies (Chapter 5) or the siting of hospitals (Chapter 6) or the building of schools. Its effects are more subtle, yet arguably even more pervasive. It is a government service that virtually every citizen has to deal with at crucial points in their lives. It provides registration documents and/or identity cards that the citizen needs in his or her transactions with many other government agencies, and often with other social and economic actors too (lawyers, banks, and so on). It awards membership of the national community, and symbolizes a state that enumerates and tracks its citizens, in order both to control them and to provide them with a variety of benefits and services.

Civil registration may not have undergone the high-profile technological makeovers that both the hospital sector (see Chapter 6) and the police (see Chapter 8) have experienced, but the service is nevertheless right in the middle of a period of profound change. Bit by bit, two things are happening in all three of the countries we have examined. First, the place at which the citizen accesses the civil registration process is shifting, with more and more citizens able to access more and more parts of the registration process from anywhere where they can gain access to the Net (obviously including, but not at all being confined to, home). In Belgium and England there currently remain strong requirements for citizens to show up for a face-to-face interview at the municipal/local offices, but one has the impression that this centrepiece of the old system is being gradually nibbled away at around the edges. First came the automatic registration of hospital births (throughout Finland, and in some places in England), then access to one's registration details via an eID, and so on. However, as 'registration-at-a-distance' grows, so does the requirement for new means of authentication, and the more politically controversial issues of identity management are imported to the hitherto placid world of civil registration.

Alongside and allied with this, a second trend is for more and more horizontal linkages between services—for the benefit of the citizen and/or for the convenience and better information of different public agencies. Thus, for example, the English police are now able to access death records in order to catch criminals who have adopted the identity of a dead person. The local registration service also helps immigrants to apply for UK citizenship by checking and certifying their application documents. Administratively, the General Register Office (GRO) has since 2008 been brigaded as part of the Identity and Passport Agency. Previously it had been either a free-standing office, or part of the self-consciously independent Office for National Statistics (Pollitt and Op de Beeck 2010: 292–3). This organizational realignment also symbolized the drawing closer together of civil registration and identity issues. In Belgium, citizens use their eIDs to access a range of services, not only their population register entry. Finnish citizens may use the personal identity code issued to them at birth by the national population register to claim social security or authenticate their identity when using their bank accounts or purchasing insurance.

Why is all this happening? Clearly the availability of digital, electronic technologies has been an important facilitator. What is more, these technologies are not merely 'available'; they are often strongly marketed to governments by major IT companies and consultancies. Yet it is clear that this cannot be the only dynamic, since in some countries the digitalization of civil registration has gone much further and faster than others (so other factors must also be at work). Another driver has been the increased mobility of citizens (and non-citizens). In a society where the overwhelming majority of citizens live in one locality, and interact face-to-face with the civil registration officer in that locality, authentication of identity may be quite a small problem. In a society where many citizens move homes and jobs regularly, and where international migration in the direction of the rich countries has greatly increased (Arnold 2010), authentication of identity becomes a much more complex and prominent task. Indeed, it is a vital task as far as public services are concerned, because identification is commonly the first step in gaining access to a wide range of these services. 'We can also observe that these identification categories increasingly became the basis for registering taxpayers, refugees, voters, schoolchildren and benefit claimants, for example' (Lips et al. 2009a: 722). Again, though, this 'push' for intensified and modernized identification and authentication procedures explains a good deal, but not everything; big differences between countries remain to be explained, although differential immigration pressures may be one element in this. A third factor has been the continuing pressures—in most Western countries at least—to restrain public expenditure. These increase the attractiveness of digitalized solutions where the citizen does most of the work him- or herself and local staff and offices can be downsized. As noted earlier, central databases can be sited anywhere, and can therefore take advantage of lower building and labour costs in certain parts of a country. Yet, once more, we are left with some significant international differences that cannot convincingly be attributed to national expenditure pressures.

To these various pressures and trends we need to add a more subjective, or cultural factor. Trust—both in government in general and in particular public services—varies a good deal between one country and another (Van de Walle et al. 2008). Why is it that popular reactions to the idea of a national identity card have been so aggressively negative in the UK and the USA, whereas there has been so little fuss in Belgium or Finland? It does seem to have something to do with the media-amplified, generalized distrust of government in the first two countries as compared with the latter pair. Thus two American authors can assert that 'citizens' pessimism about privacy and security and their more general distrust of government overwhelm their desire for technology that will improve service and information dissemination' (Jae Moon and Welch 2005: 259). It is also, no doubt, partly just a matter of history and familiarity. Belgians and Finns have long had identity cards, without any great catastrophe befalling their civil liberties. In the UK, however, identity cards are seen as 'foreign' (the Second World War experience of them having now been largely forgotten), and in the USA they are bound up with deep- and long-running civil liberties and anti-federal movements (Gates 2008; Thompson 2008).

Overall, therefore, it seems as though the historically place-based nature of civil registration services is gradually being eroded. Place remains prominent, and is not going to disappear tomorrow, but in the longer run it is threatened by the cheaper, but essentially placeless, e-government, in combination with the declining significance of place within contemporary concepts of multiple, digital identities. Much of the huge boom in amateur genealogical research is now conducted on the Web (indeed it provides the UK GRO with a buoyant source of revenue). There seems no strong reason why most civil registration should not eventually migrate to the Web as well.

Whether new systems of Web-based registration, identification, and authentication will achieve the same levels of public trust and administrative accuracy as traditional systems remains, however, to be seen. The locally knowledgeable, keen-eyed registrar was (and remains) a sharp form of face-to-face verification. Web-based digital systems substitute 'codified, abstract, decontextualised representations' for tacit local 'nouse' (Tsoukas 2005: 15 ff.). The first may be cheaper, but is not automatically always superior to the second. What is more, the public organizations that are responsible for maintaining digital identity management systems are in an unceasing technological struggle against those who, for criminal or personal reasons, wish to subvert them. (This same, endless competition will be encountered again in Chapter 8, when we discuss the police.)

Although change in civil registration has been relatively slow in the three countries reviewed here, the service does seem to be an example of the gradual substitution of virtual citizen–state relationships for actual face-to-face relationships. Even if the service remains familiar and trusted, it is edging incrementally towards a situation in which citizens do most of their business with it via a screen. Bit-by-bit it becomes more convenient but also more faceless and distant. By itself, this shift may not have a terribly significant effect on citizens' attitudes towards government. However, taken together with similar shifts across a range of other services, it is at least possible that it will contribute to a more general loss of government's material, 'human' face. What effects that will have is, as yet, almost entirely unresearched and unknown.

8

The Police

Policing, until the 1960s, was a locally structured and funded service which, for the most part, addressed local crime and disorder.

(Association of Chief Police Officers 2008: 22)

Communications have been transformed, and that fundamentally influences the ways in which operations can be planned and carried out.

(TPT interview 21, senior Belgian police officer)

e-crime is a non-geographical problem.

(Association of Chief Police Officers 2009: 2)

We have it—we do not manage it—we undergo it...Technology has made the distance between the police and the citizens bigger.

(TPT interview 19, very senior Belgian police officer,
asked about technological change)

Police think they steer, but in reality they don't.

(TPT interview 22, senior UK police adviser, asked
about technological change)

8.1 Introduction

Territoriality has always been fundamental to policing—'the beat', 'his patch', 'gang territory'. More recently we have come to know about, *inter alia*, 'neighbourhood policing', 'crime hotspots', and 'geographical profiling'. And, as one profiler said in interview: 'There is one certain thing about violent crimes, and that is that the victim and the perpetrator were in the same *place* at the same *time*' (TPT interview 28, emphasis in original). On the other hand, an increasing amount of crime—and

172

therefore an increasing body of police staff—seems to be detaching itself from localities and operating either internationally or in virtual space.

In this chapter we will look at how the police attempt to shape localities, and how different types of locality themselves affect how the police are organized. Part of this story concerns the need for police operations at different *scales*, and how changes in policy and technology have altered the way these scales are conceived and translated into organizational structures and processes. We will draw on empirical material from Belgium and England, including a number of interviews with senior police officers and politicians with particular responsibility for the police.

8.2 Technological Change and Police Operations

It would not be an exaggeration to say that, over the last half century, new technologies have transformed police operations. In particular, they have transformed *where* police officers and other police staff carry out various activities, as well as *who* exactly gets to do *what*. Police are much more mobile than they were (first cars and motorbikes, then helicopters and aeroplanes, and now pilotless drones and even miniature robot submarines). Yet at the same time they are far more closely and continuously in touch with each other than they were previously able to be (phones, and nowadays secure radio communications systems such as AIRWAVE in England or ASTRID in Belgium, plus the Internet). These systems have, incidentally, helped to reduce the significance of the territorial demarcations between different local police forces, because, whereas previously forces often used different equipment, now they have 'interoperability', and can talk to each other (TPT interviews 1 and 31). Reducing such internal frontiers has—as will be seen in Section 8.3—been a recurrent goal in government policies towards the police in a number of countries, including the two that we particularly focus on in this chapter, Belgium and England.

At the same time, the places where police officers get their information have changed fundamentally. Today they have far, far more information than they did only a short time ago, and most of it comes from a screen or through an earpiece rather than through their own eyes. In Belgium, more than 20,000 terminals now input data to the central police database (TPT interview 21). In the UK, the Police National Computer (PNC) contains nine million criminal records, the National Firearms Licensing Managing System (NFLMS) holds 1.2 million records and the Violent and Sexual Offenders Register (VISOR) contains both factual records and intelligence on 70,000 serious offenders (TPT interview 22). All the senior UK police I interviewed identified the ongoing development of the PNC as a fundamental technological change during their careers. The rhythm of police patrol work often now revolves around information streams coming from such databases through personal radios and mobile data terminals (Sørensen and Pica 2005). Senior officers believe that some police at operational levels may even have lost a little 'fieldcraft' because they now rely so heavily on the screen rather than on what they see and hear on the street. 'If there is a downside, it is that perhaps it means that patrol officers don't have to use their "nous" so much—in the old days they could find out a lot by asking what was in the boot of a car' (TPT interviews 1 and 22). 'There is a clear evolution from the field to the desk (but also from the individual to the team) compared to a few decades ago. An investigator now spends a lot of time behind his desk' (TPT interview 19).

To a growing extent, the police do not even need to be in a place in order to see what is going on. CCTV cameras are becoming ever more common, and some English city centres now have very extensive coverage indeed. Some of these cameras are becoming 'intelligent' in the sense that they can alter direction and track moving things, either on instruction from an operator at police headquarters, or according to a predetermined computer program. During one interview (TPT interview 4) I was told a tale of how CCTV picked up thieves breaking into the storage area at the back of a supermarket, in broad daylight. This was clearly visible in the police control room several miles away. It so happened that a couple of police officers were actually inside the store at the time, to discuss security with the management! So the control room called the officers and told them to go round the back and arrest the thieves—which they duly did. In England, and also in Belgium, though as yet to a lesser extent, cameras are fitted with automatic numberplate recognition (ANPR), so that, if a vehicle with a registration number that is on the police database as being of interest crosses the field of vision, a beep tells the police operator to pay attention. The first UK pilot of ANPR began in 2003. Indeed, some of the new technology can literally see through walls. Infrared detection systems can see in the dark, under water, or sometimes though solid structures. Other technologies detect disturbances in the ground or spaces behind apparently solid panels. It is harder than ever before to 'bury the evidence'.

Crime *scenes* are very particular places, and any regular TV viewer will by now be familiar with such acronyms as CSI (crime scene investigation) and SOCO (scene of crime officer). Technological advance has made an enormous difference to what actually happens at crime scenes. If the crime is serious enough (and in England and Wales in 2008 only about 17 per cent of recorded crimes *were* serious enough), a crime scene is officially established, and a small army of experts, many of them not police officers, go to work. The processes for the taking of fingerprints and many other details have been immeasurably improved over the years, but one forensic technique has captured the public imagination and media attention more than any other, and that is DNA analysis. DNA will identify an individual uniquely and with only an infinitesimal amount of uncertainty (except for identical twins, who share their DNA—hence one or two improbable plots in TV crime series). Forensic DNA analysis was pioneered in the UK, and at the time of writing the UK 'leads' the world, in the sense of having the biggest and most sophisticated national DNA database in relation to its population size. In 2009 the National DNA Database held 4,859,934 individual profiles, and during 2008/9 almost 60 per cent of crime scene DNA profiles loaded onto the database produced a match. The National Database report contains vivid details of a number of murders and rapes that have been solved with substantial help from DNA evidence (National DNA Database 2010).

Technological change has also changed the very appearance of the police—what they wear and what they carry. An early example in the UK was the move from the traditional short truncheon to a longer one. This made quite a difference to both the police and the policed. For the police it meant that it was less risky to tackle an assailant with a knife. For the assailant it meant that there was a reduced chance that they would be hit hard over the head (a target that was often the only one available with a short truncheon, but one where serious injuries were more likely to be caused (TPT interview 1)). The police also benefit from bulletproof vests and far better riot gear, meaning that they sustain fewer injuries and can hold back for longer in violent situations before launching aggressive action. The advent of tasers—electric stun guns—and other 'sub-lethal' weapons give police the possibility to tackle armed criminals at a distance without having to shoot them (Leppard 2008; TPT interview 9). All these devices lead directly to alterations in police training and tactics.

All this, however, is only one side of a multi-sided story. Technological improvements for the police frequently have large financial implications. They may also require extensive retraining and/or new types of staff. They may have effects on innocent citizens. And the less innocent citizens—the criminals themselves—will certainly react. They may have means of avoiding or suppressing the new technology. They may adopt new technologies themselves. 'Technology is great, but the challenge is managing the expectations and the outcomes' (TPT interview 9). Several of our English police interviewees, unbidden, conceptualized technological progress as an unceasing race between the police and the criminals. Similarly, a Belgian federal police report comments: '[The police] are permanently confronted with technological developments, especially in telecommunications and computer matters, and with criminal organizations which continuously adapt to progress' (Federal Judicial Police 2009: 7).

CCTV, for example, has multiple implications (many TPT interviews). It provides endless images, mainly of innocent people doing innocent things. While it has often proved useful in reconstructing episodes of crimes, it also ties down significant manpower if lots of tapes have to be gone through and analysed ('a huge information overburden' (TPT interview 1)). It raises issues of privacy. For example, in Leuven, CCTV has been installed in the main market square, but, at the request of residents, the cameras are not able to look at the first floors or above (mainly residential accommodation), only at the busy street level (TPT interview 31). The good Belgians did not want police HQ to be able to see into their living quarters. Other evidence suggests that public reactions to CCTV vary considerably—and may shift over time. In the Leuven case, police surveys indicate that initial public apprehensiveness concerning the cameras in the market-place diminished as residents became used to them (TPT interview 31). Nevertheless, other scholars argue that CCTV tends to 'leave the public as passive subjects' and to put them 'under control' rather than 'in control' (Koskela 2000: 250, 259). (One might, of course, ask what the previous state of 'in control' actually consisted of, if one was assaulted or had one's bag snatched.) There are also issues over ownership and accountability—as one walks around many European cities, for example, there is usually no way of telling which cameras are privately owned and which public, while the precise conditions under which the police may have access to private tapes varies from country to country. CCTV also provokes various responses from criminals. They may take to wearing hoods to obscure their faces, or they may simply shift their criminal activities to another part of town, where cameras have not been installed ('displacement').

DNA analysis is similarly complex. While DNA analysis can be startlingly useful and determinative, it can also reveal other sensitive information, such as someone's true parentage, or the fact that an individual suffers from a particular disease or genetic predisposition. In the UK, controversy has also arisen over the police practice, under certain circumstances, of using the National DNA Database to conduct 'familial searches', where millions of records are trawled in an effort to find partial matches that might indicate family relationships to the sample taken from a crime scene ('New fears that innocent people will get caught up in investigations' (*Mail on Sunday*, 2010)). In Belgium, a far more restrictive policy than in the UK has been adopted towards storing DNA samples. One has to be convicted of a serious crime before one's DNA can be put on the national database. The result is that that database is proportionately far smaller than the one in the UK, and that the chances of getting a match are also smaller. 'Our political people are afraid of DNA because DNA might be open to abuse' (TPT interview 19). One Belgian interviewee described DNA analysis as a 'Pandora's box'.

A final issue in relation to new technologies and the police is whether the latter are able to plan and control the former, or not. In interviews with both Belgian and English police officers (including several who were specifically responsible for technological development), the majority thought not, although one individual was marginally more optimistic. In both countries attempts were being made to look ahead, and in both countries steps had been taken to improve the assessment and procurement of new technologies. But the idea that the police could significantly shape the direction of technological development to suit their needs was seen as unrealistic. (See the last two quotations at the head of this chapter.) Sometimes new devices were developed first for the (burgeoning) private security sector and were subsequently adopted by the police. One Belgian police officer spoke of the police going to trade exhibitions to see if there was anything that might be useful (TPT interview 31). Sometimes the police would realize that criminals were using a particular technology and would then try to commission an 'antidote' (for example, certain kinds of financial analysis software that helped in the identification of fraud or money laundering). The picture drawn in the interviews was a fairly consistent one—that the business world spewed forth all manner of new technologies, and the police could do little more than try to keep abreast of this, to identify what might help them in their activities, and to keep a wary eye on what new technologies the criminals were using. One argument for the expensive new twenty-first-century communications systems (AIRWAVE in the UK and ASTRID in Belgium) was that criminals had been able to listen in to their previous radio communications, so they needed new systems that were secure (TPT interviews 1, 19, 22, and 31).

8.3 Territorial Units: An Anglo-Belgian Comparison, 1960–2010

Size matters in the police. Larger administrative units tend to have more staff, to support more specialized personnel and equipment, and to be able to tackle larger-scale and more complex crime without heavy external assistance. Yet, however strong these organizational and technological arguments, historically the actual size of police forces has varied enormously between countries—often between neighbouring countries—and still does. It has also varied over time, and, just as we saw was the case with units of local government in Europe, the dominant recent direction of travel has been towards larger units (see Section 4.2). In this section we will briefly review the history of police scale in Belgium and England since 1960. In both countries the relevant police organizations evolved considerably over the period of study, and some quite new ones emerged. And in both there are echoes of the general observations concerning boundary-drawing made in Section 4.2—namely that there are always conflicting or at least competing criteria at work, that technocratic arguments often point to the advantages of larger size, and that there are always winners and losers in any rescaling—in whichever direction.

8.3.1 England

In England there has never been a national police force—a fact that has now acquired a positive political charge, as though it somehow guarantees a more democratic and responsive force. Each local force long enjoyed a high degree of autonomy, with the chief constable granted firm job security and effectively answerable to nobody for his or her operational decisions (although the Metropolitan Police, responsible for the capital, has been something of an exception, in so far as the Commissioner reported directly to the Home Secretary). At the time of writing, the Coalition government is implementing proposals to make chief constables answerable in certain respects to elected police and crime commissioners, but it is too early to say how significant a change that will turn out to be. At the moment it appears to leave chief constables' operational autonomy intact.

To summarize the history in England, there was a round of force mergers following the 1964 Police Act, but, since then, there has been no comprehensive restructuring of force boundaries. Between 1970 and the present there have been forty-something forces, many of them coterminous with the boundaries of the old English counties (the Sussex Police, the Yorkshire

Police, and so on). These forces varied very considerably in terms of equipment and culture. Speaking of his early experiences of being sent to the north of England during the 1984–5 miners' strike, one senior policeman told me that he had 'witnessed big differences between police forces, both north versus south and urban versus rural' (TPT interview 4). In 2005–6 the Labour government did attempt to launch a programme of mergers, hoping to reduce the numbers possibly to as low as seventeen in order to create more 'strategic' commands, but this met stiff resistance, and the government lost office before it could make any substantial progress with the idea. 'The Home Office told the police to amalgamate, and it failed' (TPT interview 3).

The most obvious innovatory trend in England was the creation (or enhancement) of a series of national-level bodies to deal with the perceived gap left by the famous absence of a national force (see Savage 2007: ch. 3). These included a National Reporting Centre (1972), a strengthened and more inquisitive HM Inspectorate of Constabulary, an Audit Commission (created in 1983 and abolished in 2011—it carried out a number of influential performance audits of different aspects of policing (see, e.g., Audit Commission 1996)), the National Criminal Intelligence Service (1992), National Police Training (1993), the National Crime Squad (1997), the National High-Tech Crime Unit (2001), the National Policing Improvement Agency (NPIA) (2004) and the Serious Organized Crime Agency (SOCA) (2006). Savage (2007: 113) sees this trend as follows:

British policing had traditionally been locally-based and locally-accountable, however fragile that accountability might have been. The formation of national policing bodies moves the process of accountability to other levels, allowing major decisions about policing to be made some distance away, both geographically and structurally, from localities.

Alongside these national bodies, the role of the (national) Association of Chief Police Officers (ACPO) has expanded considerably: 'The Home Office has . . . encouraged [ACPO] to develop a much higher profile and expand its role, as a means of enhancing the standardization and centralization of policing' (Reiner 2000: 192; see also Jones 2008: 7–8). By 2004 ACPO appears repeatedly on the face of government planning documents, cited as a partner and guarantor of the professionalism of the proposed measures (see, e.g., Home Office 2004).

In parallel with the appearance of these national bodies, central governments progressively erected a detailed framework of targets, incentives, and penalties around the forty-three police forces. The drive for greater efficiency and value for money (VFM) went hand in hand with the centralizing measures referred to above. 'The balance of power between the police, the Police Authority and the Home Office has shifted hugely'—in favour of the Home Office (TPT interview 3). A main means for requiring efficiency became centrally orchestrated systems of performance indicators backed up by performance audits and inspections (see, e.g., Audit Commission 1990, 1996; Her Majesty's Chief Inspector of Constabulary 1998a, b; Home Office 1999; Collier 2006). VFM was not a sudden innovation, but rather a steady tightening and elaboration of controls, beginning with Home Office Circular 114 of 1983 and running on to climax in the first National Policing Plan of 2003.

The theme of local accountability, control, and responsiveness obviously sits in a potentially tense relationship with the centralizing measures described in the previous two paragraphs. (The contrast with Belgium was stark: there the municipal police were, if anything, too intimately under the control of the local mayor, whereas in England chief constables exercised real operational independence and increasingly tended to look to the Home Office and ACPO for guidance.) The police authorities, with their nominated local authority representatives, were usually only a weak influence. In 1981 the Greater London Council (GLC) took matters into its own hands by setting up a police committee to monitor local police practice. At the time this was often depicted (negatively) as 'bringing politics into the police', but quite a few other councils followed the GLC example, and by the early 1990s most such committees had been able to establish more settled relationships. In 1994, however, the Police and Magistrates Court Act, if anything, took power away from the local authorities. The new structures and membership of police authorities made them more independent of local authorities and gave the Home Secretary the authority to determine 'national key objectives' (Loveday 2000; Reiner 2000). Some ground was perhaps regained when the 1998 Crime and Disorder Act set a statutory requirement for police to work in partnership with local authorities. Overall, however, almost all the senior officers and politicians I interviewed agreed that central government control over the police had grown considerably from the late 1980s onwards. 'This has all gone slightly over the top,' said one, referring to the framework of performance targets and inspections (TPT interview 4; see also Pollitt and Bouckaert 2009: 113–14).

Local responsiveness is different from accountability to local authorities (in theory at least, a police force could be highly responsive to local communities at a grass-roots level without being at all formally accountable to local elected representatives). The theme of 'community' and later 'neighbourhood' policing has been a recurrent one since the 1970s. It has been plagued both by multiple models and definitions and by a certain cultural reluctance within the police to give this kind of activity high status (see McLaughlin 2007: 133–8; Tilley 2008; Tuffin 2008). Nevertheless, in the early twenty-first century the government launched a new programme to 'roll out' neighbourhood policing (Home Office 2004). It is still too early to say how far this will actually take hold: 'There is the strong impression that underneath the new "going local" rhetoric, the formation of a much stronger centrally controlled government matrix is taking place' (McLaughlin 2007: 195).

English police forces themselves are mid-scale organizations—they are more than local but less than national. We have already commented on the tension between the national government and this mid-level, but to complete the picture we also need to look at the micro-scale. Here the traditional picture was of local police stations with a considerable presence in the community, including associated police houses and social clubs (TPT interview 4). From the early 1990s, however, a new concept took flight— the Basic Command Unit (BCU). The idea was to create a unit at 'the lowest level in the command structure which can provide a 24-hour policing service, able to respond to all incidents and deal fully with most of them without frequent external support' (Audit Commission 1991). As a term, the BCU seems to have originated in work done by HM Inspectorate of Constabulary (HMIC) and the Audit Commission. It comprises the basic territorial, operational unit below the level of the police force. By the 2001 police reform white paper it was seen as being the key recipient of the devolution of powers, as well as a central player in neighbourhood policing (Home Office 2001; McLaughlin 2007: 192–3). Since then: 'In many ways the BCU notion has been the most resilient of the police reform measures to emerge in the early 1990s, as it has remained a cornerstone of the management of the police organization and of operational delivery of policing in Britain' (Savage 2007: 105). In the later stages of the New Labour administration of 1997–2010 enthusiasm for neighbourhood policing grew and grew. By 2008 every locality was to be served by a multi-functional Neighbourhood Policing Team (NPT). However: 'To make NPT a reality, chief constables will be required to devolve more resources and operational decision-making powers to BCU commanders' (McLaughlin 2007: 192).

Thus, what we have seen in terms of the territorial organization of the police since the 1960s has been a mixture of the incremental and the radical. Radical change has taken place at national level, with the flowering of a profusion of national-level bodies and national-level regulatory frameworks, some of them fairly short lived (such as the 2001 National Centre for Policing Excellence), but others having embedded themselves and developed over the long term (such as the PNC). Incremental change has proceeded at the meso, force level, where government attempts to enforce more radical amalgamations came to naught. Meanwhile, at the local level, BCUs emerged in the early 1990s and seem to have acquired the useful property of being all things to all men. They fitted the 'neighbourhood and community' themes of New Labour and they can also claim to fit the 'new localism' theme of the Conservative/Liberal Democrat Coalition government from 2010. At any event, in so far as crime remains local, they are the coordinators of the local response.

8.3.2 Belgium

We now turn to territorial issues in the Belgian police. From the end of the First World War there were three main police forces in Belgium: the Rijkswacht/Gendarmerie (national, hierarchical, somewhat militaristic), the Judicial Police (attached to public prosecution offices and organized in judicial districts), and the municipal police (under local mayors, and with a somewhat 'softer' and also less 'professional' image than the Rijkswacht). In effect, there are no police forces at the meso-level occupied by the British forces, unless one counts the regional divisions of the federal police.

In 1976–7, a local government restructuring reform reduced 2,359 municipalities (each with its own police force) to 589. Some of these were still very small by UK standards (589 forces in a country with a 2010 population of fewer than eleven million). In 1998 a major legislative reform redrew the boundaries between the forces. Basically the municipal forces were enlarged by merger, and absorbed some elements of the Rijkswacht/Gendarmerie. From 2001 there were 50 single municipality forces and 146 joint municipality forces, a total of 196. Even so, in 2011 the Belgian municipal forces remain much smaller than the average English 'county' police force, and require assistance from the national police for a wide range of more serious or complex types of crime. Much recent emphasis has therefore also been placed on better coordination between the national and municipal forces, although the reality of achievement here is hard to assess (Bergmans 2005: 29; see also Lippens and Van Calster 2002; PZ Leuven 2006). In 2008 there were in total about 28,500 municipal police and about 12,150 national/federal police. Historically, the municipal police forces have been closely supervised by the mayors—indeed, not infrequently local political leaders have intervened in operational details and appointments in ways that would be regarded as inappropriate in an English context. A background theme since the late 1980s has been the increased professionalization of the municipal police (one outcome of the 1998 reform was a joint training programme for the national and municipal police).

The Police Reform Act of 1998 took a long time to arrive, against a background of sustained public criticism and mistrust, not only of the police but of the criminal justice system more generally. A sequence of scandals and failures continued for more than a decade before the political elite finally agreed on the 1998 Act (Maesschalck 2002). When it came, the reform was predominantly structural—some of the national police were integrated with the municipal police, and the judicial police and the Rijkswacht/Gendamerie were merged.

The 1998 reforms also reinforced the priority for community policing and community safety. In each municipality there was to be a local crime prevention panel, chaired by the mayor. However, the 'mix of personnel often results in both an overcrowded setting and agency tensions created by individual agendas' (Goris and Walters 1999: 646). These panels have worked reasonably well in some localities, but not in others. In general there have been structural, especially political concerns, 'which have produced impediments to a constructive partnership approach and hindered implementation' (Goris and Walters 1999: 648).

As in many other countries, the Belgian police have needed to improve training and upgrade their managerial and technical skills. There has been a particular problem here with some of the smaller municipal forces, especially in Wallonia (Maesschalck 2002: 182–3). So part of the reform agenda that evolved from the late 1980s through to the 1998 legislation concerned the upgrading of these local forces. Both in training and in community orientation, therefore, there has been considerable variation from one municipality to another. Local politics (and regional politics, as between Flanders and Wallonia) have made a difference. In 2010, for example, a big political row broke out over the lack of coordination between the six police zones in Brussels. Four police unions announced strike plans after a number of violent acts against the police, and a lack of back-up from adjacent police zones. But the political struggle parlayed into yet another version of the ongoing language wars between Dutch- and French-speakers. Flemish-speaking politicians supported a zonal merger, but the (mainly French-speaking) mayors of Brussels opposed it (Hope 2010). Place continues to matter in the sphere of Belgian law and order—both politics *and* policing are highly territorial.

A few general remarks may serve as a conclusion to this section. It might seem that, compared with the dramatic operational impacts of new technologies described in Section 8.2, the setting and resetting of administrative borders to particular police jurisdictions is fairly dry and inconsequential stuff. Dry it may sometimes be, but hardly inconsequential. Issues of local political control and citizen 'ownership', economies of scale, complexity of operational coordination, police career structures, and even, to some degree, public trust—all these and more are directly affected by the size and 'distance' of the jurisdiction, and its coterminosity (or otherwise) with the units of political authority and service provision (especially emergency services such as fire brigades and ambulances). All these factors will have some influence on police management.

Furthermore, the topographical and socio-demographic make-up of places will affect both how the police operate and, in all probability, their organizational culture. One does not attempt to police a multi-ethnic, economically depressed inner-city district in the same way as a prosperous, largely mono-ethnic rural area (in TV terms *The Wire* versus *Midsomer Murders*). In the UK, middle-class people—especially those with lots of insurance—report incidents to the police at a higher rate than working-class people. There are also systematic differences between different ethnic groups. The famous British TV policeman of the 1960s, Dixon of Dock Green, was very much a product of his time, place, and class (McLaughlin 2007: 10–25), whereas the more recent TV series *Life on Mars* hinged almost entirely on the humour to be extracted from a confrontation between the police culture of the twenty-first century and that of the early 1970s (McLaughlin 2007: 112–13). One does not need to be a social scientist to understand that the ways in which the police carry out their jobs are deeply affected by the places in which they are operating.

8.4 Crime Goes Global: The Police Response

Although robust statistics for international crime are even harder to come by than those for domestic crime, it is almost certainly on the increase. In the EU, in particular, organized criminals have taken advantage of the easier transport of people and goods between states precisely in order to transport people and goods between states—for criminal purposes. For example, in Belgium in 2008 the federal police spent 85,712 hours on projects and cases to do with human trafficking, and carried out 162 arrests (Police Fédéral 2009: 3). Also in Belgium: '50,000 to 60,000 burglaries are committed each year, mainly by gangs from Eastern Europe. It is hard to assess the exact proportion of burglaries committed by itinerant criminal groups, but, according to us, it exceeds 25%' (Federal Judicial Police 2009: 15). Meanwhile in England the human trafficking problem was deemed to be serious enough to warrant the formation of a special unit within SOCA (see www.soca.gov.uk/about-soca/about-the-ukhtc (accessed 7 February 2011)). In the year 2009/10 over 700 cases of suspected human trafficking were referred, 74 per cent of them female.

In such a situation, all national police forces are being obliged to have more to do with their counterparts in other countries. This process intersects with the development of new police technologies, as described earlier. For example: 'The adoption of common quality standards for forensic science across Europe has become ever more important as the international exchange of DNA profiles offers greater potential to increase public safety in a significantly more mobile society' (National DNA Database 2010: 4).

In this context, one major development has been the Treaty of Prüm, signed in 2005 by Austria, Belgium, France, Germany, Luxembourg, the Netherlands, and Spain. It provided a framework for enhanced cross-border cooperation, particularly in combating terrorism, cross-border crime, and illegal migration. More specifically, it included arrangements for international matching of DNA profiles, vehicle registrations, and other information. Core parts of the Treaty were formally adopted into EU law in 2008, meaning that all EU member states are supposed to comply with this Decision by August 2011 (which would mean that some, who do not yet have national DNA databases, would have to set them up).

The Treaty of Prüm has proved controversial among academics, if rather less so among the (mainly supportive) politicians and practitioners. One group of lawyers has argued that the treaty creates a hierarchy within the EU, separating the original seven signatories from the other seventeen member states. They see it as going against the spirit and practice of the EU, and as being undemocratic because it is not subject to scrutiny by the European Parliament (see, e.g., Balzacq et al. 2006). Another set of academics has seen the Prüm arrangements as symptoms of the 'big brother' surveillance state—threats to civil liberties and a harbinger of a police superstate (Guild and Geyer 2008; Kirkegaard 2008). This all seems rather gloomily one-sided, especially since in some important respects the Treaty 'will probably decrease and regularize rather than increase the amount of personal data that travels across borders' (Prainsack and Toom

2010: 1124). This debate has strong echoes of the two opposing camps already referred to in the discussion of identity management (Section 7.3; see also Lyon 2002).

Alongside Prüm there have been ongoing developments in the Schengen Information System (SIS). The SIS originated in the 1985 Schengen Agreement, and became operational in 1995. Originally it covered only France, Germany, and the three Benelux countries, but by 2005 at least twenty-eight states were taking part (Brouwer 2005). By 2005 SIS comprised a database of more than fifteen million records, of which more than one million concerned persons who were wanted for arrest or extradition or in connection with various crimes or misdemeanours. The largest single category has been third-country nationals, who, it is considered, should be refused entry to the EU. Various additions and alterations have been made to the original scheme, including data on lost or stolen passports, stolen car registrations, and arrest warrants (Brouwer 2005). Overall, a UK House of Lords committee found that 'the System raises fundamental questions concerning the balance between, on the one hand, the operational effectiveness of immigration control and public security by law enforcement authorities, and on the other hand the protection of civil liberties' (House of Lords 2007: 6).

A second generation system (SIS II) was launched in 2001 and was planned to become operational in 2007, but suffered repeated delays and complications. It was not yet up and running when this book was being completed in the spring of 2011. Negotiations for the UK to use some but not all its functionalities had proven both lengthy and convoluted (see House of Lords 2007). (The UK and Ireland remained outside the Schengen Agreement, largely because they wanted to be able to continue to control their own borders in particular ways.) Like Schengen I, Schengen II was pushed forward by the EU Commission without either clear evaluations or precise commitments on some issues of data handling and definition. Referring to this, the Programme Director of the UK initiative to link in with Schengen said: 'My personal view is that they could have been more open about those arrangements' (House of Lords 2007: Minutes of Evidence, 11 Oct. 2006, p. 5). An academic perspective arrives at a similar assessment:

Until now, the EU policy on the use and amendments of EU databases, is characterised by a lack of transparency, which is enhanced by the piecemeal approach by which the decisions are actually taken...It is very difficult on the basis of the different decisions which have been adopted, to get an overall picture of the EU architecture for the future collection and sharing of personal information.

(Brouwer 2005: 11)

These EU databases (and there are more of them than have been mentioned here) illustrate the complexity of interactions between new technologies and old borderlines. This is hardly the sometimes-fantasized 'borderless world' (Houtum et al. 2005b). Prüm, Schengen, and the like undoubtedly offer improved chances of catching criminals and undesirable would-be entrants to EU territory. At the same time, they accentuate the twin needs of protecting privacy and ensuring the highest possible levels of accuracy and uniformity in data. So it is not simply a matter of a UK police force being able to tap into an EU database and see if some other member state has data on a suspect. It is also a question of the reliability of that (French/Polish/Estonian, and so on) data, and of what use the French, Polish, or Estonian authorities will make of data that they, reciprocally, extract from the UK PNC. Answering these questions entails solving problems of different national legal systems, different organizational practices and standards, and the interoperability of different technologies. Such questions also raise basic problems of trust. One of my interviewees (who in respect of this remark shall remain wholly anonymous) said: 'we don't want to share our data on criminals with them because in some cases the organizations we are sharing with contain some of the criminals'. It is perhaps unsurprising that the development of Schengen I and II have been such long-drawn-out sagas.

At least burglaries and crimes of violence (and illegal immigration and human trafficking) involve real places, where criminals have been and may have left traces that CCTV or the new forensic techniques can pick up and use as evidence. But what if the 'burglar' may be thousands of miles away, and leaves no physical trace? In a sense, e-crime, where someone, somewhere, taps into your bank account, could be thought of as 'the new burglary'. 'E-crime transcends borders' (TPT interview 22). While much of it involves the use of false identities to defraud or steal money from accounts, e-crime also intertwines with many other types of crime. Money laundering, to hide money used by criminal gangs or terrorist cells (or kleptomaniac rulers), frequently involves the Internet. So do people trafficking and prostitution. Indeed, virtually any crime can be organized, in whole or in part, over the Net.

The first signs of the importance of e-crime included the setting-up of special police teams or units to tackle it (including an Interpol European

Working Party group on IT Crime). Policy papers soon followed (see, e.g., Association of Chief Police Officers 2009). It turns out that e-crime is one of those types of crime that is significantly under-reported (because of embarrassment or fear of damage to reputation, or even lack of awareness that a crime has taken place). Yet, despite this, the sheer scale of the (reported) malfeasance is impressive (for example, globally, there was perhaps £52 billion of online fraud in 2007, including more than a quarter of a million cases in the UK (Association of Chief Police Officers 2009: 4)). 'The Internet allows criminals to target potential victims from anywhere in the world and enables mass victimization to be attempted with relative ease—a single e-mail infected with malware can be sent to millions of recipients' (Association of Chief Police Officers 2009: 3).

Indeed, the scale of the problem soon indicated to the police that specialist units would not be enough: 'building specialist e-Crime capability is not enough—all police officers need to have an understanding of e-Crime' (Association of Chief Police Officers 2009: 5—precisely echoed in Belgium in TPT interview 21). This further implies that police must re-skill frequently—as the technology moves on (TPT interview 19). 'The pace of technological development provides criminals with a continuing stream of new opportunities and new methods of attack, as well as challenging the Police service and other law enforcement agencies to ensure their own knowledge and expertise are kept up to date' (Association of Chief Police Officers 2009: 3).

8.5 Policing from a GAP Perspective

Policing remains a profoundly territorial, place-based activity. It shapes places and is shaped by places. It shapes because, first, it overtly and covertly exerts the state's authority within its territorial boundaries, and helps to maintain those boundaries (GAP modality A). It also shapes (modality B) by locating its 'own things' within its areas of jurisdiction—not only police stations but also public notices, barriers, marked and unmarked vehicles, uniformed personnel, surveillance devices, and so on. It directly regulates the use of space (modality C), not by 'planning' but by coercive force—demonstrations are channelled and controlled, sensitive locations are sealed off, traffic is directed. Indeed, the maintenance of order in public places is a central goal for the police, and shows every sign of remaining so. To some extent the police negotiate and bargain with other placemakers (modality E), especially when it comes to agreements with the organizers of marches and protests about routes and spaces. And policing most certainly uses symbolism to reinforce the affective dimensions of certain, special places (modality G). Consider the seemingly eternal policeman standing under the light outside No. 10 Downing Street, or the German equivalent on duty outside Chancellor Merkel's apartment in Berlin, or, indeed, those prominently visible at most important public buildings—palaces and parliaments all over the developed world.

Policing is shaped by place because topography, the built environment, the local social and cultural mix, and particular histories all affect both what crime is 'produced' and what police strategies and tactics are most likely to yield good results. (Commenting on the current police strategy of concentrating resources on particular crime 'hotspots', one local politician I interviewed speculated on what might happen if the tactic were (counter-intuitively) reversed, and police resources were reallocated to the lowest crime areas. Possibly, he thought, this would almost eliminate crime from these blessed places, thus rewarding their law-abiding residents and increasing their attractiveness, while the 'hotspots' would then become so bad that people would either leave them or insist that their leaders did something decisive about it! (TPT interview 3; the respondent lived in one of the low crime areas.)) Crime maps often show extraordinarily local concentrations of certain types of crime, and strong patterning even of more common crimes such as burglary. Geographical profilers pay great attention to the physical detail of local places—where is the nearest railway station or bus terminal (if it looks like a 'commuter crime'), which places are overlooked and which not, whether the movements of the criminal indicate that he or she knows the area, and so on (TPT interview 28).

Yet at the same time important aspects of policing are becoming less and less place-bound. That is partly, but not entirely, because the police, like almost everyone else, have been drawn steadily deeper and deeper into the Internet. The police now attempt to police 'virtual space' (modality H) by tracking paedophiles and money launderers and those who try to steal identities and break into bank accounts. The 2008 annual report of the Belgian federal judicial police, for example, is almost entirely taken up with these types of activity (Police judiciaire fédéral 2008). In these and other senses, policing is becoming 'more virtual'. One could plausibly argue that the traditional investigatory methods of extracting information face-to-face, by interviewing people, has become steadily less and less central to police operations. DNA matches, mobile phone data, and evidence taken from the hard discs of suspects' computers stand up in court better than witnesses' statements. More and more police officers find it more productive to sit in front of screens than to pad the streets, even if there is little recognition of this in the newspapers—'Bobbies on the Beat for Just 6 Hours a Week' screamed a *Daily Telegraph* front page headline in 2009 (Whitehead 2009).

However, it is not only the technology of the Internet that has increasingly uprooted some police from their local concerns. It is also the growth of mass, cheap international transport, the loosening of borders within the EU, and the consequent internationalization of organized crime. This has led to the sharing of national databases, exchange of personnel, joint training schemes, and a generally heightened awareness of the techniques and technologies used by police forces in other countries. The development of the specific technique of geographical profiling, for example, depended initially on an academic base in North America, which then spawned an international network of trained specialists who continue to swap experiences and assist in the solution of each other's crimes (TPT interview 28). The UK has been one of the leaders, but Belgium subsequently developed its own specialists.

Overall it could be said that, of all the examples of public-service place-making examined in this book, policing is the one that shows the most intense and diverse impacts on specific localities. Its impacts on localities are intense, in the sense that they are often directly connected to high-profile, sometimes dramatic events, and they have an obvious salience for residents' basic feelings concerning orderliness and safety. Police action can sometimes transform a particular locality—at least temporarily—for example, by clearing out drug dealers or prostitutes from a particular street or by banning inflammatory marches through ethnically sensitive areas. The impacts are widespread, in the sense that police intervention may be called for at any place at any time (unlike hospitals, schools, or civil registration).

It is also the case that policing is the activity that exhibits the most obvious, and occasionally spectacular, impacts of technological change. New diagnostic technologies have not merely fuelled a seemingly endless series of TV dramas; they have also profoundly changed the way the police (or rather, increasingly, other professions allied to the police) organize and work at crime scenes. These diagnostic investigations feed into an increasingly large and sophisticated range of national databases, which can themselves increasingly be accessed from data terminals in police vehicles or even mobile devices carried by individual officers. In the UK, not only does one have the now-familiar Police National Computer databases on criminals and vehicle registrations, but also the Missing Persons Bureau, the Central Witness Bureau, the National DNA database, and even a National

Footwear Reference Collection, as well as, internationally, the second generation Schengen Information System (National Policing Improvement Agency 2009). Meanwhile, new crowd-control technologies (protective clothing, instant, secure radio communications, helicopter and drone surveillance, specialized vehicles) have permitted police to face more dangerous public-order situations with fewer injuries and less temptation to make an early resort to offensive tactics. Likewise tasers and other sub-lethal weapons have enabled police to tackle dangerous adversaries without resorting to lethal firearms. The sum total of all these technological advances is not merely a better-equipped police officer. They have meant a huge increase in training and specialization—in short a further professionalization of police officers, with evident consequences for their cost and capability (Pollitt and Bouckaert 2009). Nor have the effects of technological changes been confined to internal police affairs. As this book was being written, the first release of crime maps broken down by local areas proved wildly popular with the British public (see www.police.uk/crime (accessed 15 Feb. 2011)), although it immediately triggered complaints that the (unprecedentedly detailed) data were . . . not detailed enough.

Thus we may conclude that the role of 'place' in police work is changing. The 'power geometries' affecting that work have been transformed by technological as well as social developments. The police can 'see' more places than before (new surveillance techniques) and see more *in* places than before (new diagnostic techniques), and they can move from one place to another *more quickly* than ever before. Unfortunately, to a considerable extent so can the criminals, or, at least, the organized, professional sort. To some extent, mobile, organized, international crime can be countered by the real-time international data exchanges that have been the goals of programmes such as Schengen II. At the same time, however, new categories of 'placeless' criminal have emerged—individuals and organizations who could be anywhere in the world as they offer you false or illegal services, or hack into your bank account, or penetrate confidential government records, or move 'dirty' money from country to country, or organize a terrorist attack. The early idealists who envisaged the Internet as a free, democratic, and unregulated space now appear rather naive. The traditional debates between freedom and security, transparency and privacy, and democracy and efficiency are being played out anew in cyberspace.

9

Discussion and Conclusions

The process of reforming any governmental system is contingent because so many [of these other] factors are the product of long historical processes. They are peculiar to a place.

(Roberts 2010: 147)

The questions are no longer 'Are you going to disappear soon?' 'Are you the telltale sign of something new coming to replace everything else?' 'Is this the seventh seal of the Book of Apocalypse that you are now breaking?' An entirely new set of questions has now emerged: 'Can we cohabit with you?' 'Is there a way for all of us to survive together while none of our contradictory claims, interests and passions can be eliminated?' Revolutionary time, the great Simplifier, has been replaced by cohabitation time, the great Complicator. In other words, space has replaced time as the main ordering principle.

(Latour 2005: 40)

9.1 Summing up

Time and place are the fundamental elements of contextualization. They can be defined loosely ('in the twentieth century'/'in the developing world') or tightly ('the news arrived five minutes before he was due to speak'/'No Canberra resident should be more than fifteen minutes' walk from a tram stop'). Together they situate any statement or claim, and begin to outline the likely extent of its domain.

Where public services are placed has many effects on many different people and groups. Within mainstream public policy-making and management, this significance of place has often been underestimated. Within the academic world, apart from some geographers, it has likewise remained neglected, or even (especially in the case of generic public-management writing) totally ignored. For some—seemingly rather a lot of—management professors, the world is, metaphorically at least, flat and rather uniform. The dominant tendency has been the quintessentially modernist search for 'disembedded', abstract types of knowledge that 'empty out' both time and space (Giddens 1990: 17–22). To halt this march away from the specificities of time and place—even within a small academic field such as public policy-making and administration—would be a major task, and by itself one book cannot do more than hope to provide a few insights and tools.

Beyond merely halting decontextualization and disembedding, what would be quite revolutionary would be actually to invert the modernist view of knowledge. By inversion, I mean to begin from the assumption that, for explanatory purposes, 'context' was usually *primary*, and generalized, abstract mechanisms (such as 'strategic planning' or 'innovation') were commonly subordinate or ancilliary—to be modified, or abandoned, according to circumstances. That is at least an interesting thought experiment, although let me hasten to say that the main thrust of this book has been to advance claims that are more qualified and nuanced, less imperial, than such a whole-scale inversion.

More cautiously then, one point to be made is that spatial relations are particularly dependent on material particularities. The idea of 'spatial relations', by itself, is a content-free abstraction. Actual spatial relations always involve things: '*space can exist in and through objects.*' However, paradoxically, space '*is independent of the particular types of object present*' (Sayer 1985: 52; emphasis in original). Furthermore: 'The spatial is *partly* constituted by the social, but it is reducible neither to natural nor to social constituents' (Sayer 1985: 59; emphasis in original). Attempts to render such broad ontological statements into more prosaic language are usually dangerous, but one version might go as follows. First, the idea of place can be operationalized only by specifying particulars, and some of those particulars will have to do with material features—roads, buildings, rivers, mountains, and so on. There is no general model of a place (except, tautologically, that a place is somewhere with a particular and special set of spatial relationships!). Second, places are socially shaped, but not *only* socially shaped— they have other constituent elements, including material factors such as landscape and climate. And, as we have said at several points in the book, these material factors interact with and channel the social construction of a place. Furthermore, the ongoing interaction of material heritage and the current processes of social construction are themselves conditioned by the currently available technologies. With mid-twentieth-century earth-moving equipment, it is possible, rather swiftly, to construct a large artificial lake in the middle of Canberra. That lake realizes a key element in the original design of the city, and comes to symbolize both the determination of the authorities (at last) to make it a real capital and the personality of the place (Lake Burley Griffin features in most of the many postcards sold to tourists). At a deeper level, however, the lake is possible only because of the material fact of the natural course of the river Molongo.

Place directly affects *how* and even sometimes *which* public services can be provided. Remote areas are unlikely to have tertiary hospitals or frequent public transport. Public 'bads', such as waste dumps, nuclear power plants, or prisons, tend to be sited in less wealthy, less stable, more socially diffuse areas (Aldrich 2008). In the USA, 'most [social assistance] service providers are not located in high-poverty areas. The vast majority of assistance is delivered in neighborhoods with low to moderate poverty rates' (Allard 2009: 85). In all countries, city centres will require different policing styles because of, *inter alia*, the local concentrations of wealth and poverty, and because of the high number of transient souls. The management team at a tough inner-city school will need to take a different approach to the physical security of the school buildings and equipment than that taken in a village school. During the height of the AIDS epidemic in the 1980s and 1990s, the Royal Sussex County Hospital had to adjust its services to the fact that it was situated right next to one of the largest and most vibrant gay communities in the UK (as did the local police force (several TPT interviews)). Even civil registration—a fairly routine and uniform job one might imagine—varies significantly in management terms between big city and rural offices. The inner-city offices must be prepared to deal with a wider range of cultural and linguistic issues, and they may also have greater difficulty attracting and retaining staff (TPT 5 interview). These are all management problems that are directly dependent on place.

Furthermore, place is intimately connected to culture, to levels of civic activism, and to the sense of belonging—or not—to the same political community that has elected the relevant political authority. Places are where, as Latour indicates in the second quotation leading off this chapter, we have to learn to co-habit (or not). All these things, directly or indirectly, impact on the organization of public services, and are, in turn, influenced by those services. This web of interactions and consequences is complex, and the preceding chapters have offered many examples of its density and importance. We have not, however, got right down to the micro-level that a full critical realist analysis would require (see Pawson 2006). We have stayed mainly at the middle scale, indicating the crucial relationships that seem to have been major placeshapers, but not putting precise mechanisms under the microscope. Of course, previous research has already helpfully illuminated some strands (such as issues of centralization and decentralization, or the constraints on town planning), but other connections remain largely innocent of systematic social science investigation (especially the long-run effects that shifting from face-to-face encounters with authority to virtual encounters may have on citizen attitudes towards government).

Chapter 4, and the subsequent empirical chapters, provided many examples of how the location of public services can have significant effects on local politics, the local economy, and local civic engagement—on Massey's 'power geometry'. Time after time public service facilities have become *foci* for political debate and civic engagement. However, what we have established here concerning the less obvious effects—the impact of placeshifts on citizens' perceptions of legitimacy and 'belonging'—is considerably less firm and fully evidenced. Nevertheless, there is a theoretical case—and some supporting fragmentary evidence—to suggest that there may be wider, cumulative effects on citizens' perceptions of governments, effects about which, as yet, we know remarkably little. What we are experiencing, in many countries and sectors, is essentially a 'thinning-out' of citizen-to-government contacts, in which such interactions are increasingly conducted in virtual rather than actual space, shorn of non-verbal communications (face), of individuality (personal variability), and of physical context (a government office). Furthermore, many of the surviving face-to-face encounters are with staff who are *not* state employees—they are contractors or partners or some other category of 'co-producer' or 'stakeholder' (the local refuse collection worker, the employment services adviser, the security guard, the home help, nurse, or doctor). To expect that all this will have *no* effect on the citizen's broader perceptions of government, or that the increased convenience of e-government will somehow exactly counterbalance any loss of face-to-face responsiveness, is to bank on the improbable. Yet concern about such wider effects has played almost no part in official discussions of these issues, which have instead been driven by shorter-term considerations of cost saving, technical feasibility, and strategies for encouraging the recalcitrant citizens on the far side of the digital divide to 'get on board'.

9.2 Placeless Public Services?

The year 2007 saw the publication of a fascinating book entitled *Creating Citizen-Consumers: Changing Publics and Changing Public Services* (Clarke et al. 2007). It traced the ways in which the UK New Labour government from 1997 had fostered a policy discourse founded on 'this strange figure—the demanding and skeptical citizen-consumer' (Clarke et al. 2007: 1). Evidence for the widespread existence of such an active, rational, vigorously choosing character in the population at large was, to put it mildly, thin on the ground, but he or she nevertheless served an important rhetorical purpose in helping to knit together different and potentially conflicting streams of policy ideas. Reading that book (as I was writing this one) stimulated me to ask myself what kind of discursive constructions might be underway with respect to public-service users and *place*. In recent reform discourse it often seems that the figure of the citizen is essentially placeless.

But not quite. While place has certainly not figured in recent policy discourses to anything like the same extent as consumer choice, it does creep in at the edges. Its main appearance is in the figure of the incessantly busy, mobile citizen who needs 24/7 access to public services wherever he or she may be:

Citizens and businesses expect the same levels of access and personalization from public services as they receive from leading private sector organizations such as Amazon and Tesco. They expect to be able to access information from multiple locations and in ways that suit them rather than the providers.

(HM Government 2010: 9)

This on-the-go citizen-consumer requires Web-based services, because they are ubiquitously available. He or she apparently does not have any strong allegiances to particular places or to individual professionals or officials. Their relationship with most services is dominantly virtual. Health care is certainly one of the sites where this image of a new citizen is under construction. New technologies have been seized upon by the authorities as a useful way of keeping patients at home and out of the local hospital or doctor's surgery: 'Some consultations could take place online, although patients may find email more appropriate for many minor interactions that previously required a visit' (NHS Confederation 2010: 5). And, more generally:

a key policy objective has been to shift at least some of the burden of routine illness management out of the formal health care systems altogether. Hence, the state has

sponsored major programmes of spending on developing the 'expert' ... 'resource-
ful' ... 'future' ... or even *activated*' patient, who exercises 'self-care' and connects to
health care resources purposefully and rationally.

(May et al. 2005: 1487; emphasis in original)

There are limits, and arguably inconsistencies, here. One obvious limit is
that the range of circumstances envisaged falls far short of that which most
of us experience in real life. At one time in our lives, faced with, say, the
need for an elective surgical procedure, we may wish to compare and
choose. At another, however, we may be distraught, or demented, or vulnerable in a whole variety of other ways, and we may want or need someone else to make decisions for us (Newman 2011). Then there is the
question of consistency. As we saw in earlier chapters, it is fine for citizens
to choose to be treated at home, or to file their tax returns from a Spanish
villa, or to choose this doctor or hospital over that one, from the current
menu. But it is *not* fine to choose to keep a small, old-fashioned local
hospital—both because it costs too much and because the professionals
say it is not up to contemporary clinical standards. Ditto the local sub-post
office. Similarly (Chapter 8), if only citizens would desist from their incessantly reiterated request for more police officers patrolling the streets! This
is plain irrational, because most of the evidence shows it to be a waste of
time, at least as far as crime-busting is concerned. Instead, the authorities
offer a variety of responses. One is to put a less-trained, lower-paid, but
nevertheless uniformed official on the streets (the Community Police Support Officer in the UK—with parallel developments in some other
countries). Thus budget-conscious local visibility is achieved. Another is
to develop 'neighbourhood policing' (Chapter 8), which, although often
valuable in a variety of ways, is nevertheless not exactly what the public
seemed to have been asking for, and which is anyway often disrupted, as
local officers have to be diverted to other, higher-priority tasks. Finally, the
citizen should not be too concerned about precisely what kind of organization is on the other end of the virtual communication link. If a UK citizen
applies for a provisional driver's licence, his or her demographic information is 'automatically transferred via a data link to an external information
solutions company that employs search technology to match applicant
data with a variety of public and private databases' (Lips et al. 2009a:
725). Third-party authentication of this kind is growing, and the applicant
is usually unaware that this is happening.

Thus the model citizen's choices of place must not be sentimental or
historical or even just based on familiarity and convenience, and the citizen

should not care too much about exactly who he or she is dealing with, so long as he or she begins through an official portal. He or she must instead express a particular kind of rationality—the kind that minimizes demands on the system in the name of the greater good, and the kind that, when it does make a demand, chooses a provider on the basis of officially measured performance, not personal impressions. This citizen consumer is constructed within a combination of a consumerist discourse and a responsible public discourse—that of actively helping others and doing things for oneself wherever possible (Newman 2011). Unfortunately, however, this rational, active time-and-place-chooser seems no more likely to represent the majority of actual citizens, most of the time, than the 'demanding and skeptical citizen-consumer' of Clarke et al.'s book. In fact, of course, it is the same person.

9.3 Re-placing

If placeless public services—and placeless citizens—are frequently unattainable and often actually undesirable, then what contemporary clues are there as to where and how place can be preserved or, where necessary, 're-placed'? A first (too simple but still useful) response is to say that certain services require such complex, sensitive, and individually tailored assessments that they can take place only face-to-face. Teaching small children, caring for elderly persons suffering from dementia, interviewing victims of a sexual assault—there are many examples where 'being there' is, or currently seems to be, an indispensable ingredient. 'The quality of interactions that patients experience with their clinicians has been shown to have a profound effect on health outcomes' (NHS Confederation 2010: 4). That is not, of course, to say that new technologies have no place at all in these encounters. Robots, for example, can already perform a range of useful caring tasks for elderly and handicapped persons, and a modern primary-care doctor's surgery will be bristling with technological aids.

A second response would be to point out that technology itself increasingly can ape the face-to-face situation. When a citizen has a live video link with a service provider, does it matter if the latter is 100 kilometres away? Perhaps, with the accelerating intertwining of different forms of digital communication, such 'virtual face-to-face' can be brought to home TV screens? Such linkages may have many uses, but also some limitations. They may, for example, be very effective for communications between people who already know each other from previous face-to-face encounters, but less so for those who have not met before (particularly if one 'end' of the exchange is an authority figure—doctor, professor). They may be less effective at giving reassurance as opposed to information (partly because they are virtual, not real). They may become more effective with repeated use, so that they are less appropriate for first or one-off encounters. All these facets could benefit from more focused research.

A third (also partial) response is to point out that even services that can be digitalized and distanced for most of us (for example, filling in tax forms or driving licence applications) still need to be delivered in real face-to-face situations—at least for a minority. There are, and probably always will be, some who cannot access or cannot use a computer, or who feel that they need the assistance of a real, live person in order to transact their business. Lack of equipment and/or technical competence is not (yet?) an acceptable reason for denial of service, so alternative, more 'traditional', forms of service need to be maintained in order to reach these minorities.

This kind of analysis points towards a multi-channel delivery system, with individual service users being able to choose what suits them on a particular occasion with a particular issue. And such a flexible vision seems to meet with the approval of many citizens themselves (Institute for Citizen-Centred Service 2008). It faces, however, a major problem—cost. The cost of the different channels varies widely, and governments understandably try hard to steer users towards the cheapest channel (Kernaghan 2007). It can also be very difficult to provide exactly the same standard of service through each channel, so inequities are amplified. Promises to do this are particularly vulnerable in times of fiscal austerity, and in some cases we have seen what is effectively a second-class service developing for those who will not or cannot use the Internet.

However, the question of 're-placing' goes much wider than the issue of channel choice or the strengths and weaknesses of video links. Put in the most portentous way, it involves finding some way of providing citizens with an alternative sense of the reality of the state as a presence—both controlling and supportive—in their everyday lives. Place thus becomes one component in the popular political discussion of what to do about an apparently increasingly volatile, disaffected, and mistrustful electorate. This is a subject for another book rather than this one, but one relevant observation that might be drawn from the previous pages is that the continuing local, face-to-face services such as hospitals, schools, and the police are of great importance. For many decades already they have been not merely points of service provision but also nodes of civic engagement. Publics in Brasília and Canberra alike fight to get them and then they fight to keep them. Planners plan modern cities around them. Locals make them major targets for voluntary work and charitable giving. Residents use them (when they are allowed to) for recreational and community activities. Their many effects are charted in Chapter 4 and the subsequent case studies. Managing them with a strong consciousness of this wider function does not fit easily with the cost-saving, target-achieving focus of some contemporary public-management systems. Yet, if there is a discrepancy here, then it is one that simply draws our attention yet again to the impoverished narrowness of the centralized management-by-targets-and-terror regimes that have on occasion prevailed in the UK hospitals, schools, and police forces (Bevan and Hood 2006; Pollitt et al. 2010; many TPT interviews).

9.4 Research

The ways in which changing technologies impact on public services (especially but not exclusively with respect to location) have preoccupied only a few public policy and management scholars, mainly in the 'e-government' subfield. It has been minimized by many more. The typical, minimalist treatment has been a general reference to how the new ICTs offer more management data, faster communication and transformed possibilities for public consultation. This may be accompanied by one of those statements about the diminution or disappearance of time and distance that we have logged in some of the earlier chapters. Even if a few areas (such as the police) have been extensively researched (often by sociologists or criminologists rather than public administrationists), there are vast swathes of the public sector that are almost entirely innocent of serious scholarly analysis of the effects of technological change.

As for the core focus of this book—the *interaction* between places and changing technologies—there is very little independent scholarly commentary. For academics to conclude their books and articles by stating that there is much more research to be done is almost *de rigueur*, but in this case the cliché is richly deserved.

But what kind of research would that be? The analysis presented in the preceding chapters may cast some light, but by doing so it also reveals large misty areas. Here I will mention just three.

A particularly important one is face-to-face contacts between citizens and public-sector staff, and how they influence, first, civic engagement and, second, trust in the system. It is unlikely that these connections work through some single, uni-directional process. It is also unlikely that all citizens will react in the same way. What little we know suggests that the connection is probably interactive, but how and when do those interactions occur? The model suggested here presumes that positive face-to-face contacts with officials (or politicians) are usually a stimulus to civic engagement and negative ones (such as experiences of corruption or rigid high-handedness) tend to be a disincentive. It then posits that higher civic engagement breeds higher trust. (Of course it does not assume that positive contact with public officials is the *only* factor prompting civic engagement, though it does assume that it is a significant one. Neither does it assume that civic engagement is the *only* factor promoting trust, although it does seem to be a pretty important one.) However, this model is speculative: it is arrived at by drawing together somewhat disparate pieces of research, none of which really had this whole nexus as its central focus.

A second issue is the effect that electronic contacts with governments has on the citizen-user's attitudes to government. Are e-contacts as potent as face-to-face contact with officials? Does accessing a friendly, high-quality website have a positive influence? Does wider experience of using the Internet to access services tend to increase or decrease users' satisfaction with government websites? On most of these counts the evidence so far is mixed or inconclusive (West 2004; Reddick 2005; Welch et al. 2005; Morgenson et al. 2011). Much of it is also American, raising the question of how far American attitudes, coloured as they are likely to be by the prevailing anti-government bias (and possibly by the kind of techno-optimism that is also supposed to be characteristic of the US culture) will be reflected in Europe or other parts of the world. While we can probably already say that overall satisfaction with a routine service such as filing tax returns or applying for licences is likely neither to soar nor to plummet when it 'goes digital', the elimination of these extreme scenarios still leaves a lot of detailed questions unanswered. Furthermore, very few studies in any country seem directly to compare a face-to-face service with its e-government counterpart. While there are methodological problems in setting up such a comparison, absent data of this kind, claims about the superiority of e-government, even for those who are satisfied with it, will remain fragile. Most difficult of all, does the overall shift away from local, face-to-face relationships to distant, usually virtual relationships have any accumulating or long-term effect on the way citizens conceive of public authority? Does it have little or no effect— most citizens taking it all in their stride, as these changes are similar to those taking place anyway in their commercial and social relationships? Or does it blur and weaken their image of public authorities as distinct entities with their own personnel, places, and styles, so that citizens do indeed come to regard public services as just something else they consume when it suits them? A research design that would firmly answer these questions would be a formidable undertaking, requiring an extended longitudinal study, a large and diverse population, and a variety of services. Almost certainly, the answers would vary somewhat across different types of service and different types of citizen. But as yet very little such work has even been started—most studies of attitudes to Net-based services have been based on cross-sectional surveys.

A third item on the research agenda should be the particular implications of the joined-up government 'movement' for localities. Much joining up has been driven by the attractive notion that individuals should not have to go to two or more service points, or make two or more declarations of the same information. This is the familiar 'one-stop' aspect of service integration. Without wishing in any way to diminish, still less oppose, this objective, we may note here that there could also be greater attention given to joining-up as a vehicle for increasing the leverage and coherence of the actions of public authorities in particular *places*. 'One place' is complementary to, not in contradiction with, 'one stop', but it has hitherto received rather less attention.

9.5 Final Word

The twin foci of this book—place and technology—are not equal partners. In both academic study and policy-making practice, far more attention has recently been lavished on technological possibilities than on issues of place. Technological change is seen as exciting, sexy, fast-moving, and replete with opportunities—not least those of new jobs, profits for suppliers, and efficiency gains for public organizations. Place, by contrast, is usually regarded as rather an old-fashioned kind of preoccupation— a question of traditional ties and expensive and often slow-moving 're-development' (or gentle, off-stage decline). Individuals, careers, services, organizations (and technologies themselves) are all supposed to be becoming more mobile, and the spoken or unspoken corollary is that being tied to a particular place matters less than ever before. Place is more of a 'heritage thing', a residual. Even in matters as fundamental as one's official identity, place-based elements seem to be giving way to placeless PINs and biometrics.

The case made here has been that this disparity of attention is unfortunate. Place is not just a residual. For many citizens it remains a potent focus for personal identification and civic engagement. What is more, public-service organizations often play a prominent role in anchoring communities to specific locations. There may well have emerged a group of cosmopolitan, always-on-the-move, 'rootless' business and professional people, but this group is still a tiny minority, even in the most advanced economies, and is likely to remain so. Most of us are *residents*, somewhere. And as (in Western Europe and North America) our populations age, a growing proportion of us will enjoy an extended, but often relatively sedentary, period at the end of our lives. For managers and professionals in the public services, locational factors frequently influence which types of service to provide and how to provide them. As we have seen in earlier chapters, hospitals, schools, police forces, post offices, and other public services actually vary quite a lot from one place to another—citizens and service professionals know that, even if academics have been rather slow to recognize it. And, for most politicians, politics remains a fundamentally territorial activity (although exactly how the link to territory works depends partly on voting systems and the configuration of internal boundaries). Places are, as we have shown, dynamic. Their constitutive relationships ('power geometries') are changing all the time. In all these respects, therefore, places still warrant our attention.

This is not, however, simply an argument for upgrading the status of, and attention given to, place. To set up new university institutes or departments of 'place studies', or to create 'place tanks' or 'place advisers', would be to misconstrue the present analysis. Our understanding of the significance of place is unlikely to be much enhanced by the construction of new academic ghettos or the insertion of add-on policy roles. Rather, the argument has been for a broad approach, one that embraces both place *and* technological change, and that attempts to integrate these with longer-standing, well-honed themes within politics, policy-making, and public administration. Technological relationships then become one subset of the spider's web of interactions that constitute places. Such a treatment cannot be wholly accommodated within any one of the traditional university disciplines and fields. It is not 'just' politics or geography or economics or urban studies or sociology. It is multidisciplinary and critical. It points towards the integration of place factors with more conventional analyses of the economy, efficiency, and effectiveness of public-sector organizations. It requires academics and advisers alike to wrestle with 'subjective' issues of place symbolism, affective attachment, and the accumulative influence of face-to-face relationships between citizens and representatives of the state. It also reinforces the current cry for policy-makers to try to see public services from the viewpoint of the service user. Users are usually very much concerned with physical and locational aspects—how close is it, how easy is it to find, is it clean and friendly or run-down and depressing, can I park, can I do all my business there in one go, is there somewhere for small children? Places and virtual places are where all the multifarious dimensions of public-service activity come together in particular configurations. They are not the only such locus, but they are an important one, and one that offers us a powerful opportunity to see public services 'in the round'.

'All things have their place, knew wee how to place them' was one of the folk proverbs collected by George Herbert for his 1640 omnibus of *Outlandish Proverbs* (it was proverb number 379 of 1,032). Nowadays places and things probably both change much more quickly than they did all those years ago, yet there may still be a grain of truth in the saying. The second clause remains particularly pertinent. In the twenty-first century it seems that we are embarked on a wholesale series of placeshifts of our major public services. The suggestion here is that these shifts are proceeding on the basis of rather thin analyses of where to place them and, more fundamentally, of what 'place' itself might mean.

Technology, Place, and Task (TPT): Brief Summary of a Research Programme

Overview

Technology, Place, and Task (TPT) comprised a series of linked small research projects, each one of which explored one or more aspects of the interconnections between the (changing) *technologies* used to design and deliver public services, the (changing) *places* (locations) at which the different activities making up these services are carried out, and the (changing) nature of the core *tasks* of which these services are composed.

The constituent projects have involved research in a number of countries (Australia, Belgium, Brazil, Finland, Ireland, the UK) and in a number of sectors (relocation of government administrative services, hospitals, police, population registration).

TPT was exploratory—designed to identify issues and develop relevant conceptual schemes. It aimed to describe and explain the evolutions and interactions of some of the most fundamental dimensions of public services. These three dimensions are:

- *Technology*: new technologies have frequently meant that service provision has speeded up; both the demand and the supply side of public-sector organizations are expected to operate faster and more flexibly. New technologies can also radically alter the accessibility of services (for example, by providing 24/7 online service, or by providing much more mobile service provision). In addition, changing technologies may have a range of other significant impacts.

- *Place*: the locations of public-service activity have often changed, in the sense not only of the centralization or decentralization of service provision, but also of the move into new types of environment, such as service provision that is 'joined up' to other services or offered in a 'one stop/one window', or provided in the homes or workplaces of clients, or on the Net.

- *Task*: technological developments—most obviously in ICTs but in many other respects too—have fundamentally altered the actual substance of daily work for most public-service workers. Jobs have been redefined, combined, divided. New 'products' have been developed. Tasks have changed throughout the public sector.

The project was comparative. The comparison had three dimensions:

- over time: the diachronic dynamics;
- between a range of services with different characteristics;
- between at least two countries (the development of each service was traced in at least two countries, and in some cases three or four);

Research Questions

The central research questions were:

- How have changes in technology affected what tasks are carried out and where they are carried out?

- How have changes in the locations of activities affected the citizens' experiences of 'interfacing' with the state?

- How have changes of technology and location affected the state's role as a 'placeshaper'—a set of organizations with powerful regulatory, economic and other resources that can influence the relative attractiveness of different locations within its territory?

- What theories and models best help us to understand and explain the patterns of change revealed by the empirical reviews of individual services in individual countries?

Methods

The main theoretical perspective employed has been one of historical institutionalism tinged with critical realism (see Section 2.5), although other theories and concepts—particularly those from the emerging literatures on technological change and e-government—have also been drawn upon. All the constituent projects have taken 'the long view'—thirty years or more.

A variety of methods have been employed, including:

- extensive literature reviews of previous academic work on technological change and locational policies;

- extensive analysis of organizational reports, plans, board minutes, performance data, and so on;

- extensive email and snail-mail correspondence with academics and public officials with relevant expertise;

- a programme of semi-structured interviews with senior decision-makers in each chosen sector; in total fifty TPT interviews were carried out, plus a further thirty

Table A1 Interviews for the project *Technology, Place, and Task* (*TPT*)

TPT interview number	Description	Date
1	Senior UK police officer	11 June 2006
2	Senior NHS manager	20 Nov. 2006
3	Police authority member (UK)	10 May 2007
4	Senior UK police officer	11 May 2007
5	English registrar	3 Oct. 2007
6	Senior GRO staff	3 Oct. 2007
7	Senior GRO staff	4 Oct. 2007
8	Senior GRO staff	4 Oct. 2007
9	Senior UK police officer	23 Apr. 2008
10	Senior Belgian civil servant	14 May 2008
11	Senior UK police officer	16 July 2008
12	Senior GRO staff	16 July 2008
13	Two senior Finnish population register staff	16 Feb. 2009
14*	Senior NHS civil servant	20 Mar. 2009
15	Senior NHS civil servant	12 May 2009
16	Senior GRO staff	12 May 2009
17	Belgian municipal registration officer	3 June 2009
18	Belgian municipal registration officer	9 Sept. 2009
19	Senior Belgian police officer	29 Sept. 2009
20	Senior Belgian civil servant	1 Oct. 2009
21	Senior Belgian police officer	8 Oct. 2009
22	Senior UK police manager	14 Oct. 2009
23	Senior Belgian civil servant	27 Oct. 2009
24	Belgian municipal registration officer	8 Dec. 2009
25*	Belgian municipal registration officer	12 Jan. 2010
26	Two senior UK civil servants concerned with relocation policy	24 Feb. 2010
27	Senior UK civil servant (police related)	25 Feb. 2010
28	Senior UK police officer	25 Feb. 2010
29	English registrar	26 Feb. 2010
30	Senior Belgian police officer	5 Mar. 2010
31	Senior Belgian police officer	9 Mar. 2010
32	Senior local government officer	27 July 2010
33	Canberra academic and long-term resident	16 Nov. 2010
34	Canberra academic and long-term resident	22 Nov. 2010
35	Senior Australian civil servant	22 Nov. 2010
36	Canberra activist and city planner	23 Nov. 2010
37	Canberra developer and architecture academic	24 Nov. 2010
38	Canberra civic activist	24 Nov. 2010

(continued)

Table A1   Continued

TPT interview number	Description	Date
39	Canberra planning academic	24 Nov. 2010
40	Brasília planning academic	12 Mar. 2010
41	Senior NHS clinician	20 Nov. 2010
42	Senior NHS manager	22 Aug. 2006
43	Senior Finnish civil servant	16 Feb. 2009
44	Senior Finish civil servant	17 Feb. 2009
45	Senior NHS manager	20 June 2006
46	UK NHS policy analyst and adviser	21 Jan. 2011
47	UK senior civil servant, Meteorological Office	22 Jan. 2011
48	Leading UK health-care academic	10 Mar. 2011
49	UK health-care researcher and ex-NHS manager	10 Mar. 2011
50	Leading international geographer specializing in space and place	11 Mar. 2011

* Email answers only.

Note: Some of the interviewees had retired or moved to other jobs by the time they were interviewed. In many cases the interviews themselves were augmented by subsequent correspondence.

in the pilot 'Brighton–Leuven' project, which was undertaken in 2004–8, and which was more broadly focused on time and change (Pollitt and Bouckaert 2009: 195–7).

The key questions posed in the TPT interviews were as follows:

1. What have been the key technological changes over the past few decades?
2. How have they influenced [specify service] operations and practice?
3. In particular, to what extent have they altered the locations/places in which different tasks are carried out?
4. Has technological change led to the growth of significant new tasks—or to the disappearance of old ones?
5. What issues have technological change raised for the training of officers/staff?
6. What legal and ethical issues have been raised by technological change?
7. How far can technological change be 'managed'—or does it just happen and then have to be responded to?
8. What are the most important strategies for managing technological change?
9. How have new technologies affected the relationships between [service] and citizens?
10. What are the main changes you see in the future?

All interviewees were volunteers, and were offered an explicit opportunity to ask and have answered any questions they might have about the project. The interviews are listed in Table A1. Some were retired and some still in service. Interviews were conducted either by note-taking or by digital recording. Most interviewees were given a summary copy of the record after it has been prepared and asked whether they had any factual amendments/corrections or additions to make (a minority did). In a few cases this was impracticable. The default position was that interviewees' names were not to be attributed to them, but in some cases they volunteered to be quoted by name. It was explained to them that their general position would be cited (for example, 'senior Belgian police officer') and that quotations would be used on that basis.

References

6, P. (2004). 'Joined-up Government in the Western World in Comparative Perspective: A Preliminary Literature Review and Exploration', *Journal of Public Administration Research and Theory*, 14/1: 103–38.

6, P. (2005). 'Joined-up Government in the West beyond Britain: A Provisional Assessment', in V. Bogdanor (ed.), *Joined-up Government*. Oxford: Oxford University Press, 43–106.

6, P. (2007). 'Don't Try this at Home: Lessons from England', in S. Borins, K. Kernaghan, D. Brown, N. Bontis, P. 6, and F. Thompson, *Digital State at the Leading Edge*, Toronto: University of Toronto Press, 325–54.

6, P., Leat, D., Selzer, K., and Stoker, G. (2002). *Towards Holistic Government*. Basingstoke: Palgrave.

6, P., Harris, M., and Spurgeon, P. (2005). *Technocracy or Politics? The Politics of Hospital Reconfiguration in the National Health Service: A Framework and Illustrative Evidence*. Nottingham: Nottingham Trent University.

Advisory Group on Reform of Australian Government Administration (2010). *Ahead of the Game: Blueprint for the Reform of Australian Government Administration*. Canberra: Commonwealth of Australia, Mar.

Agnew, J. (1987). *Place and Politics: The Geographical Mediation of State and Society*. Boston: Allen and Unwin.

Agnew, J., Mitchell, K., and Toal, G. (2008) (eds). *A Companion to Political Geography*. Malden, MA, and Oxford: Blackwell.

Aldrich, D. (2008). *Site Fights: Divisive Facilities and Civil Society in Japan and the West*. Ithaca, NY: Cornell University Press.

Allard, S. (2009). *Out of Reach: Place, Poverty and the New American Welfare State*. New Haven and London: Yale University Press.

Andrews, C. (2011). *Brasília Again*. Personal communication, 13 Jan.

Argyle, M., Salter, V., Nicholson, H., Williams, M., and Burgess, P. (1970). 'The Communication of Inferior and Superior Attitudes by Verbal and Non-Verbal Signals', *British Journal of Social and Clinical Psychology*, 9: 222–31.

Arnold, P. (2010). 'National Approaches to the Administration of International Migration', in P. Arnold (ed.), *National Approaches to the Administration of International Migration* Amsterdam: IOS Press, 1–7.

Arthur, W. B. (2009). *The Nature of Technology: What It Is and How It Evolves*. New York: Free Press.

Association of Chief Police Officers (2008). *Police Reform Green Paper: The Future of Policing*. London: Association of Chief Police Officers.

Association of Chief Police Officers (2009). *ACPO e-Crime Strategy*. Version 1.0. London: Association of Chief Police Officers.

Association of Higher Civil and Public Servants (AHCPS) (2007). *Public Service Deconcentration: The Need for an Immediate Review*. Report by the Executive Committee. Dublin: AHPCS, May.

Audit Commission (1990). *Effective Policing: Performance Review in Police Forces*. London: HMSO.

Audit Commission (1991). *Reviewing the Organization of Provincial Police Forces: Police Paper 9*. London: HMSO.

Audit Commission (1996). *Streetwise: Effective Police Patrol*. London: HMSO.

Australian Government: National Capital Authority (2010). *National Capital Authority Annual Report 2009–2010*. Canberra: National Capital Authority.

Auyero, J. (2006).'Spaces and Places as Sites and Objects of Politics', in R. Goodin and C. Tilly (eds), *The Oxford Handbook of Contextual Political Analysis*. Oxford: Oxford University Press, 564–77.

Baldersheim, H. and Rose, L. (2010) (eds). *Territorial Choice: The Politics of Boundaries and Borders*. Basingstoke: Palgrave/Macmillan.

Balzacq, T., Bigo, D., Carrera, S., and Guild, E. (2006). *Security and the Two-Level Game: The Treaty of Prüm, the EU and the Management of Yhreats*. CEPS Working Document 234; Brussels: Centre for European Policy Studies.

Barry, A. (2001). *Political Machines: Governing A Technological Society*. London and New York: Athlone Press.

Beer, C. (2006). 'The Production of Canberra and its National Cultural Institutions: Imagination and Practice of National Capital Space, National Leadership and Transnational and National Museum Practice, and Commonwealth Managerial Space'. Paper presented at the Australian Political Studies Association conference, University of Newcastle, 25–7 Sept.

Beer, C. (2009). 'National Capital Bureaucracy as a Spatial Phenomenon: The Place of Canberra within the Australian Public Service', *Administration and Society*, 41/6: 693–714.

Bekkers, V. (2000). 'Information and Communication Technology and the Redefinition of the Functional and Normative Boundaries of Government', in O. Van Heffen, W. Kickert, and J. Thomassen (eds), *Governance in Modern Society*. Dordrecht, Kluwer, 257–78.

Bekkers, V., and Homburg, V. (2005) (eds). *The Information Ecology of e-Government*. Amsterdam: IOS Press.

Bekkers, V., Van Duivenbonden, H., and Thaens, M. (2006) (eds). *Information and Communication Technology and Public Innovation: Assessing the ICT-Driven Modernization of Public Administration*. Amsterdam: IOS Press.

Bellamy, C., and Taylor, J. A. (1998). *Governing in the Information Age*. Buckingham: Open University Press.

References

Bennett, C., and Lyon, D. (2008) (eds). *Playing the Identity Card: Surveillance, Security and Identification in Global Perspective.* London and New York: Routledge/Taylor and Francis.

Berger, J. (1972). *Ways of Seeing.* London: British Broadcasting Organization and Penguin Books.

Bergmans, D. (2005). 'Police and Gendarmerie Reform in Belgium: From Force to Service'. Paper presented to the Geneva Centre for the Democratic Control of Armed Forces international conference 'Democratic Horizons in the Security Sector', Ankara, 3 Feb.

Bevan, G., and Hood, C. (2006). 'What's Measured Is What Matters: Targets and Gaming in the English Public Health Care System', *Public Administration,* 84/3: 517–38.

Bin Wong, R. (2006). 'Detecting the Significance of Place', in R. Goodin and C. Tilly (eds), *The Oxford Handbook of Contextual Political Analysis.* Oxford: Oxford University Press, 534–46.

Bogdanor, V. (2005) (ed.). *Joined-up Government.* Oxford: Oxford University Press.

Bolton, R. (1992). '"Place Prosperity vs People Prosperity" Revisited: An Old Issue with a New Angle', *Urban Studies,* 29/2: 185–203.

Booth, P., Breuillard, M., Fraser, C., and Paris, D. (2007) (eds). *Spatial Planning Systems of Britain and France: A Comparative Analysis.* London and New York: Routledge/Taylor and Francis.

Borins, S. (2007). 'What Keeps a CIO Awake at Night? Evidence from the Ontario Government', in S. Borins, K. Kernaghan, D. Brown, N. Bontis, P. 6, and F. Thompson, *Digital State at the Leading Edge.* Toronto: University of Toronto Press, 69–101.

Borins, S., Kernaghan, K., Brown, D., Bontis, N., 6, P., and Thompson, F. (2007). *Digital State at the Leading Edge.* Toronto: University of Toronto Press.

Bouckaert, G. (1993). 'Efficiency Measurement from a Management Perspective: A Case of the Civil Registry Office in Flanders', *International Review of Administrative Sciences,* 59/1: 11–27.

Bovens, M., and Zouridis, S. (2002). 'From Street-Level to System-Level Bureaucracies', *Public Administration Review,* 62/2: 174–84.

Bowen, C. (2009). 'Service Delivery Reform: Designing a System that Works for you'. Address to the National Press Club, Canberra, ACT, 16 Dec.

Boyd, R. (1964). 'The Canberra Virus', *London Magazine,* 4/4 (July), 78–82.

Brasilmar, F., and Costa, A. (2007). 'Distrito federal e Brasília: Dinâmica urbana, violência e heterogeneidade social', *Caderos Metrópole,* 17/1: 35–57.

Brenner, N. (2004). *New State Spaces: Urban Governance and the Rescaling of Statehood.* Oxford: Oxford University Press.

Breuillard, M., and Fraser, F. (2007). 'The Purpose and Process of Comparing British and French Planning', in P. Booth, M. Breuillard, C. Fraser, and D. Paris (eds), *Spatial Planning Systems of Britain and France: A Comparative Analysis.* London and New York: Routledge/Taylor and Francis, 1–14.

Breuillard, M., Stephenson, R., and Sadoux, S. (2007). 'Institutional Frameworks and Planning Processes', in P. Booth, M. Breuillard, C. Fraser, and D. Paris (eds), *Spatial Planning Systems of Britain and France: A Comparative Analysis*. London and New York: Routledge/Taylor and Francis, 55–66.

Brighton Hospitals Health Bulletin (1967a). 'Introduction to the Hospital World', 7 (Sept.), 3.

Brighton Hospitals Health Bulletin (1967b). 'Introduction to the Hospital World', 9 (Nov.), 3.

Brighton Health Bulletin (1976). 'Revolutionary Scanner Gift for Brighton', 24 (Sept.), 4.

Brighton Health Bulletin (1991a). 'MP Challenges Single Site Hospital Plan', 257 (Apr.), 2.

Brighton Health Bulletin (1991b). 'The Single Site Debate Continues', 258 (May), 7.

Brouwer, E. (2005). *Data surveillance and border control in the EU: balancing efficiency and legal protection of third country nationals*, www.libertysecurity.org/article289. html (accessed 12 Feb. 2011).

Brown, D. (2007). 'The Government of Canada: Government on-Line and Citizen-Centred Service', in S. Borins, K. Kernaghan, D. Brown, N. Bontis, P. 6, and F. Thompson, *Digital State at the Leading Edge*, Toronto: University of Toronto Press, 37–68.

Brown, T. (2003). 'Towards an Understanding of Local Protest: Hospital Closure and Community Resistance', *Social and Cultural Geography*, 4/4: 489–506.

Brunsson, N., and Jacobsson, B. (2002). *A World of Standards*. Oxford: Oxford University Press.

Business and Enterprise Committee (2009). *Eighth Report, Session 2008–09: Post Offices—Securing their Future*, 23 June, www.publications.parliament.uk/pa/ cm200809/cmberr/371/37102.htm (accessed 11 Sept. 2009).

Callanan, M. (2003). *Local Government in Ireland: Inside Out*. Dublin: Institute of Public Administration.

Cameron, K. (2005). *The Laws of Identity*, www.identityblog.com (accessed 20 Apr. 2009).

Cairncross, F. (1997). *The Death of Distance: How the Communications Revolution will Change our Lives*. Boston, MA: Harvard Business School Press.

Camille, M. (2000). 'Signs of the City: Place, Power and Public Fantasy in Medieval Paris', in B. Hanawat and M. Kobialka (eds), *Medieval Practices of Space*. Minneapolis: University of Minnesota Press, 1–36.

Carmona, M., Tiesdell, S., Heath, T., and Oc, T. (2010). *Public Places, Urban Spaces: The Dimensions of Urban Design*. 2nd edn. Amsterdam: Elsvier.

Carroll, B., and Siegel, D. (1999). *Service in the Field: The World of Front-Line Civil Servants*. Montreal and Kingston: McGill-Queen's University Press.

Carter, L., and Belanger, F. (2004). 'Citizen Adoption of Electronic Government Initiatives', *Proceedings of the 37th Hawaii International Conference on System Sciences*. Washington: IEEE Computer Society, 1–10.

References

Casey, E. (1993). *Getting Back into Place: Towards a Renewed Understanding of the Place-World*. Bloomington, IN: Indiana University Press.

Castells, M. (1989). *The International City*. Oxford: Blackwell.

Castells, M. (2001). *The Internet Galaxy: Reflections on the Internet, Business, and Society*. Oxford: Oxford University Press.

Castells, M. (2010). *The Rise of the Network Society*. 2nd edn. Chichester: Wiley-Blackwell.

Castles, F. (2007) (ed.). *The Disappearing State: Retrenchment Realities in an Age of Globalization*. Cheltenham: Edward Elgar.

Catney, P. (2009). 'New Labour and Joined-up Urban Governance', *Public Policy and Administration*, 24/1: 47–66.

Chan, J. (2001). 'The Technological Game: How Information Technology Is Transforming Police Practice', *Criminology and Criminal Justice*, 1/2: 139–59.

Christensen, T., and Lægreid, P. (2007). 'The Whole-of-Government Approach to Public Sector Reform', *Public Administration Review* (Nov.–Dec.), 1059–66.

Christensen, T., and Lægreid, P. (2011) (eds). *The Ashgate Research Companion to New Public Management*. Farnham: Ashgate.

Christou, G., and Simpson, S. (2009). 'New Governance, the Internet, and Country Code Top-Level Domains in Europe', *Governance*, 22/4: 599–624.

Clarke, J., Newman, J., Smith, N., Vidler, E., and Westmarland, L. (2007). *Creating Citizen-Consumers: Changing Publics and Changing Public Services*. London: Sage.

Coetzee, J. (2008). *Diary of a Bad Year*. London: Vintage.

Cole, M., and Talbot, C. (1997). 'The Geographical Distribution of Civil Servants: The Politics of Change', *Teaching Public Administration*, 17/2: 41–53.

Collier, P. (2001). 'Police Performance Management: An Ethical Dilemma?', in P. Neyroud and A. Beckley (eds), *Policing, Ethics and Human Rights*. Portland, OR: Willan Publishing, 94–123.

Collier, P. (2006). 'Policing and the Intelligent Application of Knowledge', *Public Money and Management*, 26/2: 109–16.

Collier, P., Edwards, J., and Shaw, D. (2004). 'Communicating Knowledge about Police Performance', *International Journal of Productivity and Performance Management*, 53/5: 458–67.

Cowen, H. (1990). 'Regency Icons: Marketing Cheltenham's Built Environment', in M. Harloe, C. Pickvance, and J. Urry (eds). *Place Policy, and Politics: Do Localities Matter?* London, Unwin Hyman, 128–45.

Craig, D. (2006). *Plundering the Public Sector: How New Labour Are Letting Consultants Run off with £70 Billion of our Money*. London: Constable.

Crampton, J., and Elden, S. (2007) (eds). *Space, Knowledge and Power: Foucault and Geography*. Aldershot: Ashgate.

Crompvoets, J., Rajabifard, A., Van Loenen, B., and Fernández, T. (2008) (eds). *A Multi-View Framework to Assess Spatial Data Infrastructures*. Wageningen: Space for Geo-Information (RGI), Wageningen University.

Cullingworth, J., and Nadin, V. (1994). *Town and Country Planning in Britain*. 11th edn. London and New York: Routledge.

Damiani, M., Dixon, J., and Propper, C. (2005). 'Mapping Choice for the NHS: Analysis of Routine Data', *British Medical Journal*, 2 Feb.

Davies, J. (2009). 'The Limits of Joined-up Government: Towards a Political Analysis', *Public Administration*, 87/1: 80–96.

Denton, J. (2007). 'Walter Burley Griffin Memorial Lecture'. Canberra, ACT, 7 Nov.

Derlien, H.-U., and Peters, G. B. (2008) (eds). *The State at Work: Public Sector Employment in Ten Western Countries*. 2 vols. Cheltenham: Edward Elgar.

Dewett, T., and Jones, G. R. (2001). 'The Role of Technology in the Organization: A Review, Model and Assessment', *Journal of Management*, 27: 313–346.

Dittrich, Y., Ekelin, A., Elovaara, P., and Hansson, C. (2003). 'Making e-Government Happen: Everyday Co-Development of Services, Citizenship and Technology', *Proceedings of the 36th Hawaii International Conference on Systems Sciences*. Washington: IEEE Computer Society, 1–12.

Dunleavy, P. (1996). 'The Globalization of Public Services Production: Can Government Be "Best in World"?', in A. Massey (ed.), *Marketization and Globalization of Government Services*. London: Macmillan, 16–46.

Dunleavy, P. (2010). *The Future of Joined-up Public Services*. London: 2020 Public Services Trust at the RSA, June.

Dunleavy, P., Margetts, H., Bastow, S., and Tinkler, J. (2006). *Digital Era Governance: IT Corporations, The State and e-Government*. Oxford: Oxford University Press.

Edwards, J. (1990). 'What is Needed from Public Policy', in P. Healey and R. Nabarro (eds), *Land and Property Development in a Changing Society*. Aldershot: Gower.

Elden, S. (2005). 'Missing the Point: Globalization, Deterritorialization and the Space of the World', *Transactions of the Institute of British Geography*, NS 30: 8–19.

Fainstein, S. (2009). 'Planning and the Just City', in P. Marcuse, J. Connolly, J. Novy, I. Olivio, C. Potter, and J. Steil (eds), *Searching for the Just City: Debates in Urban Theory and Practice*. London and New York: Routledge/Taylor and Francis, 19–39.

Farrington-Douglas, J., and Brooks, R. (2007). *The Future Hospital: The Politics of Change*. London: Institute of Public Policy Research.

Federal Judicial Police (2009). *Our Commitment in the Fight against Crime*. Brussels: Federal Judicial Police.

Ferguson, J., and Gupta, A. (2002). 'Spatializing States: Towards an Ethnography of Neoliberal Governmentality', *American Ethnologist*, 29/4: 981–1002.

Ferlie, E., Lynn, L., Jr, and Pollitt, C. (2005) (eds). *The Oxford Handbook of Public Management*. Oxford: Oxford University Press.

Foucault, M. (1986). 'Space, Knowledge and Power', in P. Rabinow (ed.), *The Foucault Reader*. Harmondsworth: Penguin, 239–56.

Fountain, J. (2001). *Building the Virtual State: Information Technology and Institutional Change*. Washington: Brookings Institution.

References

Francis, C. (2009). *Independent Inquiry into Care Provided by Mid Staffordshire NHS Foundation Trust, January 2005–March 2009*. HC375-1. London: The Stationery Office.

Fulop, N., 6, P., and Spurgeon, P. (2008). 'Processes of Change in the Reconfiguration of Hospital Services: The Role of Stakeholder Involvement', in L. McKee, E. Ferlie, and P. Hyde (eds), *Organising and Reorganising: Power and Change In Health Care Organisations*. Basingstoke: Palgrave/Macmillan, 19–32.

Galey, M., and Booth, P. (2007). 'Land Law, Land Markets and Planning', in P. Booth, M. Breuillard, C. Fraser, and D. Paris, D. (eds), *Spatial Planning Systems of Britain and France: A Comparative Analysis*. London and New York: Routledge/Taylor and Francis, 34–49.

Gaston, H. (2008). *Brighton's County Hospital, 1828–2007*. Brighton: Southern Editorial Services.

Gates, K. (2008). 'The United States Real ID Act and the Securitization of Identity', in C. Bennett and D. Lyon (eds), *Playing the Identity Card: Surveillance, Security and Identification in Global Perspective*. London and New York: Routledge/Taylor and Francis, 218–32.

Gavrilis, G. (2008). *The Dynamics of Interstate Boundaries*. Cambridge: Cambridge University Press.

Geels, F. (2004). 'From Sectoral Systems of Innovation to Socio-Technical Systems: Insights about Dynamics and Change from Sociology and Institutional Theory', *Research Policy*, 33: 897–920.

Giddens, A. (1990). *The Consequences of Modernity*. Cambridge: Polity Press.

Goodsell, C. (1977). 'Bureaucratic Manipulation of Physical Symbols: An Empirical Study', *American Journal of Political Science*, 21/1: 79–91.

Goodsell, C. (1988). *Social Meaning of Civic Space: Studying Political Authority through Architecture*. Kansas: University Press of Kansas.

Goris, P., and Walters, R. (1999). 'Locally Oriented Crime Prevention and the "Partnership Approach"', *Policing: An International Journal of Police Strategies and Management*, 22/4: 633–45.

Graham, S. (1998). 'The End of Geography or the Explosion of Space? Conceptualizing Space, Place and Information technology', *Progress in Human Geography*, 22/2: 165–85.

Gregory, D., and Urry, J. (1985) (eds). *Social Relations and Spatial Structures*. Basingstoke: Macmillan.

Greig, A. (2006a). 'The Accommodation of Growth: Canberra's "Growing Pains" 1945–55', *Canberra Historical Journal* (July), 1334.

Greig, A. (2006b). 'Canberra', in P. Beilhartz and T. Hogan (eds), *Sociology: Place, Time, and Division*. Oxford: Oxford University Press, 47–50.

Guild, E., and Geyer, F. (2008) (eds). *Security versus Justice? Police and Judicial Cooperation in the European Union*. Farnham: Ashgate.

Hall, E. (1968). 'Proxemics', *Current Anthropology*, 9/2–3: 83–108.

Halligan, J. (2010). 'Post-NPM Responses to Disaggregation through Co-Ordinating Horizontally and Integrating Governance', in P. Lægreid and K. Verhoest (eds), *Governance of Public Sector Organizations: Proliferation, Autonomy and Performance*. Basingstoke: Palgrave/Macmillan, 235–54.

Halligan, J., Skelly, L., and Wettenhall, R. (2002). 'Patterns of Representation and Community Governance in the City-State', *Canberra Bulletin of Public Administration*, 103 (Mar.), 47–57.

Halligan, J., and Wettenhall, R. (2002). 'A City State in Evolution', *Canberra Bulletin of Public Administration*, 103 (Mar.), 3–10.

Halligan, M. (2008). *Murder on the Apricot Coast*, Crows' Nest, NSW: Allen and Unwin.

Hamelin, F. (2010). 'Renewal of Public Policy via Instrumental Innovation: Implementing Automated Speed Enforcement In France', *Governance*, 23/3: 509–30.

Hardman Report (1973). *The Dispersal of Government Work from London*. Cmnd 5322. London: The Stationery Office, June.

Harloe, M., Pickvance, C., and Urry, J. (1990) (eds). *Place, Policy, and Politics: Do Localities Matter?* London: Unwin Hyman.

Harman, R., L'Hostis, A., and Ménerault, P. (2007). 'Public Transport in Cities and Regions: Facing an Uncertain Future', in P. Booth, M. Breuillard, C. Fraser, and D. Paris (eds), *Spatial Planning Systems of Britain and France: A Comparative Analysis*. London and New York: Routledge/Taylor and Francis, 188–204.

Harvey, D. (1989). *The Condition of Postmodernity: An Enquiry into the Origins of Cultural Change*. Oxford: Blackwell.

Harvey, D., and Potter, C. (2009). 'The Right to the Just City', in P. Marcuse, J. Connolly, J. Novy, I. Olivio, C. Potter, and J. Steil (eds), *Searching for the Just City: Debates in Urban Theory and Practice*. London and New York: Routledge/Taylor and Francis, 40–51.

Hay, C., and Wincott, D. (1998). 'Structure, Agency and Historical Institutionalism', *Political Studies*, 46: 951–7.

Healey, J., and McKee, M. (2003). 'The Evolution of Hospital Systems', in M. McKee and J. Healy (eds), *Hospitals in a Changing Europe*. Buckingham: Open University Press, 14–35.

Henman, P., and Adler, M. (2003). 'Information Technology and the Governance of Social Security', *Critical Social Policy*, 23/2: 139–64.

Her Majesty's Chief Inspector of Constabulary (1998a). *Annual Report for 1997/98*. London: The Stationery Office.

Her Majesty's Chief Inspector of Constabulary (1998b). *What Price Policing? A Study of Efficiency and Value for Money in the Police Service*. London: HMSO.

Herbert, S. (1996). 'The Geopolitics of the Police: Foucault, Disciplinary Power and the Tactics of the Los Angeles Police Department', *Political Geography*, 15/1: 47–57.

Hirst, P. (2005). *Space and Power: Politics, War and Architecture*. Cambridge: Polity.

HM Government (2010). *Government ICT Strategy: Smarter, Cheaper, Greener*. Cabinet Office. London: HMSO.

HM Treasury (2010). *Total Place: A Whole Area Approach to Public Services*. London: HM Treasury, Mar.

Holanda, F. de (2007). *Be Aware of Local Properties*. Proceedings, 6th International Space Syntax Symposium, Istanbul.

Holanda, F. de (2010). *Brasília: Cidade moderna, cidade eternal*. Brasília: Livraria Cultura.

Holanda, F. de, Mota, A., Leite, A., Soares, L., and Garcia, P. (2001). 'Eccentric Brasília'. Updated version of paper presented to the Space Syntax – III International Symposium, Atlanta, 7–11 May.

Holanda, F. de, Ribeiro, R., and Medeiros, V. (2008). 'Brasília, Brazil: Economic and Social Costs of Dispersion'. Paper presented to the 44th ISOCARP (International Society of City and Regional Planners) Congress, Dalian, China, 19–23 Sept.

Holston, J. (1989). *The Modernist City: An Anthropological Critique of Brasília*. Chicago: University of Chicago Press.

Homburg, V. (2008). 'Red Tape and Reforms: Trajectories of Technological and Managerial Reforms in Public Administration', *International Journal of Public Administration*, 31: 749–70.

Home Office (1999). *Ministerial Priorities, Key Performance Indicators and Efficiency Planning for 1999/2000*. London: Home Office.

Home Office (2001). *Policing for a New Century: A Blueprint for Reform*. Cm 5326. London: HMSO.

Home Office (2004). *Building Communities, Beating Crime: A Better Police Service for the 21st Century*. Cm 6360. London: HMSO.

Hood, C. (1976). *The Limits of Administration*. London: Wiley.

Hood, C. (2005). 'The Idea of Joined-Up Government: A Historical Perspective', in V. Bogdanor (ed.), *Joined-up Government*. Oxford: Oxford University Press, 19–42.

Hood, C., and Lodge, M. (2006). *The Politics of Public Service Bargains: Reward, Competency, Loyalty—and Blame*. Oxford: Oxford University Press.

Hood, C., and Margetts, H. (2010). 'Cyber-Bureaucracy: If It Is So Central to Public Administration, why Is It So Ghetto-ized?', in J. Pierre and P. Ingraham (eds), *Comparative Administrative Change and Reform: Lessons Learned*. Montreal and Kingston: McGill-Queen's University Press, 114–38.

Hope, A. (2009). 'Prisoners to Move to Dutch Jail: Overcrowding Forces Export of 500 Inmates', *Flanders Today*, 27 May, pp. 1, 3.

Hope, A. (2010). 'Police Announce Strike Plans: Brussels Officers Protest Lack of Action in the Face of "Extreme Violence"', *Flanders Today*, 10 Feb., pp. 1, 3.

House of Commons Debates (1979). *Civil Service Dispersion*, cols 902–22, 26 July.

House of Lords (2007). 'Schengen Information System II (SIS II)'. 9th Report of the House of Lords European Union Committee, Session 2006–7, HL Paper 49, 2 Mar.

Houtum, H. van, Kramsch, O., and Zierhofer, W. (2005a). 'Prologue: B/*ordering* Space', in H. van Houtum, O. Kramsch, and W. Zierhofer (eds), *B/ordering Space*. Aldershot, Ashgate, 1–13.

Houtum, H. van, Kramsch, O., and Zierhofer, W. (2005b) (eds). *B/ordering Space*. Aldershot: Ashgate.

Humphreys, P., and O'Donnell, O. (2006). *Public Service Decentralisation: Governance Opportunities and Challenges*. Dublin: Institute of Public Administration.

Humphries, R., and Gregory, S. (2010). *Place-Based Approaches and the NIS: Lessons from Total Place*. London: King's Fund.

Huxley, M. (2007). 'Geographies of Governmentality', in J. Crampton and S. Elden (eds), *Space, Knowledge and Power: Foucault and Geography*. Aldershot: Ashgate, 185–204.

Institute for Citizen-Centred Service (2005). *Citizens First 4*. Ottawa: ICCS.

Institute for Citizen-Centred Service (2008). *Citizens First 5*. Ottawa: ICCS.

Jacobs, A., Helft, J., and Markoff, J. (2010). 'Beijing Stifles News of Google's Defiance', *International Herald Tribune*, 14 Jan., pp. 1, 15.

Jae Moon, M., and Welch, E. (2005). 'Same Bed, Different Dreams? A Comparative Analysis of Citizen and Bureaucrat Perspectives on e-Government', *Review of Public Personnel Administration*, 25/3: 243–64.

Jefferson, C., and Trainor, M. (1996). 'Public Sector Relocation and Regional Development', *Urban Studies*, 33/1: 37–48.

John, P. (2010). 'Larger and Larger? The Endless Search for Efficiency in the UK', in H. Baldersheim and L. Rose (eds), *Territorial Choice: The Politics Of Boundaries and Borders*. Basingstoke: Palgrave/Macmillan, 101–17.

Jones, K. (2008). 'Association of Chief Police Officers (ACPO)', in T. Newburn and P. Neyroud (eds), *Dictionary of Policing*. Cullompton: Willan Publishing, 7–8.

Jorgensen, D., and Klay, W. (2001). 'Technology and Public Administration', in K. Liou (ed.), *Handbook of Public Management Practice and Reform*. New York: Marcel Dekker, 75–96.

Kakihara, M., and Sørensen, C. (2002). 'Mobility: An Extended Perspective', in *35th Proceedings of the Hawaii International Conference on Systems Sciences*. Big Island, Hawaii, January 7–10.

Kaplan, C. (2006). 'Mobility and War: The Cosmic View of US "Air Power"', *Environment and Planning A*, 38: 395–407.

Kaufmann, D., Kraay, A., and Mastruzzi, M. (2009). 'Governance Matters: Governance Indicators for 1996–2008'. World Bank Research Working Paper No. 4978. Washington: World Bank, 29 June.

Kay, A. (2006). *The Dynamics of Public Policy: Theory and Evidence*. Cheltenham: Edward Elgar.

Keele, L. (2007). 'Social Capital and the Dynamics of Trust in Government', *American Journal of Political Science*, 51/2: 241–54.

Kennedy, M. (2007). 'Family Historians Aghast as Paper Records Locked away before Online Version Ready', *Guardian*, 29 Oct., p. 12.

References

Kernaghan, K. (2007). 'Beyond Bubble-Gum and Goodwill: Integrating Service Delivery', in S. Borins, K. Kernaghan, D. Brown, N. Bontis, P. 6, and F. Thompson, *Digital State at the Leading Edge.* Toronto: University of Toronto Press, 102–36.

Kerschot, H., Steyart, J., and Van Gompel, R. (2006). *Fed-e View Citizen: Longitudinal Study of the Internet and e-Government in Belgium. What Citizens Think.* Brussels: Indigov/Fedict.

Kingdon, J. (1995). *Agendas, Alternatives and Public Policies.* 2nd edn. New York: Harper Collins College Publishers.

Kirkegaard, S. (2008). 'The Prüm Decision: An Uncontrolled Fishing Expedition in "Big Brother" Europe', *Computer Law and Security Report*, 24: 243–52.

Klein, R., and Plowden, W. (2005). 'JASP Meets JUG: Lessons of the 1975 Joint Approach to Social Policy for Joined-up Government', in V. Bogdanor (ed.), *Joined-up Government.* Oxford: Oxford University Press, 107–13.

Knox, P. (2005). 'Creating Ordinary Places: Slow Cities in a Fast World', *Journal of Urban Design*, 10/1: 1–1.

Koppell, J. (2010). 'Administration without Borders', *Public Administration Review*, 70 (Dec.), suppl., S46–55.

Koskela, H. (2000). 'The Gaze without Eyes: Video-Surveillance and the Changing Nature of Urban Space', *Progress in Human Geography*, 24/2: 243–65.

Kurki, M. (2008). *Causation in International Relations: Reclaiming Causal Analysis.* Cambridge: Cambridge University Press.

Latour, B. (2005). 'From Realpolitik to Dingpolitik: Of How to Make Things Public', in B. Latour and P. Weibel (eds), *Making Things Public: Atmospheres of Democracy*, Cambridge, MA: MIT Press, 14–41..

Leadership Centre for Local Government (2010). *Places, People and Politics: Learning to do Things Differently.* London: Leadership Centre for Local Government.

Lefebvre, H. (1991). *The Production of Space*, trans. D. Nicholson-Smith. Oxford: Blackwell.

Lefebvre, H. (2009). *State, Space, World: Selected Essays*, ed. N. Brenner and S. Elden. Minneapolis and London: University of Minnesota Press.

Leppard, D. (2008). 'Police to Get 10,000 Taser Guns', *Sunday Times*, 23 Nov., p. 1.

Lewis, J. (2010). 'New Fears that Innocent People Will Get Caught up in Investigations: Detectives Trawl DNA Database 60 Times a Year—Hunting for Criminals' Relatives', *Mail on Sunday*, 28 Feb., p. 22.

Liddell, A., Adshead, S., and Burgess, E. (2008). *Technology in the NHS: Transforming the Patient's Experience of Care.* London: King's Fund.

Lippens, R., and Van Calster, P. (2002). 'Policing as Forestry? Re-Imagining Policing in Belgium', *Social and Legal Studies*, 11/2: 283–305.

Lips, M., and Schuppan, T. (2009). 'Editorial: Transforming e-Government Knowledge through Public Management Research', *Public Management Review*, 11/6: 739–49.

Lips, M., Taylor, J., and Organ, J. (2006). 'Identity Management as Public Innovation: Looking beyond ID Cards and Authentication Systems', in V. Bekkers, H. Van Duivenbonden, and M. Thaens (eds), *Identity Management as Public Innovation: Looking beyond ID Cards and Authentication Systems*. Amsterdam: IOS Press, 204–16.

Lips, M., Taylor, J., and Organ, J. (2009a). 'Identity Management, Administrative Sorting and Citizenship in New Modes of Government', *Information, Communication and Society*, 12/5: 715–34.

Lips, M., Taylor, J., and Organ, J. (2009b). 'Identification Practices in Government: Citizen Surveillance and the Quest for Public Service Improvement', *Identity in the Information Society*, 1/1: 135–54.

Longley, P., and Goodchild, M. (2008). 'The Use of Geodemographics to Improve Public Sevice Delivery', in J. Hartley, C. Donaldson, C. Skelcher, and M. Wallace (eds), *Managing to Improve Public Services*. Cambridge: Cambridge University Press, 176–94.

Loveday, B. (2000). 'New Directions in Accountability', in F. Leishman, B. Loveday, and S. Savage (eds), *Core Issues in Policing*. 2nd edn. Harlow: Pearson Education, 213–31.

Low, S., and Smith, N. (2006) (eds). *The Politics of Public Space*. New York and London: Routledge/Taylor and Francis.

LSE (2005). 'The Identity Project: An Interim Assessment of the UK Identity Cards Bill and its Implications'. The LSE Identity Project Interim Report, London School of Economics, London, Mar.

Lucas, H. (2001). 'Information Technology and Physical Space', *Communications of the ACM*, 44/11: 89–96.

Lupton, R. (2003). 'Secondary Schools in Disadvantaged Areas: The Impact of Context on Schools, Processes and Quality', Ph.D. thesis, London School of Economics/University of London.

Lyon, D. (2002). 'Editorial. Surveillance Studies: Understanding Visibility, Mobility and the Phonetic Fix', *Surveillance and Society*, 1/1: 107.

Lyons, G., and Urry, J. (2005). 'Travel Time Use in the Information Age', *Transportation Research Part A*, 39: 257–76.

Lyons Review (2004). *Well-Placed to Deliver? Shaping the Pattern of Government service*. Independent Review of Public Sector Relocation. London: HMSO, Mar.

McDonald, F. (2005). 'Using Public Servants as Political Pawns'. Keynote address to the Association of Higher Civil and Public Servants, 6 May (accessed 6 May 2009).

McKee, M., and Healy, J. (2003) (eds). *Hospitals in a Changing Europe*. Buckingham: Open University Press.

McKee, M., Healy, J., Edwards, N., and Harrison, A. (2003). 'Pressures for Change', in M. McKee and J. Healy (eds), *Hospitals in a Changing Europe*. Buckingham, Open University Press, 36–54.

McLaughlin, E. (2007). *The New Policing*. London: Sage.

Maesschalck, J. (2002). 'When do Scandals Have an Impact on Policymaking? A Case Study of the Police Reform Following the Dutroux Scandal in Belgium', *International Public Management Journal*, 5/2: 169–9.

Mahoney, J., and Thelen, K. (2010) (eds). *Explaining Institutional Change: Ambiguity, Agency and Power*. Cambridge: Cambridge University Press.

MailOnline (2007). 'Fears over Innocent Britains' DNA being Given to European Police Forces', 9 May, www.dailymail.co.uk/news/article-453739 (accessed 2 Feb. 2010).

Mann, M. (1984). 'The Autonomous Power of the State: Its Origins, Mechanisms and Results', *European Journal of Sociology*, 24/2: 109–36.

Mann, M. (1993). *The Sources of Social Power*, ii. *Rise of Classes and Nation States, 1860–1914*. Cambridge: Cambridge University Press.

March, J., and Olsen, J. (1998). 'The Institutional Dynamics of International Political Orders', *International Organization*, 52/4: 943–69.

March. J., and Olsen, J. (2006). 'Normative Institutionalism', in R. Rhodes, S. Binder, and B. Rockman (eds), *The Oxford Handbook of Political Institutions*. Oxford: Oxford University Press, 3–22.

Marcuse, P., Connolly, J., Novy, J., Olivio, I., Potter, C., and Steil, J. (2009) (eds). *Searching for the Just City: Debates in Urban Theory and Practice*. London and New York: Routledge/Taylor and Francis.

Maricato, E. (2009). 'Fighting for Just Cities in Capitalism's Periphery', in P. Marcuse, J. Connolly, J. Novy, I. Olivio, C. Potter, and J. Steil (eds), *Searching for the Just City: Debates In Urban Theory and Practice*. London and New York: Routledge/Taylor and Francis, 194–213.

Markus, M., and Robey, D. (1988). 'Information Technology and Organizational Change: Causal Structure in Theory and Research', *Management Science*, 34/5: 583–99.

Massey, D. (1985). 'New Directions in Space', in D. Gregory and J. Urry (eds), *Social Relations and Spatial Structures*. Basingstoke: Macmillan, 9–19.

Massey, D. (1992). 'Politics and Space/Time', *New Left Review*, 196: 65–84.

Massey, D. (2005). *For Space*. London: Sage.

Mathiason, N. (2009). 'Two Days after the General Motors Takeover is Agreed, Brussels Throws a Spanner in the Works', *Guardian*, 12 Sept., p. 17.

Matos, R., and Baeninger, R. (2001). 'Migration and Urbanization in Brazil: Processes of Spatial Concentration and Deconcentration and the Recent Debate'. Paper presented at the XXIV General Population Conference, International Union for the Scientific Study of Population, Salvador, Bahia, Brazil, 18–24 Aug.

Marcuse, P., Connolly, J., Novy, J., Olivio, I., and Steil, J. (2009) (eds). *Searching for the Just City: Debates in Urban Theory and Practice*. London and New York: Routledge/Taylor and Francis.

May, C., Finch, T., and Mort, M. (2005). 'Towards a Wireless Patient: Chronic Illness, Scarce Care and Technological Innovation in the UK', *Social Science and Medicine Journal*, 61/7: 1485–94.

Moran, M., Rein, M., and Goodin, R. (2006) (eds). *The Oxford Handbook of Public Policy*. Oxford: Oxford University Press.

Morgeson, F., III (2011a). 'Comparing Determinants of Website Satisfaction and Loyalty across the e-Government and e-Business Domain', *Electronic Government: An International Journal* (forthcoming).

Morgeson, F., III (2011b). 'Do They All Perform Alike? An Examination of Perceived Performance, Citizen Satisfaction and Trust with US Federal Agencies', *International Review of Administrative Sciences*, 77 (forthcoming).

Morgeson, F., III, Van Amburg, D., and Mithas, S. (2011). 'Misplaced Trust? Exploring the Structure of the e-Government–Citizen Trust Relationship', *Journal of Public Administration Research and Theory* (forthcoming).

Murray, E., Kerr, C., Stevenson, S., et al. (2077). 'Internet Interventions Can Meet the Emotional Needs of Patients and Carers Managing Long-Term Conditions', *Journal of Telemedicine and Telecare*, 13 (suppl. 1): 42–4.

Murtagh, B. (2002). *The Politics of Territory: Policy and Segregation in Northern Ireland*. Basingstoke: Palgrave.

National Audit Office (2000). *The Cancellation of the Benefits Payments Card Project*. HC 857, Session 1999–2000. London: The Stationery Office.

National Audit Office (2009). *Department for Business, Enterprise and Regulatory Reform: Oversight of the Post Office Network Change Programme*. HC 558, Session 2008–2009, Norwich: The Stationery Office.

National Capital Development Commission (1970). *Tomorrow's Canberra*. Canberra: Canberra ACT, NCDC.

National DNA Database (2010). *Annual Report 2007–2009*, www.npia.police.uk (accessed 15 Feb. 2010).

National Health Service Executive (1998). *Information for Health: An Information Strategy for the Modern NHS 1998–2001*. London: National Health Service Executive.

National Institute for Health Research (2010). *Evaluating Models of Service Delivery: Reconfiguration Principles*. SDO Project 08/1304/063. London, HMSO.

National Museum of Australia (2010). *Yiwarra Kuju: The Canning Stock Route*. Canberra: National Museum of Australia Press.

National Policing Improvement Agency (2009). *Business Plan 2009/10*. London: NPIA.

Negroponte, N. (1995). *Being Digital*. London: Hodder and Stoughton.

Newman, D. (2008). 'Boundaries', in J. Agnew, K. Mitchell, and G. Toal (eds), *A Companion to Political Geography*. Malden, MA, and Oxford: Blackwell, 123–37.

Newman, J. (2011). 'Serving the Public: Users, Consumers and the Limits of NPM', in T. Christensen and P. Lægreid (eds), *The Ashgate Research Companion to the New Public Management*. Farnham: Ashgate, 349–60.

NHS Confederation (2010). *Remote Control: The Patient–Practitioner Relationship in a Digital Age*. London: NHS Confederation.

Nissel, M. (1989). *People Count: A History of the General Register Office*. London: HMSO.

Nordlinger, E. (1981). *On the Autonomy of the Democratic State*. London: Harvard University Press.

Norris, P. (2001). *Digital Divide: Civic Engagement, Information Poverty, and the Internet Worldwide*. Cambridge: Cambridge University Press.

Nunn, S. (2001). 'Cities, Space, and the New World of Urban Law Enforcement Technologies', *Journal of Urban Affairs*, 23/34: 259–78.

Oborn, E. (2008). 'Legitimacy in Hospital Reconfiguration: The Controversial Downsizing of Kidderminster Hospital', *Journal of Health Service Research Policy*, 13/2, suppl. 2 (Apr.): 11–18.

OECD (2008). *Ireland: Towards an Integrated Public Service*. OECD Public Management Review. Paris: OECD.

OECD (2009). *Government at a Glance*. Paris: OECD.

Office for National Statistics (2003). *Civil Registration: Delivering Vital Change: A Public Consultation Document*. London: Office for National Statistics.

Orlikowski, W., and Barley, S. (2001). 'Technology and Institutions: What Can Research on Information Technology and Research on Organizations Learn from Each Other?', *MIS Quarterly*, 25/2: 145–65.

Osborne, S. (2010) (ed.). *The New Public Governance: Emerging Perspectives on the Theory and Practice of Public Governance*. Abingdon and New York: Routledge.

O'Toole, P., and Were, P. (2008). 'Observing Places: Using Space and Material Culture in Qualitative Research', *Qualitative Research*, 8/5: 616–34.

Paasi, A. (2005). 'The Changing Discourses on Political Boundaries: Mapping the Backgrounds, Contexts and Contents', in H. van Houtum, O. Kramsch, and W. Zierhofer (eds), *B/ordering Space*. Aldershot: Ashgate, 17–31.

Paasi, A. (2008). 'Territory', in J. Agnew, K. Mitchell, and G. Toal (eds), *A Companion to Political Geography*. Malden, MA, and Oxford: Blackwell, 109–22.

Paddison, R. (1983). *The Fragmented State: The Political Geography of Power*. Oxford: Basil Blackwell.

Page, E. (2005). 'Joined-up Government and the Civil Service', in V. Bogdanor (ed.), *Joined-up Government*. Oxford: Oxford University Press, 139–55.

Painsack, B., and Toom, V. (2010). 'The Prüm Regime: Situated Dis/Empowerment in Transnational DNA Profile Exchange', *British Journal of Criminology*, 50: 1117–35.

Parkes, D., and Thrift, N. (1980). *Times, Spaces and Places: A Chronogeographic Perspective*. New York: Wiley.

Pawson, R. (2002). 'Evidence and Policy and Naming and Shaming', *Policy Studies*, 23/3–4: 211–30.

Pawson, R. (2006). *Evidence-Based Policy: A Realist Perspective*. London: Sage.

Pawson, R., and Tilley, N. (1997). *Realistic Evaluation*. London: Sage.

Peers, J. (1994). 'Vijftig jaar ziekenhuiswezen in Belgie', *Tijdschrift voor Geneeskunde*, 50/1: 17–24.

Pegrum, R. (1983). *The Bush Capital: How Australia Chose Canberra as its Federal City.* Sydney: Hale and Iremonger.

Pennington, M. (2000). *Planning and the Political Market: Public Choice and the Politics of Government Failure.* London and New Brunswick, NJ: Athlone Press.

Peters, G. B. (1999). *Institutional Theory in Political Science: The 'New Institutionalism'.* London and New York: Continuum.

Peters, G. B., and Pierre, J. (2003) (eds). *Handbook of Public Administration.* London: Sage.

Peters, G. B., Pierre, J., and Stoker, G. (2008) (eds). *Debating Institutionalism.* Manchester and New York: Manchester University Press.

Peterson, J., and Shackleton, M. (2002) (eds). *The Institutions of the European Union.* Oxford: Oxford University Press.

Pica, D., Sørensen, C., and Allen, D. (2004). 'On Mobility and Context of Work: Exploring Mobile Police Work', *Proceedings of the 37th Hawaii International Conference on System Sciences*, Washington: IEEE Computer Society, 1–11.

Pickvance, C., and Preteceille, E. (1991) (eds). *State Restructuring and Local Power.* London and New York: Pinter Publishers.

Pierre, J., and Peters, G. B. (2008) (eds). *Debating Institutionalism.* Manchester: Manchester University Press.

Pinch, S. (1985). *Cities and Services: The Geography of Collective Consumption.* London: Routledge and Kegan Paul.

Police Fédéral (2009). *Rapport d'activités de la police federal 2008.* Brussels: Police Fédéral.

Police Judiciaire Fédéral (2008). *Rapport annuel 2008.* Brussels: Police Judiciaire Fédéral.

Pollitt, C. (2003a). *The Essential Public Manager.* Maidenhead: Open University Press; Philadelphia: McGraw Hill.

Pollitt, C. (2003b). 'Joined-up Government: A Survey', *Political Studies Review*, 1/1: 34–49.

Pollitt, C. (2005). 'Decentralization', in E. Ferlie, L. Lynn Jr, and C. Pollitt (eds), *The Oxford Handbook of Public Management.* Oxford: Oxford University Press, 371–97.

Pollitt, C. (2008). *Time, Policy, Management: Governing with the Past.* Oxford: Oxford University Press.

Pollitt, C. (2009a). 'Bureaucracies Remember, Post-Bureaucratic Organizations Forget?' *Public Administration*, 87/2: 198–218.

Pollitt, C. (2009b). 'Structural Change and Public Service Performance: International Lessons?', *Public Money and Management*, 29/5: 285–91.

Pollitt, C. (2011). 'Mainstreaming Technological Change in the Study of Public Administration: A Conceptual Framework', *Public Policy and Administration*, 26/5: 377–97.

Pollitt, C. and Bouckaert, G. (2009). *Continuity and Change in Public Policy and Management.* Cheltenham: Edward Elgar.

225

References

Pollitt, C., and Bouckaert, G. (2011). *Public Management Reform: A Comparative Analysis*. 3rd edn. Oxford: Oxford University Press.

Pollitt, C., and Hupe, P. (2011). 'Talking about Government: The Role of Magic Concepts', *Public Management Review*, 13/5: 641–58.

Pollitt, C., and Op de Beeck, E. (2010). 'Hyper-Stability in an Age of Hyper-Innovation: A Comparative Case Study', *Public Policy and Administration*, 25/3: 289–304.

Pollitt, C., Talbot, C., Caulfield, J., and Smullen, A. (2004). *Agencies: How Governments Do Things through Semi-Autonomous Organizations*. London: Palgrave/Macmillan.

Pollitt, C., Harrison, S., Dowswell, G., Jerak-Zuiderent, S., and Bal, R. (2010). 'Performance Regimes in Health Care: Institutions, Critical Junctures and the Logic of Escalation in England and the Netherlands', *Evaluation*, 16/1: 13–29.

Prainsack, B., and Toom, V. (2010). 'The Prüm Regime: Situated Dis/Empowerment in Transnational DNA Profile Exchange', *British Journal of Criminology*, 50/6: 1117–35.

Putnam, R. (1993). *Making Democracy Work: Civic Traditions on Modern Italy*. Princeton: Princeton University Press.

PZ Leuven (2006). *Protocols en samenwerkingsakkorden vanaf 24–04–1996* ('Protocols and Cooperation Agreements from 24–04–1996'), Leuven, 1 June.

Raco, M. (2003). 'Remaking Place and Securitizing Space: Urban Regeneration and the Strategies, Tactics and Practices of Policing in the UK', *Urban Studies*, 40/9: 1869–87.

Rajabifard, A., Crompvoets, J., Kalantari, M., and Kok, B. (2010) (eds). *Spatially Enabling Society: Research, Emerging Trends and Critical Assessment*. Leuven: Leuven University Press.

Reddick, C. (2005). 'Citizen Interaction with e-Government: From Streets to Servers?', *Government Information Quarterly*, 22: 38–57.

Reed, M. (2009). 'Critical Realism: Philosophy, Method or Philosophy in Search of a Method?', in D. Buchanan and A. Bryman (eds), *Sage Handbook of Organizational Research Methods*. London: Sage, 430–8.

Reiner, R. (2000). *The Politics of the Police*. 3rd edn. Oxford: Oxford University Press.

Richardson, J. (2001) (ed.). *European Union: Power and Policymaking*. 2nd edn. London and New York: Routledge/Taylor and Francis.

Roberts, A. (2010). *The Logic of Discipline: Global Capitalism and the Architecture of Government*. Oxford: Oxford University Press.

Rothstein, B., and Teorell, J. (2008). 'What is Quality of Government? A Theory of Impartial Government Institutions', *Governance*, 21/2: 165–90.

Royal College of Surgeons (2006). *Delivering High-Quality Surgical Services for the Future*. London: Royal College of Surgeons of England.

Sahay, S. (1997). 'Implementation of Information Technology: A Time–Space Perspective', *Organization Studies*, 18/2: 229–60.

Savage, M. (2005). 'The Popularity of Bureaucracy: Involvement in Voluntary Associations', in P. Du Gay (ed.), *The Values of Bureaucracy*. Oxford: Oxford University Press, 309–34.

Savage, S. (2007). *Police Reform: Forces for Change*. Oxford: Oxford University Press.

Sayer, A. (1985). 'The Difference that Space Makes', in D. Gregory and J. Urry (eds), *Social Relations and Spatial Structures*. London: Macmillan, 49–65.

Scott, J. (1998). *Seeing like a State: How Certain Schemes to Improve the Human Condition Have Failed*. New Haven and London: Yale University Press.

Schuppan, T. (2009). 'Reassessing Outsourcing in ICT-Enabled Public Management', *Public Management Review*, 11/6: 811–31.

Self, P. (1975). *Econocrats and the Policy Process: The Politics and Philosophy of Cost–Benefit Analysis*. London: Macmillan.

Sennett, R. (1998). *The Corrosion of Character: The Personal Consequences of Work in the New Capitalism*. New York: W. W. Norton.

Sennett, R. (2005). *The Culture of the New Capitalism*. New Haven: Yale University Press.

Sharp, E. (1986). *Citizen Demand-Making in the Urban Context*. Montgomery, AL: University of Alabama Press.

Simmons, R., Birchall, J., Doheny, S., and Powell, M. (2007). ' "Citizen Governance": Opportunities for Inclusivity in Policy and Policymaking?', *Policy and Politics*, 35/3: 457–78.

Smith, A., Schlozman, K., Verba, S., and Brady, H. (2009). *The Internet and Civic Engagement*. Pew Internet, Sept. (accessed 3 Feb. 2010).

Smith, J. S. (2006). *Building New Deal Liberalism: The Political Economy of Public Works 1933–1956*. Cambridge: Cambridge University Press.

Snellen, I., and Van de Donk, W. (1998) (eds). *Public Administration in an Information Age: A Handbook*. Amsterdam: IOS Press.

Sørensen, C., and Pica, D. (2005). 'Tales from the Police: Rhythms of Interaction with Mobile Technologies', *Information and Organization*, 15: 125–49.

Sparke, E. (1988). *Canberra 1954–1980*. Canberra: Australian Government Publishing Service Publication.

Staeheli, L. (2008). 'Place', in J. Agnew, K. Mitchell, and G. Toal (eds), *A Companion to Political Geography*. Malden, MA, and Oxford: Blackwell, 158–70.

Starr, P. (2010). 'The Liberal State in a Digital World', *Governance*, 23/1: 1–6.

Story, E. (2006). 'Constructing Development: Brasília and the Making of Modern Brazil'. Ph.D. dissertation, Graduate School, Vanderbilt University.

Sudjic, D. (2006). *The Edifice Complex: How the Rich and Powerful—and their Architects—Shape the World*. London and New York: Penguin.

Sutherland Inquiry (2008). *An Independent Inquiry into the Delivery of the National Curriculum Tests in 2008*. Report to Ofqual and the Secretary of State for Children, Schools and Families, HC62, 16 Dec., London: The Stationery Office.

Sykes, O., and Motte, A. (2007). 'Examining the Relationship between Transnational and National Spatial Planning: French and British Spatial Planning and the

European Spatial Development Perspective', in P. Booth, M. Breuillard, C. Fraser, and D. Paris (eds), *Spatial Planning Systems of Britain and France: A Comparative Analysis*. London and New York: Routledge/Taylor and Francis, 99–118.

Taylor, J., Lips, M., and Organ, J. (2007). 'Information-Intensive Government and the Layering and Sorting of Citizenship', *Public Money and Management*, 27/2 (Apr.), 161–4.

Taylor, J., Lips, M., and Organ, J. (2009). 'Managing Citizen Identity Information in e-Government Service Relationships in the UK: The Emergence of a Surveillance State or a Service State?', *Public Management Review*, 11/6: 833–56.

Therborn, G. (2006). 'Why and how Place Matters', in R. Goodin and C. Tilly (eds), *The Oxford Handbook of Contextual Political Analysis*. Oxford: Oxford University Press, 509–33.

Theroux, P. (2008). *Ghost Train to the Eastern Star*. London: Penguin.

Tholen, B. (2010). 'The Changing Border: Developments and Risks in Border Control of Western Countries', *International Review of Administrative Sciences*, 76/2: 259–78.

Thomas, J., and Streib, G. (2003). 'The New Face of Government: Citizen-Initiated Contacts in the Era of e-Government', *Journal of Public Administration Research and Theory*, 13/1: 83–102.

Thompson, S. (2008). 'Separating the Sheep from the Goats: The United Kingdom's National Registration Programme and Social Sorting in the Pre-Electronic Era', in C. Bennett and D. Lyon (eds), *Playing the Identity Card: Surveillance, Security and Identification in Global Perspective*. London and New York: Routledge/Taylor and Francis, 145–62.

Thrift, N. (2006). 'Space, Place and Time', in R. Goodin and C. Tilly (eds), *The Oxford Handbook of Contextual Political Analysis*. Oxford: Oxford University Press, 547–63.

Thubron, C. (1998). 'Siberia', *Granta*, 64 (Winter), 8–35.

Till, K. (2008). 'Places of Memory', in J. Agnew, K. Mitchell, and G. Toal (eds), *A Companion to Political Geography*. Malden, MA, and Oxford: Blackwell, 289–301.

Tilley, N. (2008). 'Community Policing', in T. Newburn and P. Neyroud (eds), *Dictionary of Policing*. Cullompton: Willan Publishing, 40–1.

Treasury Board Secretariat (2004). *Service Delivery Network Profile Summary Report*. Toronto: Borins Collection, Mar.

Tsoukas, H. (2005). *Complex Knowledge: Studies in Organizational Epistemology*. Oxford: Oxford University Press.

Tuan, Yi-Fu (1977). *Space and Place: The Perspective of Experience*. Minneapolis: University of Minnesota Press.

Tuffin, R. (2008). 'Neighbourhood Policing', in T. Newburn and P. Neyroud (eds), *Dictionary of Policing*. Cullompton: Willan Publishing, 178–9.

Turkle, S. (1995). *Life on Screen: Identity in the Age of the Internet*. New York: Simon and Schuster.

Urry, J. (1990). 'Conclusion: Places and Policies', in M. Harloe, C. Pickvance, and J. Urry (eds), *Place Policy and Politics: Do Localities Matter?* London: Unwin Hyman, 187–204.

Van de Walle, S., Roosbroek, S., and Bouckaert, G. (2008). 'Trust in the Public Sector: Is there any Evidence for Long Term Decline?', *International Review of Administrative Sciences*, 74/1: 47–64.

Vigoda-Gadot, E., Shoham, A., and Vashdi, D. (2010). 'Bridging Bureaucracy and Democracy in Europe: A Comparative Study of Perceived Management Excellence, Satisfaction with Public Services, and Trust in Governance', *European Union Politics* 11/2: 289–308.

Wanna, J., and Craik, J. (2010). 'Committed Cities and the Problems of Governance: Micromanaging the Unmanageable', in S. Kallidaikurichi and B. Yuen (eds), *Developing Living Cities: From Analysis to Action.* Singapore: World Scientific, 47–75.

Walsh, E. (2004). 'Public Service Relocation Programme: Optimizing the Opportunity'. Keynote address to the Annual Delegate Conference, Association of Higher Civil and Public Servants, Dublin, 15 May.

Welch, E., Hinnant, C., and Jae Moon, M. (2005). 'Linking Citizen Satisfaction with e-Government and Trust in Government', *Journal of Public Administration Research and Theory*, 15/3: 371–91.

West, D. (2004). 'E-Government and the Transformation of Service Delivery and Citizen Attitudes', *Public Administration Review*, 64/1: 15–27.

Wettenhall, R. (2009). 'Twenty Years of ACT Self-Government: Some Governance Issues', *Public Administration Today* (Jan.–Mar.), 58–71.

Whitehead, T. (2009). 'Bobbies on the Beat for Just 6 Hours a Week', *Daily Telegraph*, 3 Oct., p. 1.

Wiener, A., and Diez, T. (2004). *European Integration Theory.* Oxford: Oxford University Press.

Winner, L. (1997). *Autonomous Technology.* Cambridge, MA: MIT Press.

Yakhlef, A. (2009). 'We Have Always Been Virtual: Writing, Institutions, and Technology', *Space and Culture*, 12/1: 76–94.

Yanow, D. (1993). 'Reading Policy Meanings in Organization-Scapes', *Journal of Architectural and Planning Research*, 10/4 (Winter), 308–28.

Yanow, D. (2005). 'How Built Spaces Mean: A Semiotics of Space', in D. Yanow and P. Schwartz-Shea (eds), *Interpretation and Methods: Empirical Research Methods and the Interpretive Turn.* Armonk, NY: M. E. Sharpe, 349–66.

Index